Isabella Blow

ALSO BY LAUREN GOLDSTEIN CROWE

The Towering World of Jimmy Choo:
A Glamorous Story of Power, Profits, and the Pursuit of the Perfect Shoe
(with Sagra Maceira de Rosen)

Isabella Blow

A Life in Fashion

LAUREN GOLDSTEIN CROWE

Thomas Dunne Books · St. Martin's Press ⚏ New York

THOMAS DUNNE BOOKS.
AN IMPRINT OF ST. MARTIN'S PRESS.

www.thomasdunnebooks.com
www.stmartins.com

ISBN 978-0-312-59294-3

First Edition: November 2010

10 9 8 7 6 5 4 3 2 1

For my parents

Contents

Author's Note

Did I know Isabella?

That, invariably, was one of the first questions people asked when I put forward my request for an interview. Of course I knew *of* Isabella. Anyone who had done their time in fashion's trenches while she was working knew of Isabella. And we'd met a couple of times—backstage at Valentino, at a dinner in Milan. Most memorably in the front row of a fashion show in London in the autumn of 2004. I was eight months pregnant with twins and weighed nearly 200 pounds. Even other pregnant women were staring at me, but Isabella seemed not to notice. She sat down next to me, introduced herself, and said, "I need a man. I am getting a divorce and I am not very good on my own." She asked if I knew anyone. It wasn't yet 10 a.m. I flipped through my internal list of the usual suspects, simultaneously thinking how hard it must be for someone as nonconformist as her to meet someone. Little did I know that she'd already cut a wide swath through some of the UK's best-looking men. The comment encapsulated the Isabella who I discovered while writing this book: provocative with sexual overtones ("I *need* a man"), but endearing, and ultimately, openly very vulnerable.

This book would not have been possible without two people. Lucy Birley and Philip Treacy were not just two of her best friends, they were the epitome of each of the worlds she lived in. Both put up with months of questioning, made all the more difficult by the fact that in my haste to learn as much as I could about Isabella's colorful life, in as much detail as I could, I would often forget that it wasn't just a character we were talking about but someone's best friend. They were emotional sessions punctuated with much laughter and occasional tears.

I conducted more than one hundred interviews for this book, and easily could have conducted another fifty. It seems there isn't a person in London who hadn't had a brush with Isabella that they wanted to share. Donald McPherson, Haluk Akakce, Kamel Belkacemi, and Matthew Mellon also stand out for the sheer number of hours they devoted to the project as well as their enthusiasm and kind words of encouragement. Gigi Solomon, Benjie Fraser, Lord David Cholmondeley and his mother Lady Lavinia Cholmondeley, Natasha Grenfell, Hon. Geraldine Harmsworth, Celia Lyttelton, Tim Willis, Michael Roberts, Sarah St. George, Richard Neville-Rolfe, Nick Ashley, Nicky Haslam, Lady Liza Campbell, Kate Bernard, Zara Colchester, Toby Young, and Joe McKenna helped me understand the girl who existed before she became famous. Her husband, Detmar Blow, is writing his own book about Isabella and didn't wish to be interviewed for this one, which makes the contributions from his mother, Helga de Silva Blow Perera, his sister Selina Blow, his uncle Sir Desmond de Silva, and his cousin Simon Blow all the more important. The ups and downs of working with Isabella were patiently explained by editors Nicholas Coleridge, Geordie Greig, and Jeremy Langmead; stylists Katie Grand, Daphne Guinness, and Laurie Schechter; her former assistants Chloe Beeney, Jessica Walsh, Anna Bromilow, Marie Petit du Thouras, Stefan Bartlett, and Daniela Paudice; photographers David LaChapelle, Sean Ellis, and Julian Broad; model turned author Sophie Dahl; designers Julien Macdonald, Rifat Ozbek, and Jeremy Scott and Nadja Swarovski from Swarovski and Sarah Doukas of Storm Models. Stuart Shave, Sue Webster and Tim Noble, Amanda Eliasch, Stefan Brüggemann,

Stephanie Theobald, Noelle Reno, John Maybury, and Margarita Wennberg were all part of the social scene in which she spent so much of her time. I had hoped to interview Alexander McQueen, but I was not able to convince him before his untimely death. In telling his story I relied in part on an interview I did with him in 2002 when I was working for *Time* magazine. I was disappointed to be told that Isabella's mother, Lady Helen Delves Broughton, would not speak for the book, but the openness of her stepmother, Lady Rona Delves Broughton, was a pleasant surprise. Many others, too numerous to mention, answered niggling questions throughout. Several people who had never discussed Isabella publicly before did so with me, but on the strict condition that I did not name them. They know who they are, and I thank them for making this a more accurate book.

Two bright young students stepped forward to answer my desperate plea for last-minute assistance. Both Winnie Herbstein and Joanne Kernan had studied art, but were familiar with Isabella's story. They ably assisted me in the gathering of photographs, fact-checking my copy, and conducting interviews when I was otherwise occupied. My mother proofread the book at various stages and took over child-care duties for long periods of time. This book was the idea of Karyn Marcus at Thomas Dunne Books, and she proved herself to be something I thought the world of books had left behind—an editor who actually edits. Elizabeth Sheinkman, my agent at Curtis Brown, has been a supportive cheerleader as well as deal broker.

Isabella was a great wit and a great writer. I've tried to use her words wherever possible, but nearly all the words here are ones she spoke in interviews and are therefore public domain. I wish I could share with you the way she described her father on vacation in a letter to a girlfriend, but the strange and confusing world of intellectual property rights makes that impossible. She also lived her life as a story, one that she frequently made up on the fly. It made for captivating conversation, but also made it tricky to know where the truth ended and her fantasy began. That Isabella kept various sides of her life separate did not help. Frequently there were different versions told of the same incidents. Where I couldn't confirm which was the truth, I either printed all versions or selected the one I felt was most plausible.

Did I know Isabella? I did not. Did anyone really know Isabella? In the wake of her death, even her oldest friends began to wonder. But everyone whose life she touched knows one thing for sure: They loved her and they miss her desperately.

Cast of Characters

Haluk Akakce — A Turkish artist. He lived with Isabella following her first stay at The Priory Hospital, and the two became close friends. He now divides his time between New York and Istanbul, and remains friends with many of the people he met through her.

Majed al-Sabah — A nephew of the Emir of Kuwait. He launched Villa Moda, a designer emporium in the Middle East, and collaborated with Isabella on several projects.

Jessica Andrews (now Walsh) — One of Isabella's longest-lasting assistants. She worked at *Tatler* magazine for Isabella from fall 2003 to summer 2005 and was promoted from intern to full-time paid employee after Isabella demanded she bare her breasts in the famous "Nipples in Naples" shoot.

Bernard Arnault — The founder and chairman of LVMH (Moët Hennessy–Louis Vuitton). He hired Alexander McQueen to design for the house of Givenchy in 1996.

Nick Ashley — A friend of Isabella's from her teenage years. His mother launched the brand Laura Ashley. Nick has his own clothing company with a store in Notting Hill, London.

Stefan Bartlett — Formerly an assistant of Isabella's. He is now Philip Treacy's trusted partner in both his personal and his private life. He is the son of industrial designer David Bartlett and was a key member of Isabella's inner circle.

Kamel Belkacemi — A young, good-looking Frenchman who worked in one of London's most chic boutiques, the Dover Street Market. Belkacemi became friends with Isabella in 2004 after two chance meetings — one on the Eurostar and another in a grocery store in Belgravia. He soon became one of her closest friends, traveling with her and visiting her nearly every night when she was interned in mental health hospitals. He is now working for Daphne Guinness on creating an archive of Isabella's clothes.

Lucy Birley (née Helmore) — A friend of Isabella's from their teenage years. She is the daughter of a barrister and grew up in Kensington in the home of her maternal grandfather, Sir Hurbert Hull, a judge. She was married to musician Bryan Ferry for twenty-one years during which time she worked occasionally as a model and had four sons. Isabella was godmother to her eldest son, Otis Ferry, who was also a pageboy at her wedding as well as a pallbearer at her funeral. Lucy is now married to Robin Birley, the son of Mark Birley (founder of Annabel's nightclub) and Lady Annabel Goldsmith.

Manolo Blahnik — The famous shoe designer who started his business in the 1970s. He was one of Isabella's close friends. He carried her over the mud to her wedding in 1989 lest she ruin the gold shoes he had made for her special day.

Amaury Blow — Isabella's brother-in-law.

Detmar Blow — Isabella's husband.

Detmar Jellings Blow (Detmar J.) — The grandfather of Isabella's husband. He was a famous architect in his day and the man who designed and built Hilles, the stately home in Gloucestershire that Isabella and Detmar considered their primary residence.

Jonathan Blow — Isabella's father-in-law. He committed suicide thirty years before Isabella by drinking weed killer, the same method she would later employ.

Selina Blow — Isabella's sister-in-law. She is a designer with a shop off Sloane Street in Knightsbridge. Isabella introduced her both to the world of fashion and to her now former husband, Dr. Charles Levinson, who was Isabella's general practitioner.

Simon Blow — Detmar's cousin and a writer. He first met Isabella when she was working at American *Vogue* in the 1980s. He lives in London.

Winifred Blow (née Tollemache) — Detmar's grandmother. She came from the aristocratic Tollemache family, which can trace its history back to the Norman conquest.

Julian Broad — The photographer at Isabella and Detmar's wedding. He first met Isabella when she was working at *Tatler* in 1989.

Anna Bromilow — Isabella's first assistant at *Tatler*. She is the current fashion director of the magazine.

Lady Liza Campbell — A friend of Isabella's from their teenage years. She is the daughter of the twenty-fifth Thane of Cawdor, and the last child to have been born in Cawdor Castle (which featured in Shakespeare's *Macbeth*). She is now an artist and writer.

Lord David Cholmondeley — The seventh Marquess of Cholmondeley. He was a childhood friend of Isabella's. In addition to Cholmondeley Castle, he also owns Houghton Hall, in Norfolk. In 1995 under the name David Rocksavage, he directed the film *Other Voices, Other Rooms*.

Lady Lavinia Cholmondeley (née Leslie) — Isabella's godmother. She is the Marchioness of Cholmondeley and was the wife of the sixth Marquess of Cholmondeley. She lives in Cholmondeley Castle in Cheshire, minutes from Isabella's childhood home.

Zara Colchester (née Metcalfe) — A former flatmate of Isabella's. She moved to New York with her in 1979.

Nicholas Coleridge —The editorial director of Condé Nast UK, Isabella's last employer.

Sophie Dahl — A model whose career was launched by Isabella. She met Isabella on a London street. Born Sophie Holloway, she is the daughter of actor Julian Holloway and the writer Tessa Dahl, and now writes and stars in a UK TV cooking program. She is married to singer Jamie Cullum.

Sir Desmond de Silva — Detmar's uncle. He is one of the most famous barristers in the UK.

Helga de Silva Blow Perera — Isabella's mother-in-law. She now runs a hotel called Helga's Folly from her childhood home in Kandy, Sri Lanka.

Domenico De Sole — The former chairman of the Gucci Group. He bought the Alexander McQueen brand in 1999 when McQueen was still designing for the LVMH-owned Givenchy label.

Sir Evelyn Delves Broughton — Isabella's father. He was the twelfth Baronet of Broughton.

Lady Helen Delves Broughton (née Shore) — Sir Evelyn's second wife and Isabella's mother. Before meeting Evelyn she was the youngest woman barrister called to the bar.

Sir Jock Delves Broughton — Isabella's grandfather. He was accused of murder in Kenya in what has become known as the White Mischief case. He was responsible for the careless spending that depleted a vast amount of the family's fortune.

Julia Delves Broughton — The second child of Sir Evelyn and Helen, Isabella's sister. She now works at Christie's in London.

Lady Rona Delves Broughton (née Clifford-Johns) — Sir Evelyn's third wife. She is a senior figure in Lloyd's insurance syndicate and the current owner of Doddington Hall, the Delves Broughton stately home in Cheshire.

Lady Vera Delves Broughton (née Griffith-Boscawen) — Isabella's grandmother. She was a famous society figure in her day and a photographer who sought excitement in exotic foreign travel and big-game hunting.

Sarah Doukas (née Chambers) — The founder of Storm modeling agency. She is an old friend of Isabella's who launched the careers of the models Isabella brought to her. She is most famous for discovering Kate Moss.

Sean Ellis — A fashion photographer who met Isabella when he was working for Nick Knight. He and Isabella did several highly acclaimed shoots for *The Face* magazine in the 1990s.

Katy England — A London-based stylist. She worked closely with Alexander McQueen until shortly before his death.

Tom Ford — The former creative director of the Gucci Group. He sat next to Isabella at a dinner party and she urged him to buy the Alexander McQueen label. He now has his own line of menswear and accessories and in 2009 directed the Oscar-nominated film *A Single Man*.

Benjie Fraser — A cousin of Isabella's. He became a close friend when she began to regularly visit her aunt in the Scottish Highlands. The eldest son of writer Lady Antonia Fraser and the former Member of Parliament Hugh Fraser, he inherited Eilean Aigas upon the death of his father. In order to help him raise funds, Isabella urged him to rent it out and became his first tenant.

Honor Fraser — A cousin of Isabella's. She was encouraged by Isabella to model and became the face of Givenchy when it was being designed by Alexander McQueen. She now owns an art gallery in Los Angeles.

John Galliano — The chief designer at Christian Dior and one of the most famous fashion designers to come out of the UK. Isabella had hoped that he would make her wedding dress.

Katie Grand — One of London's most successful stylists. She met Isabella through Alexander McQueen in 1992. Grand went on to launch two magazines, *Pop* and *Love*, and to work for a host of major brands including Prada and Louis Vuitton, which led Isabella to dub her "Katie Grand-a-minute."

Geordie Greig — The editor of London's daily newspaper the *Evening Standard*. He was Isabella's boss at *Tatler* magazine during her second stint there. He also went to prep school with Detmar, Isabella's husband, when they were eight.

Natasha Grenfell — The daughter of Peter Grenfell (Lord St. Just) and Maria. She was a friend Isabella made in her teens. Grenfell was a close friend of Fred Hughes, Andy Warhol's manager, and introduced Isabella to Andy when they were all living in New York. Isabella lived for a time in Natasha's mother's house on Gerald Road in Belgravia and also spent many weekends at Wilbury House, St. Just's country home.

Daphne Guinness — An heiress noted for her own arresting dress sense and work in the world of fashion, art, and film. She first met Isabella in the mid-1980s but the two didn't become friends until 1997. Daphne's great-grandfather Lord Moyne and Isabella's grandmother famously had an affair and traveled the world on his yacht collecting rare species of animals. As an heir to the Guinness fortune and ex-wife to the Greek billionaire, Spyros Niarchos, Daphne was one of Isabella's most wealthy friends and helped her out financially in many ways over the course of their friendship, including paying for some of her stays in various private mental hospitals. She and Isabella collaborated on many projects. In April 2010 she bought the entire archive of Isabella's clothes from her sisters, thereby stopping an auction that was scheduled to take place at Christie's that autumn.

Geraldine Harmsworth — A friend of Isabella's from their teenage years in London. She is the daughter of Viscount Rothermere, a media baron credited with turning the *Daily Mail* newspaper into a financial success, and Pamela Brooks, an actress. Isabella called her journalist boyfriend "The Rep" for "The Reptile" which was, she said, Geraldine's father's term for journalists.

David LaChapelle — A noted fashion and celebrity portrait photographer. He met Isabella on the set of a *Vanity Fair* shoot when he was photographing her and Alexander McQueen for what became known as the "Cool Brittania" story. He now focuses primarily on art photography.

Karl Lagerfeld — The chief designer at Chanel. He was introduced by Isabella to several of her protégées including milliner Philip Treacy and knitwear designer Julien Macdonald, both of whom subsequently designed for Chanel.

Jeremy Langmead — Isabella's boss at *The Times*. He hired her in 1997 in an unusual move to bring high fashion to its mass-market newspaper supplement. He is now the editor of British *Esquire*.

William Leigh — An early boyfriend of Isabella's. He was part of the Oxford set.

Julien Macdonald — One of Isabella's discoveries, he met her through Alexander McQueen. She introduced him to the house of Chanel, where he worked as a knitwear designer. He has had his own line since 1997 and succeeded Alexander McQueen as chief designer at Givenchy, remaining in the post for three years.

Joe McKenna — Now a New York–based stylist. He and Isabella worked together at *Tatler* in the 1980s and collaborated on the "London Babes" shoot for British *Vogue*.

Donald McPherson — A fashion photographer and a close friend of Isabella's since 2002. They shared an apartment in Paris. He now lives and works in New York.

Alexander McQueen — An English designer who attracted Isabella's devotion when she saw his student graduation collection at Central Saint Martins. He committed suicide in February 2010.

Matthew Mellon — An heir to the Mellon Bank fortune. He and Isabella had a brief love affair during her separation from Detmar. He is now married to the American Nicole Hanley, with whom he has launched a new clothing line, Hanley Mellon. He recently raised $10 million for research into Ibogaine, a new treatment for drug addiction.

Suzy Menkes — The fashion correspondent for the *International Herald Tribune*.

Richard Neville-Rolfe — A teenage friend of Isabella's. He was part of the Oxford set.

Tim Noble — A London-based artist. He and his partner, Sue Webster, were the first artists to sign up with the gallery Isabella and Detmar were partners in, the Modern Art Gallery.

Rifat Ozbek — A famous Turkish designer. He became friends with Isabella in the 1980s.

Noelle Reno — A former girlfriend of Matthew Mellon's. She lives in London and has partnered with British designer Zandra Rhodes to launch a clothing line, Z by Zandra Rhodes.

Michael Roberts — Now fashion director for *Vanity Fair*. He hired Isabella for her first job at *Tatler* and remained a close friend and confidant throughout her life.

Laurie Schechter — Anna Wintour's first assistant at American *Vogue* when Isabella was hired. She is now a freelance stylist and fashion editor in New York.

Jeremy Scott — An American designer whom Isabella championed when he lived and worked in Paris. He now has a studio in Los Angeles.

Stuart Shave — A cofounder of the Modern Art Gallery with Detmar and Isabella. He bought them out in 2003, five years into their partnership, and continues to run the business from a new location in Central London.

Gigi Solomon (née Callander) — Isabella's best childhood friend from Cheshire. The two remained close until their teenage years.

Sarah St. George — A friend of Isabella's from Heathfield. Her family owns 50 percent of the Grand Bahama Port Authority, and her father was instrumental in developing that island, where they still own a large estate.

Maria St. Just — Natasha Grenfell's mother, she was Isabella's frequent host in London. She was the muse to Tennessee Williams (it is said the character Maggie the Cat in *Cat on a Hot Tin Roof* was based on her) and was the executor of his estate.

Nadja Swarovski — A descendant of the family that makes the famous Swarovski crystals. She gave Isabella a contract to consult for the firm and to attract young designers to its wares.

André Leon Talley — Briefly Isabella's boss at American *Vogue*. Talley recommended her to Michael Roberts for the *Tatler* job when she wanted to return to London. He still works at *Vogue* as one of Anna Wintour's chief lieutenants.

Nicholas Taylor — Isabella's first husband. He was part of the Oxford set. He and Isabella lived in Midland, Texas, and then New York together before breaking up in the late 1980s.

Philip Treacy — An Irish hat designer Isabella met when he was a student at the Royal College of Art. She was an enthusiastic promoter of his work and famously wore his fantastic millinery creations. They were loyal friends until her death. He is now creative director on a film about her life.

Lavinia Verney (née Delves Broughton) — Isabella's youngest sister, whom she called "Baby." Following the death of her first husband, Lavinia moved into a cottage on Detmar's estate and lived there until 2010.

Sue Webster — A London-based artist. She and her partner, Tim Noble, were the first artists to sign up with the gallery Isabella helped set up, the Modern Art Gallery.

Tim Willis — A journalist and one of Isabella's most serious boyfriends. She dated Willis from 1986 to 1988, prior to meeting Detmar Blow, who would become her second husband.

Anna Wintour — The editor of American *Vogue*. Wintour hired Isabella to be one of her assistants when she first came to the magazine as its creative director.

Toby Young — A journalist living in London. Young proposed what became known as the "Cool Brittania" story to *Vanity Fair* magazine and hired Isabella as consultant on the project. The article appeared in the magazine's March 1997 issue.

What is exhilarating in bad taste

is the aristocratic pleasure

of giving offense.

CHARLES BAUDELAIRE

Those who are easily shocked

should be shocked more often.

MAE WEST

Dressing Issie

Introduction

It wasn't that they hadn't dressed her before. They had, many times—more times than they could possibly recall.

Isabella Blow, known to the public as a muse, an artist, a stylist, an eccentric, and even a national treasure, had committed suicide at the age of forty-eight. Above all else, she had been a style maverick, pushing designers to make the most inventive clothes they could—then wearing them, no matter how unusual, as further encouragement. She had, in her heyday, gone to the Paris collections in a hot pink sheer burka, suffering abuse from French journalists as a result. She'd flown to Kuwait in a cape and a mask, like a female Zorro. She'd worn on her head everything from antlers, a crystal-studded lobster, a boat, and a wooden model of a Chinese garden to a sign reading simply, "Blow." Now the job of dressing the world's most daring and original wearer of clothes fell, for the very last time, to the two men who were her closest co-conspirators in all matters sartorial.

Although there were hundreds of items made by Philip and Alexander in her wardrobe—items she had begged, pleaded, teased, taunted, bought, and even stolen to possess—Philip and Alexander had never dressed Isabella together. *She* had always been the one who would decide which of Philip Treacy's sculptural handmade hats would go with what from

Alexander McQueen's precisely tailored collections. That, in fact, was her surest claim to fame. By wearing clothes in a way that no one else would have considered, she had succeeded in making herself her own work of art.

But now she was gone, and it would be up to the two of them to decide which combination would be the last to adorn her. Some of the items on the rails in her flat on Eaton Square were easily discounted. The Givenchy suit with glowing pinstripes came with a power source to light the stripes, which might explode when it came time to cremate her. And although McQueen himself had designed it when he'd been employed by the legendary French house, he had hated his time there. Would he really want Isabella's last outfit to bear the name Givenchy? The Jeremy Scott cape with a hump on the back looked great on her (and pretty much only on her, the hunchback look not being an easy one to pull off), but it would make it awkward to lay her in the wicker willow casket she'd requested. And it was most definitely "Not McQueen." The coat of colorful trash bags that looked so beautiful when she ran to and fro across various streets and courtyards in Paris in order to show off how it inflated and ballooned behind her would have none of the same appeal lying beneath her in a coffin. And of course, done by an obscure Japanese designer, it, too, was out on the "Not McQueen" grounds.

There were plenty of McQueen garments from which to choose. Isabella's wardrobe was a microcosm of his entire career. One of her greatest McQueen hits was the "bull dress" made of calf and tulle that she loved because "people drew blood making [it]"[1]—you could still see the hole where the dagger went in and killed the bull. There would have been a certain poetry to using something from McQueen's *Icarus* collection of 1997, but the one piece she still possessed, a feathered corset, seemed too sexy for a casket. The white monkey fur jacket she had once worn around her waist when the zipper on her skirt broke lacked gravitas. Philip Treacy had been going through her clothes with Lucy Birley, one of her oldest and closest friends, considering the pieces when Alexander McQueen arrived. After the briefest of hellos, McQueen walked to the rails and, without hesitation, pulled out a multicolor beaded coat with ocelot fur tips. "Fucking hell," he said. "This weighs a ton." Then he paused. "Well, she ain't going to be walking in it, is she?" Underneath it would go a pale green dress with a pleated skirt and gold brocade embroidery.

The hats could have provided an even larger challenge. Isabella had been wearing Philip Treacy creations on her head since 1989, when she convinced the designer to make the hat for her wedding. Her collection was vast, but a large number of the hats were unsuitable in a very mundane way: they were simply too large. For instance, the tricorn hat she had urged him to make wider and then even wider, was, when finished, too wide to fit through the doorway of the party for which it was intended. She had to enter sideways and scuttle through the crowd like a crab. Also too large was Gilbert and George, a cloudlike confection with neon pink and green accents that hovered over her head when she opened the door to a shocked group of firemen who'd come to her house expecting a sedate thank-you cocktail party. There was no way either would fit into a coffin. Fortunately, Isabella herself had already chosen the hat she would wear: the Pheasant. A headless brown, black, and white bird body would sit on her head in the coffin. "I love the exotic Chinese cock," she had said many times over the years she owned the piece. "I wear it. I eat it. I want to be buried in it."[2] Treacy added to it a veil of black feathers.

The funeral was held in Gloucester Cathedral, one of the oldest places of worship in the Western world, with a history that goes back thirteen hundred years. The building embodies its noble past. Boasting the tallest spire in England, it was the place where Henry III was coroneted and Edward II was buried. A stained-glass window and intricately carved stone tomb created to memorialize each are two of the historical highlights inside the imposing structure.

Philip Treacy had spent the preceding weeks gathering together the things he knew Isabella would want to see at her last party, starting with the means of transport. He knew she would have hated the idea of a traditional shiny black hearse. Instead, he hired a glass-sided Victorian carriage that would be pulled by horses. Atop her coffin went a swath of black velvet and, on top of that, dozens and dozens of white roses mixed with her favorite flower, the white lily. Treacy and two of Isabella's friends had spent the night before dipping the lilies in crystals to emulate dew. "Many people wouldn't see it," said Treacy. "But she would have seen it."

Nestled on the fragrant flowers was a black female bust, and on its head sat Isabella and Treacy's favorite hat, the Ship, a replica of a seventeenth-century multi-sail battleship. Behind the ship, hidden from view, was a tiny motorized fan to blow wind into the ship's sails so it would look as if it were sailing on the high seas. And of course there were hats. He designed hats for the heads of her two sisters, a few select friends, and the models whose careers Isabella had boosted. Even the six horses that pulled the hearse did so with black-feathered plumes on their heads.

On the morning of the funeral, Treacy was decorating the cathedral with the dark red, almost black, lilies he'd found at the flower market near his home in London when he received a call from Alexander McQueen saying he wanted a lock of Isabella's hair. Treacy left his work and went to find Isabella's two sisters, Julia and Lavinia, and put forward the unusual request on behalf of McQueen. The sisters hesitated, more surprised than unwilling. "You know she would have given him her head," he said. They agreed to let him have some of her hair. Treacy cut off "a healthy chunk" for McQueen, who said he wanted to have it made into Victorian mourning rings for all of them. McQueen then joined Julia and Treacy to take one last look at Isabella in her splendor before the lid to the coffin was shut.

A s the procession from Stroud to the cathedral began, Treacy and Julia, Isabella's oldest sister, followed the Victorian carriage in a car. When the owner of the hearse had asked how many of the giant black-maned bay horses Treacy would like to pull the carriage, two or four, he had replied, "Six," thinking, "There was nothing budget about Isabella."

From his vantage point behind the horses, he could see it had been the right decision. When the horses with their Treacy-designed plumes hit a bit of open road, they began to trot gaily, as if they were dancing. He'd never seen horses do anything like that before. "Incredible," he said to Julia. "Isabella would have liked that."

Inside the cathedral the 300 guests divided fairly evenly into two camps. On one side were the fashion and society friends, boldface names like Sophie Dahl and Rupert Everett, whose pictures would grace the morning newspapers. On the other were some of Isabella's oldest friends, most, like Isabella, with lineages that could be traced back for hundreds of years; but they were people the paparazzi no longer hounded. Had Isabella died thirty years earlier, perhaps it would have been photos of Countess Debonnaire von Bismarck, Lord David Ogilvy, and the Seventh Marquess of Cholmondeley to make the newspapers the next day.

At the time of Isabella's funeral, some of them still lived in stately homes and had retained enough money to live comfortably without working, but aristocrats were no longer revered as the social and political leaders of their country. Their power had been stripped by a combination of economic and social forces that had been given a final push with the Second World War. Now they mostly lived anonymously. Seldom using their titles, they worked (if they had to) in jobs such as private banking, where connections are helpful and where they mingled with one another and looked with a mixture of bafflement and distaste at the rise of brash celebrity culture and the famous personalities it produced.

The two sides of the funeral mixed like oil and water. The fashion crowd was deemed a spectacle: the fashion journalist André Leon Talley swanned about in a navy blue silk taffeta cape, and numerous skinny men huddled together in shrunken suits, wearing sunglasses despite the torrential rain. The aristocrats eyed them with suspicion. No wonder Isabella had been so unhappy, if these were the characters with whom she'd had to work. The fashion crowd was less critical, viewing the hatless, conservatively dressed aristocrats as little more than a sea of nameless, faceless, shapeless blue suits, black dresses, and polite strands of pearls.

In the middle of it all was Isabella's husband, Detmar Blow, in the knee-length, black Sri Lankan jacket with gold buttons and trim he had worn to their wedding. He was eyed with a mix of sympathy and also suspicion. Had he really done enough to help her when she began on her slow decline? Certainly he'd been meticulous in the planning of her funeral and the memorial service that would follow in London. But his efforts were not beyond reproach. His lavish desires exceeded the amount of money he was willing to contribute, and Isabella's most recent employer, Condé Nast, picked up the bill for the memorial. "Condé Nast wants it to be in Hanover Square, but that church is too small," he said. "I'm thinking of the Guards Chapel."[3] Detmar got his way—Guards Chapel it was.

Detmar's seating plan at the funeral in Gloucestershire put his family before Isabella's friends. Not present was Isabella's mother. They'd had a notoriously difficult relationship and hadn't spoken in years. Many of the guests, having heard Isabella's stories, blamed the mother for not loving her daughter enough, and had she attended, a confrontation with some of them would have been possible. Would they have changed their minds if they'd known that on her most recent passport Isabella had listed her mother as the first emergency contact? Also not present was Matthew Mellon, with whom she'd had a brief but passionate affair. He stayed away out of respect for Detmar, but entertained fantasies of arriving on a white horse to throw a single rose onto her coffin before galloping away.

Detmar told a reporter that Isabella would be buried in his family plot at Hilles, the Gloucester estate she had tried to make her home. It was a place she called "Wuthering Heights on a withering budget," and the location where Detmar's father had killed himself thirty years earlier, by drinking weed killer, the same method Isabella had employed. Some friends wondered if the house were to blame for her decline. Hilles was a place she loved and sometimes loathed over the years of her marriage, and people actually thought it might be cursed. Certainly the battle for its future took its toll on Isabella's relationship with her husband. She had been raised on an estate in Cheshire, the centerpiece of which was an even more grand property called Doddington Hall, and both houses featured significantly in her life.

I sabella lived between two dying worlds—each elite, stylized, and, at least to outsiders, alluring. In the decade she was born, the 1950s, stately homes like hers were being pulled down one after another in England on a regular basis. Left without an empire to support them, the British aristocracy was finding it exceedingly difficult to keep up the kind of lifestyle it was accustomed to. Its daughters were often tossed out into the modern world with nothing in the way of preparation: little education, less money, and no one to look to for help. They could hardly ask their parents for advice; most of them had never held a job either. (As for parental love, that seemed to be doled out as randomly as good cheekbones: some were born with it, others were not.) Many of the daughters found themselves taking over the household chores that would have been performed by staff a generation earlier. Isabella was the first woman in her family's history to work for most of her life, and she was not alone among her friends in finding it a perplexing position to be in.

When she started her career in fashion, Isabella thought she'd found a place where she really belonged, a place that could fill the gaps left by her disintegrating family. A letter she wrote to her friend Liza Campbell upon getting her first job at American *Vogue* in 1982 was read at her memorial service in London weeks after her funeral: "*Vogue* is like joining the CHURCH," it said. "It is a whole new perspective on life . . . It has done a lot for the yellow fang inferiority complex syndrome & I have become quite a megalomaniac instead."

At *Vogue*, Isabella had found a place where her extreme efforts to seek out beautiful and special things were not just understood but applauded and rewarded. Still, even as she and other staffers debated passionately which of the British models was the most beautiful, even as she insisted that an architect build the entire set of a gym for a photo shoot (the real thing in New York not being up to par), the industry that supported such efforts was beginning to change. It had gone from an industry where creativity reigned supreme to one where profit margins grew to lord over all else. Serious financial players were beginning to buy fashion and luxury companies. It's unlikely Isabella knew or cared about these deals. She toiled in fashion's other extreme: her quest was for pure beauty both in her life and in her work. As someone once said of Diana Vreeland, the legendary editor of *Harper's Bazaar* and *Vogue* from 1937 to 1971, she made extravagance seem normal. But by the time she died, the slow encroachment of men in suits had changed the face of fashion. Instead of romantic souls like Madeleine Vionnet, the French designer whose technique was inspired by ancient Greek costumes, the designers who would thrive in the new luxury landscape were people like Tom Ford, creative director of the Gucci Group, who each morning would review the sales figures from the previous day and who was comfortable using the language of the men in suits.

After her death, newspaper obituaries struggled to define Isabella Blow's contribution to the world. News of her death appeared in every major newspaper in Britain and also in *The New York Times, New York* magazine, *The Wall Street Journal,* and *Time* magazine. But when it came to describing what she did, most reports fell back upon the hackneyed quip: that she had "discovered" Alexander McQueen and Philip Treacy. The reality is far more complicated.

Although people who knew her would say she belonged in another era, she lived very much in the present. She would acknowledge and dismiss childhood traumas in quick staccato sentences: "My mother rejected me. My brother drowned. My father cut me out of his will." She didn't turn to self-pity; she didn't become addicted to alcohol or to drugs. She pushed her reality to the background and created a new life, and a new persona that was intoxicating to be around. A key element of that new life was her wardrobe. Her clothes were the outward manifestation of her internal thought processes. She didn't discover these designers, but she changed their lives in ways impossible to define. And vice versa.

Her fascination with costume and clothing was with her from an early age. So was a willingness to wear things that would attract and shock. The only difference now, she'd tell Philip Treacy after she'd met him and Alexander McQueen, is that now she had *better* clothes and hats. She wasn't just a muse or a patron, though she was partly both of these things. Mostly she was a spark, an electric impulse that set their imaginations racing. She loved and encouraged a wide group of photographers, designers, stylists, and artists as a mother might, but it wasn't a completely selfless act. She was also in desperate need of what they provided. Her clothes had become the armor she used to protect herself, and she'd become addicted to the power they gave her. Philip Treacy and Alexander McQueen were her chief suppliers. She would tell her heterosexual friends, "I have to be so careful with these queens. They could cut me off entirely."

I sabella lived frenetically, so that any pain or disappointment in her life was dulled in comparison to the bright light she emitted. In the end, keeping the fire burning was just too exhausting. She succumbed to the fire she had created and was consumed.

Three years after the funeral, when a friend expressed surprise that Isabella was buried at Hilles, her sister Julia raised her eyebrows and said, "She's not." The final resting place of her remains has not yet been approved by those closest to her. Detmar wants her at Hilles and has designed a five-foot two-inch grave marker (her exact height), while a variety of friends and family members would like to see her buried on the grounds of her family's historic seat in Cheshire. Isabella would have found the debate hysterical, but a sad truth remains: Even in death, Isabella has not found a place she can call home.

The
Chatelaine
of
Elizabeth
Street

Philip Treacy sat in the basement of the Royal College of Art considering a hat he had just finished making. It bore a thistle and a rose, the symbols of Scotland and England. He had made it to be sold at Harrods, but Isabella Delves Broughton, the woman who had recently commissioned him to make her a hat for her wedding, had asked him to call should he make anything he thought would strike her fancy. She was, he thought, very English and she'd mentioned she had cousins in Scotland, so he rang her and left a message about the hat. When he didn't hear back, he sent the hat to Harrods. Isabella rang the next day wanting to see the hat. Philip explained that it had been delivered to the store. "But it's mine!" Isabella said and hung up the phone. She promptly phoned Harrods and asked if she could borrow the hat for a shoot she was putting together for Tatler *magazine. It never saw the selling floor again.*

The knocker thudded again against the heavy wooden door of 67 Elizabeth Street, a five-story house that lay in the nondescript area between London's affluent Belgravia neighborhood and the urban sprawl surrounding Victoria Station. Isabella fairly flew down the narrow staircase of the townhouse, cigarette in hand, wearing the ecclesiastical robes she'd bought the day before from Watts, a supplier of church fabrics and uniforms behind Westminster Abbey. When she swung open the door, Philip

Treacy was stunned to see her in a deep red silk robe with its accompanying white tunic. She looked rather beautiful, he thought, with her hair falling about her head in soft golden brown waves and her lips smeared with deep red lipstick. Treacy had, at the time, his own penchant for unusual dress. He was tall and thin with reddish blond hair and had taken to dressing daily in red, and only red, from his shirt down to his shoes. But he was a fashion student, and such peccadilloes were to be expected.

Isabella, on the other hand, was not a student. She was a fashion editor at *Tatler* magazine and the bride-to-be of a young barrister whose family owned a stately home outside of Gloucester. Still, though she might have come from one of the oldest families in England, though she might be on a first-name basis with members of the royal family, there was nothing fusty about Isabella—least of all the way she dressed. She was constantly looking for new things to wear or new ways to wear old things. And now she was busy planning costumes. In just a few months' time, on her thirty-first birthday, November 19, 1989, she would be able to dress an entire cast exactly as she pleased for her spectacular wedding in Gloucester Cathedral. There would be no traditional white gown for Isabella— fashion dictates of the day would be damned. Isabella wanted the wedding to be medieval—really medieval, as if Eleanor of Aquitaine were getting married, not a fashion editor from a society magazine. To accomplish this would take more than a trip to an expensive bridal boutique. It would take the help of her growing cadre of friends in fashion.

She led Treacy upstairs into a dark blue drawing room furnished with curtains, tablecloths, and lampshades all in floral Fortuny fabrics. Standing in front of a blue and gray Victorian marble fireplace was the largest black man Treacy had ever seen. André Leon Talley, then the fashion news director at American *Vogue*, was magnificent in a multicolor robe. ("If you're six feet seven inches tall, you may as well wear a beaded caftan," Talley has been known to say.)[1] Next to him was a not as tall, but tall nevertheless, gray-haired man in a bespoke Anderson & Sheppard double-breasted gray suit and spotless brown leather brogues. It was celebrated shoe designer Manolo Blahnik. Isabella introduced them only as André and Manolo. Treacy recognized neither of the men, and even had Isabella included last names in her introductions, it wouldn't have helped. He had never heard of them, either.

Similarly, Isabella didn't belabor Treacy's introduction. "This is Philip," she said. "He is making my wedding hat." She didn't mention that Treacy, unlike Manolo Blahnik, was lacking an established reputation, not to mention a decade's worth of experience. Neither did she mention that Treacy, unlike André Leon Talley, was not used to the company of fashion luminaries such as the new editor of American *Vogue*, Anna Wintour, or Diana Vreeland, who would die that August. Treacy was twenty-two, a student, and he was learning to make hats at London's Royal College of Art. Isabella didn't mention that, either. He was simply "Philip" and he was making her hat.

Philip Treacy had met Isabella when he made a hat for a shoot for *Tatler* magazine. When he came to the office to collect the hat, the magazine's art director said he should meet Isabella, who was working with Michael Roberts, the magazine's creative director. Isabella came into the room wearing a transparent cobweb top by John Galliano, an A-line skirt, flaming red lipstick, and high heels. No one else in the office looked like that. The others were all wearing the traditional beige/gray office wear of the day—and trousers dominated, even on the women. "It was evening for day before it was acceptable," Treacy recalled of Isabella's attire. "It was a little unusual." Isabella took the hat he'd made, done in a 1920s style with jagged sycamore leaves adorning it, inspected it, and returned it. Treacy then left. "I can't say it was love at first sight," he said. "She was a bit cool, actually."[2] Isabella said, "I didn't meet Philip. I met the hat. I was more interested in the work than in Philip at that point. I'd never seen anything like it. It was beautifully made and an emerald green . . . no, more grasshopper green. It was so exquisite that when we pulled it out of the box it was like we shouldn't be touching it."[3]

The next day Isabella phoned the Royal College of Art and asked what Treacy's schedule was like for the next six months. "There was a temp answering the phones," Treacy said. "She told me this woman was ringing wanting to know my schedule. I was thinking, 'What schedule?' I'm a student." When she reached him, Isabella said she wanted him to make a hat for her wedding and explained that the theme for the wedding was medieval. "I barely knew what medieval meant," Treacy said.

A flurry of phone calls followed. It seemed every time the phone rang for Treacy, it was Isabella on the other end. Sometimes she'd be asking how the hat was progressing, but increasingly it was just to ask if he was okay, or to see if he needed anything, or to tell him about a book she was reading or an exhibition she had seen. "We spent weeks courting over the headdress," he said. "It was the most incredible thing ever. It was like an affair, it was very intense. I thought all fashion people were like that."

At the time, Philip Treacy didn't really know many fashion people, but that was about to change. "Philip," Isabella now said, in her blue drawing room in 1989, presenting him to two of the most esteemed men in fashion, "show them the hat." Treacy had almost forgotten he was holding a bookbag containing his drawing of Isabella's wedding hat. It wasn't so much a hat as a headdress, two feet of swirling gold spirals held together by the finest of mesh. He had based the hat on Cecil Beaton photographs of Lady Diana Cooper in the 1930s play *The Miracle*. "Show them, Philip!" Isabella urged again. He hesitated. Why would two grown men want to see his drawing of a wedding hat? And an unusual one at that? Isabella nudged him in the ribs with her elbow. He bent and took the drawing of the golden headdress out of his bag and handed it over. He was surprised to see the two grown men go into raptures of ecstasy. He never expected anything like that. "They liked it," he said. "A lot."

At that time, English women, when they wore hats, wore hats that could almost always be described as pretty. Bows, flowers, and ribbons adorned simple round shapes that were worn primarily for tradition-laden occasions like Ascot or church weddings. The deviation of Treacy's concept from the fashion norm of the day only seemed to make the wedding headdress all the more appealing to Talley and Blahnik.

By the time of Isabella's death, eighteen years later, even the most conventional of British women were matching the pastel suits still favored for summer fêtes with towering pom-poms, horse's heads, or ice-cream cones. Camilla Parker Bowles, the second wife of Prince Charles, may not have realized it, but it was thanks to Isabella Blow that she had come to accept the more modern interpretation of headwear heralded by Philip Treacy. For the blessing service following her April 2005 wedding to the future king, her head was adorned by a Philip Treacy–designed fan of feathers.

That day in 1989, the trio went downstairs to the dining room, located in the basement. The house belonged to Helga, a Sri Lankan and Isabella's soon-to-be mother-in-law, and was decorated in a bold and colorful way that betrayed the woman's Eastern roots. Next to the dining room was a glass extension that Helga was using as a boutique of sorts, full of high-collared Sri Lankan coats of silk with handmade brass buttons as well as other curios she would periodically bring back from trips to her native country. The dining room was painted a glossy scarlet red and decorated with antique Sri Lankan spears and a Chinese wall hanging depicting, in pearls, the scene of a wedding. The quartet sat at the dining table beneath the wall hanging to talk about Isabella's wedding and eat the roasted chicken and potatoes she had prepared.

All of the things Isabella had ever wanted seemed to be falling into place. She was thirty, she had found a job as an editor at *Tatler* that she both enjoyed and was good at, and she was finally getting married in a pact that would bring her not just love, but security. Although the family of Detmar Blow, her fiancé, wasn't as grand as hers, it did possess a habitable manor house called Hilles, over which she planned to preside. A grand house like Hilles, or like her family's boarded-up Doddington Hall, in the northeast of England, wasn't just a beautiful structure in which to live. In England, as in much of Europe, the stately home embodies family pride and status. Isabella imagined she would spend her weekends entertaining guests at Hilles, her weekdays working on fashion shoots for *Tatler*, and her weeknights hosting dinners for an eclectic mix of titled friends from her past, not to mention the artists and designers who were increasingly a part of her present, and sure to be a part of her future as her stature in fashion grew. A year or two from now, she hoped, she'd be a mother and could shower all the affection on her child that she felt had been denied in her own youth.

During lunch, Treacy explained about Diana Cooper and *The Miracle* and was surprised to find that these two men knew exactly the photos that had inspired him. Manolo Blahnik said he would take his inspiration for Isabella's shoes from Treacy's hat and make them extra long, extra pointy, and from gold mesh.

But what of the dress? The dress was a problem. Isabella wanted it in purple, which the assembled agreed would be *fabulous*. (At her wedding the only person in white would be the Turkish designer Rifat Ozbek, who was wearing a suit from his own all-white collection, with mirrors on the back that spelled out, "Release It.") Isabella had hoped that Britain's most famous young designer, John Galliano, would make her dress for her, but he had pulled out. (Or Isabella pulled out when she found out the cost. When it came to Isabella, with her penchant for ignoring facts for the sake of a good story, one could never be entirely sure where the truth stopped and fiction began.)

Michael Roberts, a close friend of Talley's and Blahnik's, who was also Isabella's boss at *Tatler*, had suggested Nadia La Valle, an Italian friend and designer who had a line called Spaghetti and a shop at 32 Beauchamp Place. Isabella had asked Treacy to accompany her to the shop the week before to discuss the dress with La Valle. While there, someone Isabella later called "a grand fashion queen" asked her, in front of Treacy, why she was having a student make her headdress. "I watched Issie's response, and her face was just blank," Treacy said. "She shrugged, like, 'Why not?' She didn't give a fuck that I was a student." Isabella's instincts were right. The dress La Valle made was arresting—figure-hugging purple velvet, hand embroidered with gold trompe l'œil necklaces, and trailing a fifteen-foot train. Yet years after her death, Isabella's friends would ruminate on what the dress would have looked like had it been designed by Alexander McQueen, whose clothes she fell in love with when she saw them on the runway of his graduation show. No one would ever question Treacy's headdress.

After her guests departed, Isabella trundled upstairs to Detmar's bedroom, next to the drawing room, on the first floor. Above it was the bedroom of Selina, Detmar's younger sister, and Helga, his mother. Selina, twenty-one, had recently moved to New York, and Helga was spending increasing amounts of time in Sri Lanka, so Isabella and Detmar usually had free rein over the Elizabeth Street home. "The house," said Lucy Birley, "always had its problems. Damp, cracks in the walls, things breaking. It felt like something reaching the end of its useful life." But not to Isabella. Although she didn't own the structure, she'd taken over its soul. Whereas for much of her adult life she had been a gypsy, staying with friends rather than setting down roots, now she had a place where others could come and crash with her. "It was the most glamorous hostel ever," said Sophie Dahl, one of the models Isabella would lead into the fashion business. When Helga wasn't around, the house would usually be in a state of disarray. Guests would find packs of Benson & Hedges cigarettes and cups of tea on the various side tables. Upstairs were large wooden tea chests with Isabella's clothes spilling out of them; Manolo Blahnik shoes lying helter-skelter where she'd kicked them off; bottles of Fracas, Isabella's only fragrance, on the dressers and in the bathroom.

The guests at Elizabeth Street represented the more modern Britain that had emerged in the country's Swinging 1960s and '70s, a bohemian mix of artists, entertainers, and models, including Boy George, Naomi

Campbell, Rifat Ozbek, corset maker Mr. Pearl, and rich aristocrats united mostly by their love of a good time—and all of them attracted to Isabella's wicked sense of humor and natural ease as a host. She would stand in the kitchen, cigarette in hand, talk on the phone, make dinner (or lunch, or breakfast, as required), and keep the conversations going among the people around her. In actuality, it wasn't so much conversation that was taking place as a one-woman show, performed so arrestingly that no one noticed Isabella was doing most of the talking. A sample of her conversational style was published years later, when she was asked to describe forthcoming renovations on her home:

> We're going to have glass sculptures made especially for the hats, and the furniture is coming from a countess's palazzo in Venice. I'm going to have a bath shaped like a gondola that will be filled with Egyptian chocolate. It's very good for the skin. I hated Egypt when I went there. Too many people. But that's where you get the best chocolate for bathing in, which reminds me. I've got a corset made in the shape of a gondola. I wear it all the time. It's made by the new boy at Worth. . . . He's a genius.[4]

She peppered her talk with "Don't you agree?" "Can you believe it?" "Do you know him?" "Have you been?"—helping add to the illusion that what was happening was an interaction, not a monologue. If Isabella hadn't been fascinating, this routine would never have worked.

When Philip Treacy finished school and was looking for a place to live and work, Isabella asked Helga if he might take over the boutique in the basement. Helga loved the idea, and it was agreed he would pay £1,500 a month in rent. Isabella meanwhile found it was not only fun but also incredibly convenient to have her own milliner on the premises. She'd come home from work, bathe, dress for the evening, and then go downstairs to see what Treacy had been working on that day. Together they'd pick one of his hats to go with whichever outfit she'd selected for the evening, be it a low-cut lace dress or a pair of velvet britches. "The hats were characters to her. She would talk about them as if they were our friends or our babies," Treacy said. "I think she should come with me," Isabella would say. At the end of the evening, she'd return and bring the hat downstairs, telling Treacy, "She had a marvelous time!" or, "You wouldn't believe what so-and-so said about her." Treacy loved every minute of it. "I knew that Isabella being Isabella, that that hat had gone out. That she'd marched into Claridge's with it like she owned the place."

Isabella with a neon cloud above her head was not going to go unnoticed, but that doesn't mean it set Treacy's business booming. "The kind of hats I had were a little alarming," he said. "No one wanted them but her." Isabella would try to convince people of his talents, but "no one wanted to look like that." One customer came into Philip's basement lair in Elizabeth Street thinking it was the shop of another Philip, the more conservative milliner Philip Somerville, and fled when she saw the hats. "I tried to show her some things," said Treacy. "But she just legged it."

"In the old days people were frightened by my hats," Isabella said later. "But . . . Philip has single-handedly broken through all the barriers. And now people want what I'm wearing. It's really weird. I'm being hotly pursued for my head now. I feel like Marie Antoinette."[5]

For a young couple about to be married, life at Elizabeth Street was an atypical existence. Isabella and Detmar spent little time alone in each other's company. With flexible working hours, Isabella would spend much of the day zooming Treacy around in her VW station wagon, insisting he sit in the back and referring to the two of them as Harold and Maude, the main characters of a classic British film about a young boy having an affair with a much, much older woman. Detmar, on the other hand, spent his days at court as an apprentice, trying to impress the older and esteemed men he worked for. At night Detmar was thrilled to find himself in the company of such interesting creatures as Isabella attracted.

Detmar was a far more conservative character than Isabella. When she was living in New York, working for Anna Wintour and hanging out with Andy Warhol, he'd been diligently studying at the London School of

Economics. But this was the source of his attraction to her. If she'd fallen for him at least in part because of Hilles, it could equally be said that he fell for her because of the social networks she opened up. He'd grown up in fairly sequestered circumstances, with a father who was mentally ill and a much younger mother who came from a foreign country, overwhelmed trying to take care of her husband and their three children. Detmar's brother, Amaury, said of their father, "My mother tried to keep his illness from us, but we were aware of it. Christmas could be cancelled, birthdays deferred, because he'd go into a depression . . . My poor mother was at her wits' end."[6]

Now that many of the country's most fascinating people were practically living in his mother's house, for Detmar that troubled time must have seemed very far behind him. On the weekends, he and Isabella would take a select group of her friends to Hilles. It had been built by his grandfather, a sort of champagne socialist with the idealistic goal of building a home where honest, hardworking members of the working class could mingle happily with aristocrats. Detmar had been waiting all his life to preside over Hilles as Lord of the Manor, and now, with Isabella as Lady of the Manor, that dream was finally coming true—in the most fantastic way imaginable. His country weekends would not be filled with the boring City types with whom he had to work during the week, but with an eclectic mix of sizzling personalities who would make him feel scintillating by association and ultimately lead him to quit his career at the bar in favor of a new start as an art dealer. He'd always been immensely proud of Hilles, but when he met Isabella, he realized that a stately home wasn't much good if the right people weren't around to admire it. "It's not the grandest or the most famous house in England," Detmar said in a video to promote his book on Isabella, "but it became one of the most interesting to visit. . . . She brought the house to life."

The
Stately Homes
of England
Are
Mortgaged
to the Hilt

Even from ten thousand feet in the air the pilot could see something shining on the bottom of Doddington Lake. He took a second pass to make sure it hadn't been a reflection and then he landed to report it to the local authorities. Although Nantwich in Cheshire had not been a major—or even a minor—bomb target in World War II, nearby Manchester and Liverpool had been. So one couldn't be too careful. But what the authorities sent to investigate found was not a German explosive, but the Delves Broughton family silver, dumped there, it later emerged, by Isabella's notorious grandfather Jock Delves Broughton.

Before there was Isabella Blow, style icon, there was Issie Delves Broughton, daughter of a baronet. And before Hilles, the estate in Gloucestershire where she would live with her husband, there was Doddington Park, an estate of four thousand acres in Cheshire, a sparsely populated rural county in northeast England, some four hours by train from London. An estate in England is not just a big house with a lot of land. It also can comprise cottages in which tenant farmers live, an estate shop that sells essentials for farming, and, if the house is open to the public, a café, gift shop, and toilets. The primary feature of Doddington Park, like most estates, is the manor house, in this case called Doddington Hall. But although a few farmers remain, there are no public toilets, no café, no gift shop. And while Isabella never lived in the house, it loomed large in her life. In 1958, the year of her birth, the house, which stands empty, and its grounds were all that were left of a family legacy that once exceeded that of the Westminsters. For a young girl with Isabella's active imagination, the house was a giant hulking reminder of a lavish life she never saw, but only heard about. For a girl with a sensitive nature, particularly where aesthetics were concerned, the self-inflicted expulsion of her family from the great house alone was enough for her to base a tragic story of her life around. In reality Isabella would suffer greater losses in her childhood than not being able to live within its walls.

These days it is very quiet at Doddington Hall. At the top of the drive is a cattle gate—locked, but easily crossed. On the left of the drive is a tranquil lake, which once housed a central pavilion for dinner parties but is now used by local fishermen and sailors. It was hand-dug by French prisoners from the Napoleonic Wars and enlarged by the famous landscape gardener Capability Brown. The main house looks barren. It sits at the end of the drive, a handsome pile of Samuel Wyatt–designed gray stone. Wyatt was the brother of James Wyatt, the most famous eighteenth-century architect, and Samuel's work was known to be simpler than his brother's. Architectural critics have said of Doddington Hall that it is "Wyatt at his best in the sparing use of motif and their delicacy, and also in the easy planning."[1] Attached to the west side of the main house is a curved wing for the servants, and beyond that, a brick stable. Inside are eighteen bedrooms in the main house and another twenty in the servants' wing. Beneath the bedrooms, the layout includes a music room, a ballroom, a boudoir, a salon, a study, and two libraries (one for classical works and one for contemporary). Above the front door and the largest of the windows are giant decorative black-and-white Wedgewood plates with the signs of the zodiac on them. (Doddington Hall was, at the time, the only house to have such plates.) The 1780 house is now a Grade-I listed building, the most important class of historical building in the United

Kingdom. But even from behind the locked gate, the boards in some of the windows are visible.

Off in the distance one can see another structure, made of red stone, with a crenulated roof. It's a castle of sorts—a tower house, with one room per floor. Known as Doddington Castle, it was built in 1348 to provide protection as well as habitation. During the 1356 Battle of Poitiers, eight thousand Englishmen ultimately defeated sixty thousand Frenchmen, and on one memorable occasion, three hundred French soldiers on horseback were attacked by archers under the command of Sir James Audley. One of Audley's four squires was an ancestor of Isabella's known as Delves of Doddington. It is said that Delves carried Edward, the Black Prince of England (named so for his black suit of armor), and saved him from being taken prisoner by the French. Delves was granted a license to crenellate the roof of the tower—thereby distinguishing it from a mere house— and the title of Baronet as his rewards. (The license was key, for if one were to crenellate one's roof without license, the structure could be confiscated by the king.)

"My ancestor carried the Black Prince wounded away from the battlefield," Isabella once explained in an interview. "There were all these ponces walking around the outside wanting a title, but we got our title from work—from actually saving the king."[2]

A gray stone staircase, added in the early 1600s, leads up the front of the tower, and stone knights guard the structure. They are the carved figures of the Black Prince, Sir Audley, and the four squires that served under him. At one time an underground passage led from the castle to the manor house. Isabella would later ask Philip Treacy to make her a hat called The Castle and to use the stone knights from Doddington Castle as models.

The Delveses became the Delves Broughtons when a Delves married a Broughton who brought a great deal of land into the marriage—so much land that a merger as well as a wedding was in order. The Broughtons insisted that their name stay attached to the estate, ensuring their place in the aristocratic hierarchy. "[The name] doesn't have a hyphen. If you have a hyphen it means you did it for fun,"[3] Isabella said, referring to the subsequent practice of combining family names upon marriage simply to be able to keep using an aristocratic name.

Despite the solvency of the Delves Broughton union, the Doddington Hall of today contains no seventeenth-century Flemish tapestries, crystal chandeliers, or oil paintings, but only industrial carpet, an abandoned cabinet, and a bit of empty shelving. The house hasn't been occupied by the family since the Second World War and was last used as a girls' school called Goudhurst College. But even if the floors of the house are covered in industrial carpeting (necessary to withstand the feet of hundreds of girls running to and from classes), in the basement there remains a train track—not a toy to amuse children, but one installed in its day as a necessary means of conveying food and drink from the kitchen to the main building for the adults who ate, drank, and danced above.

It's not hard to imagine a better life for the house. The dual staircase at the entrance cries out to have ladies in jewels and long gowns ascend on the arms of men in tails, after emerging from chauffeur-driven cars and pausing to have their pictures taken for society journals. In the back of the house a semi-circle protrudes, evidence of the rotund drawing room— the most famous room in the house. It once had a gilded ceiling, mirrored bays, a marble chimney, and a Waterford crystal chandelier. "It was always a very formal room, furnished very uncomfortably with gilded 'drawing-room' furniture," said Evelyn Delves Broughton.[4] Evelyn was Isabella's father, the twelfth and, for the time being, last baronet. He was, with his sister, Rosamund (now Lady Lovat), the last of the Delves Broughtons to have been brought up in the house. If the walls could talk, it's those of the ballroom one would want to listen to. It was the site of some of the most lavish parties in the county—if not the country. Isabella would later brag to friends with stately homes they still lived in, "We could fit your house in our ballroom."

Evelyn was the only son of Jock Delves Broughton. When Jock inherited the house from his father in 1914—the same year Evelyn was born—it came as part of a package that included Broughton Hall in Staffordshire and 6 Hill Street, a townhouse in London's upscale neighborhood of Mayfair. With the three homes came some forty thousand acres and an income from the land and other investments of over £80,000 a year (£35.4 million in 2008 currency).[5]

Although Isabella's grandfather would later become famous in connection with two deaths—the murder of the Twenty-second Earl of Erroll in Kenya, for which he was tried and acquitted, and his own, by his own hand (both of which would be documented in a book and movie with the same title, *White Mischief*)—in his day Jock was known for throwing a hell of a party.

In *White Mischief*, author James Fox depicts Jock's father, Louis Delves Broughton, as notoriously cheap with his son, sending him off to boarding school at Eton with next to no money but with odd luxuries essential for his social standing, such as a horse to be stabled at the school and used for hunting. Jock's impoverished state led to schoolyard rumors that he had taken to stealing to keep up with the spending of the other boys at the school—boys who came from some of the richest families in the world.

In 1913, Jock married Isabella's grandmother, Vera Edyth Griffith-Boscawen, one of the most beautiful and best dressed women in society. She had grown up in Trevallyn Hall, Denbighshire, one of the most important Elizabethan houses in the United Kingdom. Within months of receiving his inheritance, Jock, later described by his son as having a pathological fear of being left short of cash, sold off one of the residences, Broughton Hall, as well as fifteen thousand acres. That same year, he was meant to ship out on the S.S. *Novara* to fight in World War I. But when his ship left for France, Jock wasn't on it. He had come down with a severe case of what was later deemed to be sunstroke. Whatever its cause, the disability, which left him with a limp and periods of confusion, wasn't enough to stop him from pursuing what became his next purpose in life: traveling and entertaining on a massive scale.

Just as Isabella's weekends at Hilles with her crowd would later become, Jock's postwar parties at Doddington with his were legendary. He insisted on filling all of the guest rooms every weekend—including the rooms of his children—and paid for the transport of those coming from London, even hiring entire train carriages and employing a band from Ciro's Club, the famous music hall on Orange Street in London's West End, to entertain guests on the trip. "The secretary used to ring up on Wednesday morning," Evelyn recalled, "and say, 'How many of you (us young) are there this weekend?' And then she might ring back in an hour or two and say, 'Your mother and father say there is room for six more.' We seldom sat down to dinner less than twenty."[6] The house also had a famously well-stocked wine cellar in the day. "If ever I wanted a bottle of whisky or gin," Evelyn said, "I'd just say to Martin (the butler) and I'd get anything I wanted. He said, 'It will never be missed.' I've been up (from London) and I've taken a dozen of champagne, a half dozen of port and two dozen of red wine and it was never missed. The tea used to arrive in those hundred-weight chests, great big wooden chests, because it was so much cheaper that way."[7]

In 1920, Jock wanted to sell off another two thousand acres of land, for £175,000 (about £30 million in 2008), giving only one month's notice to the ninety farmers living on it. The famers complained bitterly and vocally to the local press, and Jock rescinded the notice, urging the farmers to buy the land themselves. He called them to a Sunday morning meeting in the hall's Billiards Room and explained that he thought the days of the great estates were over, and he spelled out for them the problems facing the big landowners across the country. "When my father died," Jock said, "a large portion of the estate had to be sold to pay death duties. As time went, there came the war and everything went up in price, labor, materials, and the cost of living generally; more and more of the estate was sold otherwise . . . I would not be able to exist at all."[8]

Jock's idea of subsistence living was not everyone's. While he couldn't damage his family lineage, his extravagant lifestyle made a serious dent in the Delves Broughton fortune. At a dinner many years later, a guest told Jock that she'd like to spend a million pounds a year.

"You couldn't," he said.

"What's the most you've ever spent?" she asked.

"In a good year, I think it was 1926, I spent £120,000 [or nearly $60 million in 2008 dollars]. The first £80,000 was quite easy, but unless you gamble, it's uphill work with the rest."[9] By gambling, he was largely referring to his love of racehorses—he owned several—but he also gambled with risky investments.

In 1935, Jock Delves Broughton met the woman who would become his second wife and make him famous for something even worse than squandering his family's wealth. Diana Caldwell was twenty-two, blond, pretty, and socially ambitious. She wasn't hard up—she had her own racehorses and an airplane and was part owner of a nightclub in Mayfair—but neither was she landed gentry. It was a convenient match, particularly for Jock, who was becoming lonely. For, while he was at home spending money much, much faster than he could possibly make it, his wife, Evelyn's mother, Vera, was becoming one of the most famous explorers of her day. Throughout the 1920s her photograph had appeared in society magazines and her clothing was noted as an example of the fashions of the time. But being a society darling simply wasn't enough for her. In 1931, she went to the Belgian Congo in search of gorillas, and in 1934, she embarked on a thirty-thousand-mile trip around Burma, Malaysia, Vietnam, Papua New Guinea, Australia, New Zealand, and Indonesia on *Rosaura*, the yacht of First Baron Moyne. Lord Moyne was head of the Guinness brewing family, a chief supporter of Winston Churchill, and Vera's lover.

At the time, it was a remarkable departure for a woman of her class. In her biography of Princess Diana, only three years younger than Isabella, Tina Brown writes of the women of the elder generations:

British upper-class women of the prewar generation were tough as old boots. They had used the word obey *in their marriage ceremonies, which meant putting up with a lot. Raised in freezing country seats, given a second-class education, always playing second fiddle to their brothers, they cultivated resourcefulness and the ability to live in private worlds. It prepared them for a life of low emotional expectations and husbands who were focused on being inattentive. Social activities after marriage revolved around male sporting events, so wives spent their weekends hanging about in the rain at race meets or being left at home all day during shooting parties at which you were still expected to change for lunch, tea, and dinner.*[10]

Vera played the role of the traditional upper-class wife for a while, keeping newspaper cuttings of her and Jock's outings to sporting events in a giant leather-bound book, but when the good-looking and married Lord Moyne invited her to go exploring, she left Cheshire with barely a backward glance.

The mission of the cruise, in part, was to catch Komodo dragons—the giant meat-eating lizards that were called "land crocodiles" when discovered in 1910—and to bring them back to London. Although the instinct to explore was common among members of their class, Vera and Lord Moyne took it to new extremes. Clementine Churchill, Winston Churchill's wife, who was another passenger on the yacht with the couple, wrote to her husband:

> *Apparently it was very difficult to trap a real monster, they being few, and very cunning, but the expedition's photographer had managed to photograph a twelve-foot lizard going off with half a pig in its jaws. He & Vera Broughton have lain in wait for hours in the long grass in the blazing sun near the traps, and near dead exposed & rotting animals to get good pictures. I spent one morning watching & decided upon other life.*[11]

The lovers returned with four dragons, which lived at the London Zoo until the mid-1940s, and they later wrote two books about their travels, illustrated with photographs Vera had taken. Vera brought back to Doddington pygmy furniture, a Malayan honey bear, and Gibbon monkeys that she kept as pets. While she was off catching fish (until 2000, she held the world record for the largest tuna ever caught), taking photographs of pygmies and other wild creatures (her photographs of black-maned lions are in the British Museum), and sampling new cuisine (her entry in *Who's Who* says she was "once a cannibal"), Jock was becoming increasingly enamored of his new diversion, Diana, whom he had moved into the Garden House on the Doddington estate. The infidelity wasn't a problem—such liaisons were common among the members of their class. Jock knew and tolerated Vera's lover, and she had no choice but to do the same—but Diana's presence at the family home alienated his children and many of his friends, who thought her nothing but a gold digger. The famous parties were becoming fewer and fewer—even before the outbreak of World War II.

In 1939, Jock sold another fifteen thousand acres of land. That same year, the wife of Lord Moyne died and Vera began divorce proceedings, hoping to marry her newly widowed lover. In 1969, the *Times* of London speculated that Jock "must have made over a large sum to her [Vera] and his children."[12] Whatever the reason, the estate of the Delves Broughtons had now dwindled to a mere four thousand acres from the original forty thousand. Evelyn, twenty-four, had grown weary hearing rumors about his father's wanton spending and of the decline of his future inheritance. Despite the sale of the land, money continued to be a problem. Ironically, Jock, like *his* father before him, had also kept Evelyn on a pittance of an allowance while at Eton, but rather than steal, Evelyn resorted to taking bets on his father's horses to supplement his income. Jock would often wonder how it was that his son could afford expensive dinners and holidays when he was on such a small stipend.

Evelyn's canniness with money came too late to save the Delves Broughton fortune. In 1980, he told James Fox that in addition to keeping the money from the sale of the land, which violated the terms of the trust, Jock had made a series of "almost compulsive" mistakes with his investments, including gambling on the foreign markets and commodities, and investing in "tin pot" gold mines. He also developed an affinity for gambling heavily on cockfighting, which was illegal. Some of the trustees who were charged with managing the estate were also Jock's employees, and had therefore let him act as he wished. When he was twenty-four, Evelyn decided to confront his father.

"I told him I'd heard that there was nothing left of my eventual inheritance," Evelyn told Fox, "and asked where the money had gone. My father lost his temper. He came round the desk and chased me from his study with a riding crop."[13]

Evelyn decided to hire lawyers to make sure that Jock could not squander any more. "I tied him up to the extent of the estate in the first year of the war because he'd been a naughty boy. And whatever money there was in the kitty was practically bugger all. It was something like £50,000 (about £6 million today). All the money from the sale of the land was gone."[14]

Evelyn speculated that it was his father's desperate finances that led him and Diana to move to Kenya in November 1940. They said they were going to take up farming on the Spring Valley coffee estate Jock had bought in 1923, but there was no getting around the fact that it was also a convenient place to ride out the worst of the Second World War—something a few of his landed-gentry friends had already discovered.

Upon arriving in Nairobi, the newly married Jock and Diana checked into the Muthaiga Country Club, the center of social life for the rich British expatriates living in Kenya. One of the men who nightly took his meals there was Josslyn Hay, the Twenty-second Earl of Erroll. Joss generally lived a life of pleasure in Kenya, making a career of sleeping with the wives of married men—something his own wives had turned a blind eye to.

(The scandalous behavior of his first wife, Idina, "in front of servants," was even said to have contributed to the end of British rule in Kenya.)[15] In 1934, Joss had joined the British Union of Fascists in London and worked with Oswald Mosley to bring fascism to Kenya, although he renounced the group when the war began. He was good-looking, charming, and "on first-name terms with every important person in the colony, from the Governor down."[16]

Joss's political activities were not enough to distract him from the sight of a new potential conquest in Kenya: Diana Delves Broughton. And she was similarly smitten with him—not least because he pursued her relentlessly. By December, Jock and Diana rarely dined without Joss. By Christmas, the lovers were inseparable, and by early January, Diana was regularly staying overnight at Joss's bungalow. Jock meanwhile began to drink heavily—something he hadn't done before. It wasn't that he minded Diana having affairs—she'd done so ever since they met—but never before had she been away so frequently and for so long. He'd paired up with her to avoid loneliness, and now, left alone night after night in Kenya, he was lonelier than ever. "He only married Diana because he was lonely and wanted companionship," Evelyn said. "It would not have been in his character to get upset just because she took a lover."[17]

When Joss Hay was found shot in the head early on the morning of January 24, 1941, the cuckolded husband was the most logical suspect, although some of Joss's other lovers were also questioned. Jock was arrested and spent three months in jail awaiting trial. Despite the seriousness of the case—a guilty verdict could come with a death sentence—neither of his children made the trip to Kenya to support their father. Evelyn, who sent £5,000 to cover the cost of a specialist lawyer, was serving with the Polish Army in Iraq, and Jock had written to Rosamund asking her not to come.

The trial had an unusual result. Jock was acquitted, although few in Kenya believed him to be innocent. Worse for all of them, the attention of the world had been drawn to the louche and decadent lifestyle of the denizens of "Happy Valley." Scandalous at any time, the antics of the expat British—casual sex and a fondness for drink and hard drugs—were seen as particularly revolting given that the world was at war and there was much suffering at home.

Diana stuck by Jock during the trial, but his behavior became stranger and stranger after the verdict. He began having nightmares and was obsessed with his declining social position. He and Diana had been banned from the Muthaiga Country Club and dropped by Kenyan society. When Jock returned to England in November of 1942, he traveled alone. Diana remained in Kenya and became the lover, then wife, of Kenya's largest landowner. When Jock's ship arrived in Liverpool, a group of people were there to greet him. But instead of his daughter, son, or ex-wife, it was officers from Scotland Yard.

In the years leading up to his move to Africa, Jock had filed or intended to file several insurance claims. One was for a pearl necklace that he'd given Diana and that had been stolen from her car while she was in the south of France. Another was the loss of three paintings in a robbery at Doddington Hall. The third, a story Isabella told frequently, was the loss of the family silver in yet another alleged robbery. The officers who met Jock at the docks in Liverpool questioned him about the pearls and the pictures, but never filed a case against him. He died before they had the chance.

Jock's last few days back at Doddington Hall were lonely ones. During the war, the estate was requisitioned as one of three national training schools for the Home Guard, the millions of British men who were either too old or too young to fight abroad, but who were expected to fight any invading Germans. After Jock's death, the U.S. Fifteenth Army stayed at Doddington Hall in November and December 1944, moving out on Christmas Eve. Doddington also housed some Free French troops. Many owners of stately homes had turned those homes into hospitals or girls' schools before the war, hoping to avoid the damages that military use could cause. Although Doddington Hall was also used as an evacuation location for a girls' school, it didn't escape that fate. The original gates were destroyed when a military vehicle drove through them.

When Jock returned home, the manor house was still unavailable to him. He moved in with his butler, Martin. He also tried, and failed, to get Vera back. He'd take daily walks and talk with the people who lived on his estate, reminiscing about the trial. "He was terribly worried about the tenant farmers' and the locals' opinion of him after the trial," a close friend told the author of *White Mischief*. "They had placed bets in the pub about the verdict."[18]

Jock's eventual suicide was attributed to guilt over the Kenyan murder, although he had been acquitted of that charge. But signs of depression were evident from an early age, at least according to the descriptions of his nature given by the author of *White Mischief*. It was said that while at Eton, Jock would have "fits of ungovernable temper." Later, when ensconced in Doddington Hall, he would "sulk for a week without giving a reason." He was called "distant, lonely, somewhat humorless," "a sad, rather querulous man, who never smiled," and "vicious, cold, and cruel in more ways than one."[19]

In December of 1943, Jock and a woman friend planned to go together to Liverpool to see a show, but when her son got sick, Jock went alone. He checked into a room at the Adelphi Hotel on December 2, leaving instructions that he was not to be disturbed. Two days later he was found in a coma by hotel staff. He'd injected himself fourteen times with Medinal, a barbiturate. Isabella Blow's grandfather, Jock Delves Broughton, died in a hospital the next day, December 5, simultaneously making Evelyn the twelfth baronet and breaking the taboo of suicide within the family.

Whether a guilty conscience or dire financial straits were the cause of the suicide, its effect on Jock's family's reputation was shattering. Evelyn was asked to leave his regiment in the wake of the scandal.

White Mischief became a bestselling book and then a film that forever imbued the Delves Broughton name with the scent of scandal and made Jock far more famous than the fourteenth-century squire who had secured the family title. The book also made a convincing case that he was guilty of insurance fraud—that he had made false claims and even purposely destroyed three family heirlooms. The author discovered a confession written after Jock's death by Hugh Dickinson, one of Diana Caldwell's oldest friends. In it, he explains how, at the behest of Jock, he stole the pearls from Diana's car so that Jock could claim them on his insurance. Jock then used this knowledge to blackmail Dickinson into the second theft, that of the three paintings from Doddington Hall. Two of the pictures he destroyed were Broughton family portraits done by the eighteenth-century portraitist George Romney. In *White Mischief*, Dickinson describes how destroying priceless works of art is harder than one might imagine: "You have no idea how tough canvas is. You think it's paper thin, delicate. But I had to chop and chop and chop . . . I walked out the front door like a gentleman, found a quiet field and tried to burn them. All the petrol burned away, but the canvas just wouldn't burn."[20] He finally tied the remnants to the ladder he used to break into the house and sank it all in a small river a few hours' drive from Doddington Hall.

It was Evelyn who bore the brunt of the scandal. Following his father's death, he went to work at Lloyd's of London to repay the insurance company. When he married five years later, he returned to Cheshire and set about running what was left of the estate. He soon divorced his first wife, but the bachelor baronet wasn't alone for long. He began coming back from trips to London with a couple of prospective mates. Neighbors in Cheshire remember being invited to dine with a famous actress. But it was the unusual daughter of a Cheshire businessman, Helen Mary Shore, who struck his fancy.

Before long Evelyn was remarried and raising a family. The couple lived not in Doddington Hall, which was never turned back into a family home after its wartime commissions, but in Doddington Park House, a smaller house on the estate. Evelyn did not seem to mind that he would not be raising his family in the manor house. It hadn't been a particularly comfortable place for him to grow up in, and on at least one occasion he listed it with real estate agents to sell it. Ultimately, it was not sold, but stood instead as a backdrop for what Isabella saw as the tragic tale of her young life.

Loving Your
Parents
Is Common

The first thing Gigi noticed as Isabella walked into the twelfth-century abbey Gigi called home was that Isabella was in jeans. This was unusual. Their mothers shared a distaste for denim. Gigi didn't even own a pair and wouldn't until she went to university. But as Isabella got closer, Gigi saw something even odder. The zipper on Isabella's fly had broken and, rather than surrender the treasured trousers, she had found a handful of safety pins and used them to close the gap. This, it must be noted, was well before punk rock made such things fashionable.

The venue may have changed, but the parties thrown by Evelyn and Helen had certain similarities to those of another era. "The Kenya history still lived on," said a contemporary of Isabella's from Cheshire. Evelyn's primary daytime occupation was running the estate—in addition to the increasingly difficult task of trying to balance the books, it also meant visiting the tenant farmers, making guest appearances at Goudhurst College to give awards, and generally being the friendly face of one of Cheshire's most important pieces of property. Evelyn's new wife now focused her considerable energies on planning hunt balls and dinner parties. Every night there was a dinner, most every weekend a party—and the extroverted, flirty, often outrageously outspoken Helen was a key instigator, as Isabella would also become.

Isabella told her friends that her mother was "common"—at varying times describing her as the daughter of a butcher or a grocer. According to records held by Inner Temple in London (one of the four British Inns of Court that have had the exclusive right to appoint students to become lawyers at court), Helen, born in 1930, was the only daughter of a company director, Joseph Shore of Greenway, Wilmslow, Cheshire. The scant file on her includes the information that she attended Roedean School in Brighton and was admitted to the Inner Temple on March 17, 1948, at the age of eighteen—immediately upon graduation from the British equivalent of high school. In 1951, she was called to the bar and officially became a barrister.

For a man of this age to be called to the bar without attending university was unusual. For a woman, it was a major feat. Celia Pilkington, the archivist at Inner Temple said, "It is very unusual for a student at this period not to have attended university; she must have been a very exceptional student." That Helen attended Roedean School indicated that, in addition to being bright, she was the daughter of enlightened parents. Even if she had been a scholarship student, her attendance there would seem to indicate that someone had great ambitions for Helen—or at the very least was supportive of her ambitions.

The arrival of Helen—the blond, busty barrister with political connections—into Cheshire society in 1955 was met with a few raised eyebrows. "She looked like a brainless blonde, but was very, very clever. It was frightening to the women of Cheshire," said an old friend. "But she was brilliant. Had she remained in London she would have become a QC," meaning a Queen's Counsel or one of the top lawyers allowed to speak in court. But Helen was, depending on whom you ask, a "bright woman bored in Cheshire" or "a little bit of a joke" for she had channeled her substantial ambitions into navigating the social scene.

Isabella would later complain of her parents' taste, saying Evelyn "used to buy paintings from drugstores. Women weaving baskets. Noah's ark. It was really bad."[1] But that didn't stop Helen from entertaining.

When she issued invitations it wasn't just "do come round for dinner." It was "there will be dinner and then smoochies in the dining room." After the meal, she would turn off the dining room lights and everyone would dance with whoever took their fancy. No hard drugs, no orgies. It paled in comparison to what people used to get up to in Happy Valley, but it was enough to cause gossip about the various games that went on—all of which were far tamer than the Kenyan versions. Take "Blow the Feather." In Kenya, if a feather landed on you, you had to have sex with the person who'd blown it. In the Cheshire version, the assembled sat under a blanket and if the feather found its way to your lap, an item of clothing had to be removed.

Helen's husband loved every minute of it. "Evelyn just rubbed his hands together," said Penelope Bostock, a childhood friend of Evelyn's. "He couldn't believe his luck." While Evelyn was a flirt with "bedroom eyes," his behavior was generally regarded to have been better than Helen's. Perhaps it was his age—at forty he was fifteen years older than she. In an essay for a book called *Home*, Isabella wrote, "Neither of my parents had any interest in furnishings; they were socialites. They poured crème de menthe over each other every night."[2]

Into this lusty world came Isabella, their first child, on November 19, 1958. Isabella would later say, "My mother was expecting a boy and when I came out she didn't look at me for nine days." For a godmother, Helen and Evelyn chose Lady Lavinia Cholmondeley, their neighbor and the wife of the Sixth Marquess of Cholmondeley. Although she was a frequent visitor to their home for the dinner parties they would throw, she didn't consider herself a great friend. As it goes with godparents, the choice was likely made on the grounds that Lady Cholmondeley's husband was of a higher rank and more affluent than Sir Evelyn. But Isabella and her sisters were fond of Lady Cholmondeley, just as her children had only kind things to say about Helen, who frequently gave them little gifts.

The arrival of the first of their four children did little to stem the nocturnal activities of Evelyn and Helen. Isabella had what people of a certain age and class in Britain call a "traditional" childhood—"traditional" in the Edwardian sense—which meant that she was largely raised by nannies. Her parents were glamorous, mysterious figures who would dress the children up to pose for photographs by the famous fashion photographer of the day, Lenare, and then disappear off to their outings.

Three years after Isabella, in February 1961, came another girl, Julia. This was not good news. "Evelyn was desperate for a son," said Lady Cholmondeley. The Western world looks with distaste at the Chinese practice of favoring boy children; however, in England, even today, the female descendants of these great families are regarded as more decoration than anything else. The pride and future of the family rests upon having an heir—a male heir—to inherit the title as well as the estate. Even in the progressive 1960s, primogeniture remained the rule rather than the exception. Liza Campbell, daughter of the Twenty-fifth Thane of Cawdor and the last child to be born in Cawdor Castle in Scotland, wrote in a memoir of her childhood:

> *My father . . . always arranged to fly separately from Colin, but not from us. I vaguely understood that Colin was the "heir," but it was a wholly abstract concept . . . Girls were presumed to acquiesce innately to such bigotry, but it was like being invited to smile while swallowing gravel. There was absolutely no-one with whom I could discuss these tangled feelings. . . . If Colin and Fred had not been born or if they had died before they were able to produce sons of their own, the next nearest Cawdor male, however distinctly related, would be favored over [any girl] . . . As long as they had exterior genitalia, it was all theirs.*[3]

Isabella and Julia were tolerated by their mother and loved by their father, but their existence could in no way compensate for the lack of a son. When, on July 2, 1962, John Delves Broughton was finally born, it was no small matter. And, when, on September 12, 1964, he died, it was more than just a normal family tragedy.

When she spoke of it, Isabella almost always said the boy drowned. But he didn't. He choked. The difference is crucial. A small child drowning in this case would have been easily prevented, but a small child choking, less so. Accounts of the day vary, but the one thing that everyone present can remember is that the nanny had the day off. Other facts are easily established: Helen was four months pregnant with her fourth child. There were people coming over for dinner—or maybe a party. John had just eaten—reports say baked beans, but Helen told Lavinia Cholmondeley he was running around with a biscuit. Whatever the food, the boy choked. He was found in less than two inches of water in a shallow pool that Evelyn had been building for toy boats. Helen told Lady Cholmondeley that she thought the shock of the cold water on his bare feet caused him to breathe in sharply. Isabella later said in an interview, "It was awful. I can remember everything. The smell of the honeysuckle and him stretched out on the lawn. We were having our photographs taken and my mother had gone upstairs to put her lipstick on. I think that might have something to do with my obsession with lipstick." [4] (Julia later said she doesn't remember the incident at all; she'd read in the newspaper that she was there.) Isabella's mother later denied Isabella's account to a tabloid journalist: "This is an awful confounded lie. I'm afraid my daughter made it up. It never happened." [5] Isabella would obsess over the death of her little brother until the end of her life, bringing it up in interviews and constantly asking friends, "How can a child drown in two inches of water?" But he didn't drown. She must have known that. Isabella's husband knew it, her sisters knew it, her godmother knew it, so why did she persist in saying he drowned? Was it because she found him and felt responsible?

Whether or not Isabella was blamed directly for the boy's death, it affected relations between all of the members of the family. Until that time, the family had its dysfunctions—but within reason, within a sort of norm for families of that kind and of that time. Afterward, relations between them—particularly between Evelyn and Helen—quickly declined. Helen, as one would expect, took it particularly hard. "She [Helen] became very odd after the boy's death," said one of her former friends from Cheshire. The birth, on Valentine's Day 1965, of another girl, Lavinia, did little to lift spirits. "In Cheshire men don't value their daughters. Everything goes to the eldest son. Evelyn was particularly like that," said another Cheshire daughter. If Isabella, like Liza Campbell, with whom she would later become friends, hadn't realized it before, she couldn't escape it now. She later said, "I don't think [my parents] were so keen on us girls; they wanted a boy. We were lumped together as 'the girls.'"[6]

The psychology of a mother favoring a son over her daughters is even harder to understand given the feat Helen had achieved in being called to the bar so very young. However, her accomplishments did have an impact on her daughters: at a very young age they learned to say, "I want to be a barrister," if they needed pocket money.

In the year of Johnny's death, Isabella was attending Nuthurst Primary in nearby Nantwich, a quaint historical town with more government-protected buildings than any town in Cheshire outside of Chester, including the two-story, red brick building built in 1820 that had been used as a school since 1928. Affectionately known as "the Nuthouse," Nuthurst was a private day school for girls. "It taught you manners more than academics," said Alison Price, a former student in Isabella's era, who also claimed that one particular teacher didn't even bother grading their homework. "There was no science or anything like that. Instead we did cookery and dance." In that, it was an unremarkable education for girls of the time. The students, twelve to fifteen to a class, all came from comfortable backgrounds, the daughters of well-off farmers mixing easily with Isabella and her friend Gigi Callander, whose parents lived in a nearby twelfth-century abbey and were part of the same hunting and partying set. Gigi and Isabella were best friends into their teenage years. While Helen shared her distress over the loss of John with the parents of Isabella's friends, Isabella's friends remember nothing of the incident. "I don't remember her brother dying at all," said Callander, whose married name is Solomon. "Those days a lot was shielded from children." "I didn't realize things were quite miserable for her," said another student in Isabella's year at Nuthurst. "I just knew that she and Gigi were both from those estates." There were other differences their classmates did not notice. While most of the girls were dropped off and picked up by their parents, it was nannies who came to fetch Gigi and Isabella. "We grew up with nannies, with parents whom we saw just before they went to dinner. Our mothers would look fabulous and beautiful and our fathers were remote figures in suits," said Geraldine Harmsworth, a friend Isabella would make in her teens.

Isabella, then a wavy-haired little blonde, and the smallest in her class, would dress each day in her green uniform: a gingham check with contrasting white collar and cuffs for summer, and a green wool tunic for winter. On her head she wore a green beret until she was old enough to earn the requisite straw boater hat. Deviations were not allowed. No makeup, no jewelry. "Fashion didn't come into it," said Alison Price, Isabella's former schoolmate. "We had to wear the skirts a certain length, and that was it." Isabella had a cheerful, commanding presence that the Nuthurst school uniform could not hide. "She always seemed happy, confident and outgoing," said Price. "She was always fun and happy."

When does a little girl decide she is not beautiful? Tiny Isabella looked almost like a fairy with elfin ears and a palatable energy visible even in a photograph. Her Nuthurst classmates do not remember her being self-conscious. That would come later. It was her sense of fun and mischief that made her popular and memorable among her little peers at Nuthurst, and that was all Helen. "At Nuthurst we both had our gangs," said Solomon. "She always had many more people on her side. She was enormously popular and very cheeky."

The childhood games she'd play after school with Gigi had a fairy-tale quality to them. Yes, there were dress-up boxes, but theirs were filled with the Edwardian dresses and coats of their grandparents. There were play-houses, but Isabella's was a thirteenth-century tower. Play dates were held at Cholmondeley Castle, with a shy and terrified David Cholmondeley trying to hide from the raucous Isabella, or at the twelfth-century Combermere Abbey, where Isabella and Gigi would terrify their playmates by chasing them down its halls or darting along underground passages, beneath four hundred years of family crests, and through rooms once visited by Charles II, William of Orange, and Samuel Johnson. "We had naughty fun, lots of conspiracies," Solomon said. "We'd tell scary stories about ghosts in the house. Friends still remember us scaring them with tales."

Despite the tensions at home, these friends, these spectacular homes, made what might seem like an unhappy childhood quite fun. "If you're brought up on an estate, there's an infrastructure," said one of Isabella's friends. "It's about security. If you're out past six p.m., there's always someone around who will say 'you must go home.' It gave them [Isabella and her sisters] a sense of security and entitlement. Although they never saw their parents, ever, they didn't have an unhappy time."

But like a single cancer cell, the death of John had infected the family—and its destructive power was spreading. In the hours after school and away from her friends, it became more and more difficult for Isabella to ignore what was happening between her parents. "The death of the son had led to an estrangement between them," said an old friend of Evelyn's. A friend of Isabella's remembers Helen in the kitchen at one of the parties flirting with a man "in the most suggestive way. She had the most naughty laugh, and she was wonderfully outrageous," Isabella's friend recalled. "She was saying, 'Oh, darling!'" Her normal sort of bawdy talk ("Our parents were always talking about sex," Lavinia told a friend) took an even more outrageous tack. "She'd say the most scandalous things about the prime minister, Ted Heath," said a friend of Helen's. "I'm sure they were based on a bit of truth; she had worked in London, but it was shocking to hear someone speak about the prime minister in that way." (Ted Heath was a confirmed bachelor his entire life, and many suspected he might be gay. His biographer thought it more likely that he was asexual.)

As a way to escape from the strangeness of their home lives when they got older, the tow-headed Isabella and Gigi with her long dark locks transferred their love of the dressing-up box to a fondness for making discoveries at the local thrift shop, in part because they knew that wearing pillbox hats with veils at inappropriate occasions would vex their mothers, who wanted their daughters dressed conservatively. "Our mothers never bought us nice clothes," said Gigi. "We lived in postwar hand-me-downs." Isabella later said in an interview, "I was an anarchist at quite an early age. My mother was very bourgeois, and she hated the way I dressed. She still does."[7]

When it came time to pick a boarding school for Isabella, professional ambitions were not considered. Evelyn chose Heathfield because, he told his daughters, "it has the happiest, healthiest looking girls." Heathfield, unlike Helen's alma mater, Roedean, made little pretense at preparing girls for university. That was fine with Evelyn. "Only lesbians go to university," he said.

And it was pretty much his decision to make on his own. Relations between Helen and Evelyn never recovered after the death of John. In 1972, they decided to split for good, and Helen moved to London. "I was very angry with my mother," Isabella said. "I still am. She doesn't want to have anything to do with us."[8] Geraldine Harmsworth said, "When we talked to each other it always came back to this thing about our mothers. She knew I knew how lonely that felt." Lavinia told friends that she doesn't remember being told about the split between her parents, just that suddenly she was spending a lot more time with her mom—which wasn't necessarily a good thing. Isabella felt that Helen was preoccupied with her new suitors and setting up a new career. She'd gone back to work for her old boss, Quintin Hogg.

At Heathfield, Isabella would mingle not just with farmers' daughters but the daughters of aristocrats from the entire country. *Tatler*, the society magazine that would later employ her, says of the school, "Academically, it may not be in the top flight, but Heathfield is one of a kind. Pupils excel at smart sports: they flourish at the Inter-School Showjumping Competition, the lacrosse teams are mustard and the polo players regularly see off their rivals. . . . The upper sixth enjoy oodles of privileges, including . . . evenings in the pub across the road and the opportunity to meet urbane, well-behaved boys at socials with Eton, Harrow and Wellington."[9] Isabella was at the school when, in 1970, it made the radical decision that students would no longer be allowed to bring with them their own maids. One of Isabella's contemporaries remembers that in all her time at Heathfield, only one girl went on to university—and the whole school had an assembly to celebrate this remarkable achievement. One thing hadn't changed from her Nuthurst days: Isabella's parents did not drop her off. At age eleven, a member of the estate staff drove her to boarding school, where she would study until she was sixteen. Julia, who arrived at Heathfield three years later, was driven to school by the chauffeur of her mother's then-boyfriend. Their mother "thought us fortunate to have rides at all," Julia told a friend. From Evelyn's perspective, it wasn't a slight, just the way things were. His parents hadn't visited him once when he was at Eton, and one of his closest friends used to spend school holidays in a hotel.

Fun, outgoing, slightly naughty—these were the perfect traits for a successful boarding school career. "Isabella had a very boarding school side to her," said Sarah St. George, a friend Isabella made at the time. Other Heathfield alums found the school snobby and off-putting; not so Isabella, who thrived on the camaraderie. "It was very St. Trinian's," said St. George, speaking of the fictional boarding school from the 1950s films, where the behavior of the students was not just mischievous or capricious, but frequently criminal, and the teachers weren't much better. "We were never lonely. Everyone was always together. [Isabella] was always better if you surrounded her by people." Isabella's Heathfield school report read that she "occasionally talks too much, but it is always in a good cause."[10] She won the school cheerfulness prize three years in a row.

To indulge her growing love of costume, Isabella became the head of chapel, with the task of laying out the robes. "When I was at school, I became obsessed with God and the Church," she said. "I wanted to be a nun. I was only thinking of the habit, really—and I loved the ritual. The incense," she said.[11] The elaborate ceremony at Heathfield was the perfect conduit for her taste for pageantry. She said, "When you are little, church is the one place where your imagination can go crazy because there is nothing to do and you've got to sit in this place."[12] It provided something else: a chance to stay near the only man on campus, the priest, Richard Stride. Isabella would later write that she loved the priest Dick Stride. Sarah St. George pointed out that to call him the suggestive Dick instead of Richard was typically Issie. "He was the only man in the school," said St. George. "All the girls imagined that he was madly in love with them, that he was randy, and we'd conjecture the most outrageous things. 'Did you see what happened when Penelope dropped the pen?' " Isabella said, "I was so naughty. I used to lie in the chapel spread-eagled before the altar, all by myself. I did the most extraordinary things. I drank the blood of Christ—the wine left in the vestry—and I was sure that something dreadful would happen to me."[13]

When it came time to choose a school for Isabella's younger sister Lavinia, Helen decided against Heathfield, on the grounds that Isabella and Julia had had too good a time there—to the detriment of their studies. Instead, nine-year-old Lavinia was sent to her mother's alma mater, Roedean. Sarah St. George ran into Helen years later and told her she was a friend of Isabella's from Heathfield. "That school was the ruination of that girl," Helen snapped. By contrast, Isabella's friends claim she remembered it as a very happy time.

School breaks were spent either in Cheshire, where the teenage parties mimicked those of the adults, or in London. "We went to lots of teenage parties in Cheshire," said Gigi Solomon. "It was quite normal for our mothers to find us entwined with some handsome boy when they came to pick us up." Isabella was known among the Cheshire boys for being particularly affectionate. She'd inherited her mother's fondness for flirting—"I think inherently I'm probably a total slag,"[14] Isabella once said—traits that led to some unfortunate nicknames and, more seriously, her having at least three abortions, the first while still at Heathfield.

In London on weekends off from school, Gigi and Isabella could take advantage of the cultural offerings of the city. Gigi remembers being on the phone with Isabella in 1973, making plans to see the Steve McQueen/Dustin Hoffman film *Papillon*, when she heard a crash on the other end of the line and a yowl of horror. Isabella had stepped on the heavy curtains and pulled the valance down from the wall on top of her. From under the yards of damask silk, still holding the phone, she said, "Oh, my mother is going to kill me." "It was always chaos with Issie," said Solomon. "No matter how much she tried she was always leaving a trail of destruction."

Months before Isabella was due to graduate from Heathfield, she got another shock from home. The same year he finally divorced Helen, 1974, Evelyn announced he had met someone new. He and Rona Crammond, a divorcée, were both on trips around the Far East when they met. He was instantly taken with her. Like Helen, she was blond and busty and, although twenty-four years younger than he was, a force to be reckoned with. Evelyn had taken Isabella to Rona's house in Sussex to meet her, and the couple married two years later. "They were very much in love," said a friend. "He'd call her his Sussex chick."

The arrival of a stepmother into the lives of the teenage girls was never going to be easy, but for Isabella and Julia it meant more than just the loss of a father—they felt it meant the loss of the place they called home. Rona arrived from Sussex with three young daughters of her own. There weren't enough bedrooms in Doddington Park House for each of the six children to have her own, so Rona tried to persuade Evelyn either to extend the house—offering to pay for the addition—or turn the guest wing over to the girls. Evelyn refused both options, not seeing the point in extending the house when the children spent most of their time at boarding school, and insisting that the guest wing was for guests. "As a child he had been turned out of his room for guests," Rona said. "So that was how he wanted it."

The girls, and many of the people who had been friendly with Helen and Evelyn, thought the main attraction for Rona was Evelyn's money. But she had her own assets and, according to Rona, Evelyn didn't have much money. "All of his cash went in the divorce," she said. "He had the land and the houses on it." On their honeymoon, Evelyn decided he should have the varicose vein on his ankle removed. Back in Cheshire he had the operation—with disastrous consequences. His leg became infected with gas gangrene and ultimately was amputated above the knee. He spent months in intensive care, with only Rona to care for him. Treatment called for the wound to be left open without a bandage—something Rona didn't think the children should see, so she took care of him herself. Suddenly Evelyn was completely dependent on his new young wife—and she felt utterly alone in Cheshire. "The dynamics changed when he lost the leg," said a friend close to the couple.

However it may have appeared to the outside world, Evelyn was still very much in love with his new, young wife and vice versa. "To be with an older man . . . ," Rona said, "the way his eyes lit up when I entered a room. I hadn't had it before and I haven't had it since."

Rather than acknowledge the bond between her father and his new wife, Isabella tried to dismiss it. Isabella had been born with a naturally creative nature and as life became difficult, rather than confronting uncomfortable situations—something discouraged by her upbringing—she retreated into fantasy. Given her family dynamics, that fantasy could be exceedingly appealing. And if Isabella tended to embellish a bit for dramatic effect, what of it? Now she seized on the shortage of bedrooms and the encroaching influence of an "evil stepmother" as a way to avoid spending holidays in Cheshire. Instead, she'd go to the highlands of Scotland, where her aunt Rosamond lived with Lord Lovat, a war hero and the esteemed head of the Fraser clan. "They lived in Beauly Castle and had pipers and things. We couldn't offer anything like that," said Rona. Evelyn was upset that Isabella wouldn't be home for Christmas, but doubly upset to find she was telling people that she was no longer welcome at home. "We were very sad not to have her, but we couldn't compete," said Rona. Isabella was besotted with Scotland and the cousins she found there—and they with her. Her cousin Benjie Fraser's father was brother to Lord Lovat and remembers going to visit for Christmas to meet the head of the clan and "be the entertainment." "Not needed," he said. "Issie was already running the entertainment . . . The warmth was palpable." And also savory: Benjie found Isabella persuading her war hero uncle to put crème de menthe liqueur in his morning porridge. She'd convince her cousins to do things considered cliché by some Scots—planning hunts for the Loch Ness monster or encouraging the men to don their clan kilts.

Upon graduation from Heathfield, Isabella was at a loss as to what to do next. Had she been five years older, she almost certainly would have been paraded on the debutante circle in hopes of landing her a suitable mate. But since the end of the war, the prestige of that process had been on a downward slide. Princess Margaret explained that they had to put an end to presenting the young debs to the queen at court because "every tart in London was getting in." At only sixteen, Isabella was still too young to be married and too cool to want a coming-out party. She was from too conservative a family to consider university—and, with the shortage of bedrooms, she felt she was unwelcome at home. After a last-minute scramble, it was decided that she'd spend a year learning shorthand and typing at secretarial college in Oxford. It was a not unusual choice for girls of her background, and it had several advantages. The Oxford location meant she would be able to mingle with boys—potential husbands—who shared her background. Not just those at Oxford, but those at Oxford who had previously studied at Eton, the British private school known for educating the country's, and the world's, elite. The aristocracy in Britain may have fallen from the front pages, but Eton survives as the only place a certain set will consider sending their sons—and the only fit place for their daughters' husbands to have studied. Perhaps paradoxically, this snob appeal is matched by academic prowess: the school still turns out some of the brightest alumni in the country. (Nineteen prime ministers went to Eton, including the current, David Cameron.) The skills Isabella would learn at secretarial school would enable her to get a job in the City, London's financial district, where she might meet a husband, if she didn't leave Oxford with one. Isabella enrolled at Oxford and County Secretarial School, took a room in a house on Blenheim Road, and set about the far more entertaining task of meeting the friends she would have for the rest of her life.

"There were a group of girls who went to these secretarial colleges for about a year. They knew quite a few of the undergraduates, particularly the Etonians at Christ Church," said Richard Neville-Rolfe, who was there at the time. "They knew them socially from before they went up to Oxford. So they fitted in pretty well and were an important part of the social scene. They were really good fun. On the whole they were more fun than the undergraduates. Because the majority [of these boys] had come from an all-male background it was much easier for them to socialize with people they knew already rather than getting to know girls at the university."

The combination was a heady one. When Andy Warhol had the launch party for his book of photographs of society friends, *Andy Warhol's Exposures*, he had it not in London but in Oxford. When Nick Ashley, a friend of Isabella's, asked Warhol why, he said, "My book is all about young beautiful people and this room is filled with young beautiful people." Beautiful people who knew how to have a good time. "One didn't really go to many classes," said Neville-Rolfe. "It wasn't part of the done thing. You might meet up at lunchtime or go to a party in the evening. The parties were pretty wild. [Isabella] wasn't living a genteel life of dinner parties particularly. We weren't old fogies."

Many of the boys Isabella and her friends hung out with were part of notorious Oxford institutions—the Bullingdon Club, the Dangerous Sports Club, and the Piers Gaveston Club. All three celebrated hedonistic behavior of one kind or another. In 1913, the *New York Times* wrote that "The Bullingdon represents the acme of exclusiveness at Oxford; it is the club of the sons of nobility, the sons of great wealth; its membership represents the 'young bloods' of the university."[15] It also was famous for raucous drunken dinner parties after which, quite frequently, not a piece of glass or china was left intact. The lesser-known Dangerous Sports Club began in the late 1970s, when Oxford students began attempting feats such as bungee jumping or skiing while playing a grand piano that slid down the mountain in front of them. At the Piers Gaveston Club cross-dressing parties were attended by the likes of Hugh Grant and Valentine Guinness, son of Lord Moyne, where the men would sport hats to rival those Isabella would wear in her heyday.

Partying in England in the late 1970s, as in America, took on a new dimension with the introduction and widespread use of hallucinogenic drugs. Many of Isabella's friends and family members developed serious addictions to heroin. Nick Ashley once went to a Piers Gaveston Club party dressed as a joint. More recently he staged an exhibition of photographs he took from that era. "The key attributes of a heroin addict are too much money and too much time," he said. "Of the people in my photographs, all the ones who qualified are now dead." The drug's effects had a huge appeal for children raised with distant parents. "It's like a hug," said one of Isabella's friends. "These children were raised so badly. They were so not loved. There was nothing friendly going on." But Isabella herself didn't need heroin. She had a natural energy and imagination that negated the need for heavy-duty hallucinogens. She lived a natural fantasy life; she didn't need to partake in a chemically induced one. Others might cloak their pain with drugs and drink. Isabella would cloak hers in coats, hats, and imaginary circumstances. Sarah St. George remembers that around this time, Isabella spent £500—the last of her spending money—on a picnic basket from the luxury emporium Asprey, complete with Wedgewood plates. When St. George asked her why she would do such a thing, Isabella said, "It's for me and my lover." St. George asked, "What lover?" Isabella said, "I haven't found him yet."

Her eccentricity made her intoxicating to be around, and was also self-fulfilling. The more interesting she looked, and the more compelling her stories, the more interesting people wanted to be around her. "She was a fire starter," said Ashley. "Someone you can't pigeonhole. It's better to get behind them and enjoy the ride on their coattails."

Despite her knack for attracting friends, Isabella developed insecurities about her looks in her teenage years, at a time when she was actually very pretty. Reality had nothing to do with it—hating the way she looked was a manifestation of something else, of an internal self-loathing she would struggle against for the rest of her life. One night Isabella, Richard Neville-Rolfe, and Liza Campbell were standing in suburban Uxbridge on the side of the M40 highway waiting to hitch a ride to Oxford. Isabella, dressed in a bit of disintegrating fabric held together with a safety pin, announced to those assembled that she was going to hide, because "otherwise no one will pick us up." She claimed she was too ugly to get a lift. Neville-Rolfe hid, too—everyone knew cars were less likely to stop for men. Campbell, a pretty blonde, took her place as bait along the side of the road. Before long a car pulled over, and the other two emerged. "As soon as we were in the car, Issie was the life and soul of it," Campbell remembers. "She comes in and completely bowls over this person, who turns out to be Richard Branson. We were saying, 'What do you do?' He said, 'I have this little company called Virgin,' and we said, 'Oh, we've heard of that.' And then he asked us to a party. I think I would have been terribly shy and sat there quietly. But [Issie] was effusive, full of beans."

Even in the unlikely event that Isabella's looks might have stopped her getting a lift, it never seemed to stop her getting good-looking boyfriends.

"She was always looking for affirmation, and there wasn't enough in the world for her," said a friend. "She liked very good-looking men. She was attracted to beauty because she thought she was ugly." Her first serious boyfriend was an Oxford undergrad, William Leigh, whom almost everyone remembers as dark, handsome, and possessing an air of danger. "He was a wild creature, with long black hair and lots of swagger," said Lucy Birley, whom Isabella befriended in that era. If Isabella had a knack for finding trouble on a small scale, William took it to greater heights. She was living with him in a basement flat on Oakley Street after Oxford. One night after a dinner party, Leigh spotted a black plastic sofa in the lobby of an apartment building. "I want it," he declared. Isabella, Liza Campbell, and two other female friends were recruited to carry it from King's Road. Halfway to their destination, the police caught up with and arrested them. "I think the judge thought it had to be a prank," said Campbell. "Actually, it wasn't. We really did want that sofa. But that was what it was like with Will Leigh. You were in a lift with him and the next thing you were arrested."

In her post–secretarial school phase, Isabella took a number of jobs in London, most of them not secretarial. She worked as a house cleaner, in a shop selling scones, in a posh boutique on Sloane Street, and in Laura Ashley, the chic paradise of floral prints started by Nick's mother. Whatever the jobs were, they were never as important as her social life. In this she was not alone. One friend said, "With me, if I had a job and it interrupted something I wanted to do, then I would just quit. 'I'm out of here.'" To take a serious job as, say, an entry-level executive in advertising, would have been unthinkable to a girl of Isabella's background. To launch oneself onto a career path said to the world, "I *have* to work for a living." To take jobs that might seem lower class—such as cleaning or childcare— said, "I won't be doing this for long." The jobs had added benefits for someone as strapped and as addicted to clothes as Isabella. "We nicked things like you would not believe," said one friend. "Issie worked at a shop in Sloane Street and we came to pick her up and she said, 'There's a rubbish sack around the back. I just have to take that.' And it was absolutely full of clothes. It was a rather grown-up boutique, so it was stuff we struggled to wear." Even then (and with questionable ownership rights), Isabella displayed great generosity. Urging friends to take items they thought beyond their ability to carry off, she'd say, "Oh, that would suit you." Although her friends noticed that Isabella dressed unconventionally, she wasn't so far out of step with her time. "I deeply regret having worn some clothes, like the dungarees I wore from the early-1970s boutique Mr. Freedom," she said. "For my eighteenth birthday I wore a frilly black and electric-blue tango dress—really ugly. And I'm not proud that I once owned a fringed cowgirl jacket."[16]

Her peripatetic work life was matched by her home life. For four years after she finished her course at Oxford, she lived in London with her boyfriend William Leigh; in the homes of her girlfriends Lucy Birley, Liza Campbell, and Zara Metcalfe; or with her sister Julia in a basement flat on Horton Street that their father bought. "She called it Horny Street," said Campbell. Isabella had inherited her mother's fondness for shocking others. "She had a huge streak of vulgarity," Campbell said of Isabella. "She often made me flinch with her very bawdy streak." The "Horny Street" flat became a crash pad for the Oxford boys who were in from London. "It was a place we would all go and hang out," said Richard Neville-Rolfe. Technically inhabited by a revolving cast of teenage girls, the two-bedroom flat was messy, with no nice furniture and lots of clothes everywhere. "A lot of people from Oxford would come down and crash there for parties and stuff," said Lucy Birley. "It was extremely untidy and mad." And if there was no room at Horny Street, Isabella would arrive on a doorstep of a friend and ask to stay, bringing with her a bulging suitcase full of lace and other strange bits of fabric that, to her, constituted the makings of a wardrobe.

The bawdy streak, the insecurity, the naughtiness, the vivid imagination, and the love of clothes—they had been planted in Isabella before, but out in the world, without the protection of the estate, without

guidance from a supportive mother, without the regularity and the camaraderie of boarding school, these traits began to show themselves in
full spectrum. And all of the mechanisms Isabella had been quietly adopt-
ing to cope with her tumultuous childhood were the same characteristics
that made her so much fun to be around. She wasn't so much an eccentric
as an exhibitionist. "I think [her bawdy streak] was a way of breaking down
barriers with people," said Birley. "You wouldn't get away with it now, but
things weren't so boring then." The group of teens would often go on
shooting weekends at the home of one of their parents. When the adults
went to sleep, the cocktails would come out. Then the assembled would
begin to encourage Isabella to do her trademark dance: the dance of the
seven veils. Somewhat ironically for a woman who became famous for her
clothes, it was taking them off that first made her the center of attention.
"She was brilliant at it," said Birley. "I think she really enjoyed it. She was
excited by that kind of thing."

When Isabella would arrive at a friend's house for the weekend, the
first thing she'd do is head straight for the kitchen to talk to the staff working there. Detmar Blow would later say to friends, "Wasn't Isabella so good
with the help?" And she was. She genuinely enjoyed the company of the
people who worked at these houses and, later, at Hilles. To mingle with the
workers was normal for members of Isabella's class. Her father would often
go to the pub with the man who ran the grounds at Doddington Hall. But
would he invite the same man to his private London club? No. (On the other
hand, members of the middle class were to be strictly avoided. To be caught
having drinks with those nameless, faceless men in bad suits one saw on the
sidewalks was unthinkable.)

After her year at Oxford, Isabella moved to London where she enrolled at another secretarial school, this time with Lucy Birley. "My father
had this obsession that I should type and then I should be able to get a job,
and her father was the same," said Birley. The two were not the best students, constantly in trouble for being late to class and frequently showing
up in the clothes they had been wearing the night before. "The teacher

didn't like the way we dressed," Birley said. "We didn't follow fashion. We would go to lots of vintage shops instead. We didn't have money to go and buy expensive clothes. We had to go to Cornucopia or Kensington Market or borrow things from our parents and throw things together. There was a lot of borrowing and swapping of things." Birley had grown up in a large house on Campden Hill Road in Kensington. When Isabella was living there, Lucy's mother noticed that she had highs and lows and that there was no middle ground. "That sort of pattern was clearly there very early on, but nobody saw it," said Birley. "It took an adult to notice it."

Isabella herself didn't recognize what was happening, but that would change when she met the man who would become her first husband. After two years, she and William Leigh broke up. Within a couple of years, she fell in love with yet another Oxford man, Nick Taylor. Tayles, as Isabella called him, was, said Birley, "a star on the rise. He was an amazing tennis player. Not at all like some of his un-muscular flabby friends who would serve underarm." Taylor came from a family impressive for its accomplishments. His parents were both Oxford academics, and his older brother went on to be a professional backgammon player and commodities broker. Isabella's friends remember Taylor as being a sensitive and kind man who was somewhat in the shadow of his brother, and who would spend much of his adult life battling depression. He was very amused by Isabella, entranced by her seemingly endless amounts of energy, and he wanted to look after her. "I thought it was a very good relationship," said Birley. "He was her first true love." Isabella was mad about him, and he was mad about her. Together they'd go to the debutante balls that some of their friends were hosting at the time. When they arrived late to one black-tie dinner, at a stately home in the middle of England, Isabella rushed in and said to those assembled, "Sorry we're late. We stopped in a field for a shag. Look! There are grass stains on my knees." Taylor would stand behind her giggling as the room erupted.

When Isabella, yet again, needed a new place to live, Taylor approached a new acquaintance, Zara Metcalfe, who had a flat on The Little Boltons. "He rang and said, 'Would you mind if my girlfriend moved into your flat? She needs someplace to live.'" Metcalfe thought it a little unusual, given that she didn't know Nick all that well, but she agreed to meet the girlfriend. Isabella arrived, this "weird" creature wearing a suit, high heels, and a hat. "She was completely eccentric and original and terribly, terribly warm," Metcalfe said. "You couldn't not like her." Isabella moved in, rent-free, and would regale Metcalfe every evening with stories about Taylor and their fantastic sex life.

Upon graduation from Oxford, Taylor decided he'd go to Midland, Texas, to seek his fortune by setting up an oil business. The price of the commodity had been skyrocketing, and Midland was a key place to be if one wanted in on the action. Six months after moving in with Zara Metcalfe, Isabella announced she was going to New York to be closer to Nick. Zara was dumbfounded. She couldn't imagine life in London, much less her flat, without Isabella in it. "She said she was going to New York to be near him," Metcalfe said. "I said, 'Well, I am going to New York to be near you.'"

Biting
the
Big Apple

CHAPTER FOUR

Finally Isabella was given an assignment more interesting than answering the phones. Diana Vreeland, the director of the Costume Institute at the Metropolitan Museum of Art, was putting on an exhibition called Man and the Horse, *featuring famous people in their riding gear. Isabella's close friend Natasha Grenfell was working with Diana on the exhibition, and Isabella had been asked by her boss, Anna Wintour, to find some photographs that would work for a corresponding feature in* Vogue. *She contacted Simon Blow, another Brit who had edited a book called* Fields Elysian: A Portrait of Hunting Society, *and told him she wanted one of his pictures from it to run in* Vogue. *"The official fee was two hundred dollars," said Simon. "Issie said, 'That's far too little,' and moved it to four hundred."*

U nlike immigrants of an earlier era, when Isabella arrived in New York City in 1979 she wasn't tired or poor, or part of the huddled masses historically drawn there "yearning to breathe free." It was love, culture, curiosity, and money that drove her to America's shore. Isabella, who had been dubbed Issie the Wizzy around this time, and her London roommate Zara Metcalfe, whom Isabella had taken to calling Za Za Gabor, moved into a high-rise apartment in the West Village with Catherine Oxenberg, the daughter of Princess Elizabeth of Yugoslavia.

Catherine was then working as a model, but would go on to star in the major TV hit show *Dynasty*. Unable to work legally without a visa, Isabella enrolled at Columbia University to study Oriental Art.

On the surface, life in New York was not all that different from life in London. Days were spent doing odd jobs—the only kind they could get without visas—and nights were spent socializing with a group of expat Brits they knew from London. Of the flatmates, "Catherine was the only one who had money. The others were living on what they earned," said Natasha Grenfell, another London friend, and they weren't earning as much as the famous model.

Grenfell was living in the Upper East Side brownstone of Fred Hughes, Andy Warhol's manager. "We called it the English Hotel," said Grenfell. "It was where all the English people would go and stay." Through Grenfell they got to meet some of the most famous artists of the day: Andy Warhol and Jean-Michel Basquiat. "I knew all that set because I was Fred's date to all those flipping functions," said Grenfell. At one of those functions Andy Warhol approached Isabella, who happened to be wearing two different-colored Manolo Blahnik shoes—one pink, one purple. He said, "Wow. Do you have to buy two pairs to do that?" Isabella replied that, well, yes, she did. In actuality, it was far more likely that she'd lost one somewhere along the way and, rather than throw away a single shoe, decided to do what she could with three. In later years, when Andy would visit London, Isabella would play a hand in seeing he was properly entertained during his trip, arranging dinners and taking him to the city's hot night spots.

Most evenings were spent in the company of Lord David Ogilvy, heir to a sixteenth-century, thirty-thousand-acre Scottish estate and a god-son of the queen, and David MacMillan, heir to the publishing empire. Nights out revolved around dinner at Mortimer's, on Lexington Avenue and Seventy-fifth, a small, plain, brick-walled Upper East Side institution owned by Glenn Bernbaum and run along the lines of a private English club. People not known to the owner were often turned away. "It was full of snobby Americans and English people," said Metcalfe. Night after night the assembled would complain about how they missed England. "I was getting a bit fed up," said Metcalfe. "I didn't come to New York to talk about nannies and shoots at a snobby hamburger bar."

Isabella was getting fed up, too—of not being with Nick Taylor. She spent hours every night on the phone to him in Texas. "It was very intense and romantic," said Metcalfe. One night Isabella phoned her father with some big news: She was moving to Texas. Not Dallas, Texas—the site of the well-known, eponymous TV show that glamorized big hair and all things associated with big oil money—but Midland, originally called Midway, thanks to its being equidistant between Fort Worth and El Paso.

Despite its location in the middle of nowhere and lacking the glamorous cachet of Dallas, Texans knew that Midland was where the *real* money in the state was. It had been the administrative center of the West Texas region since 1923 when oil was discovered there. The fate of the city and the wealthy lawyers and bankers who worked there rose and fell with the fortunes of the petroleum industry.

In 1981, when Isabella arrived in Midland to be with Nick, who was trying to start his own business, the city was booming, thanks to the Arab oil embargo that had led to skyrocketing prices for crude oil. The price of a barrel of oil reached a new high of forty dollars that year, and tens of thousands of people were moving to Midland with dreams of striking gold in oil. Between 1980 and 1983, nearly twenty-two thousand people moved there. The city was unprepared for the boom, and less fortunate newcomers than Isabella and Nick were living in tents, cars, and trucks while they looked for housing—which was being rapidly built.

Although Midland shared something like a common language with London or New York, it was hard to imagine a place more culturally different. Whereas Isabella had frequently been surrounded by treasured furnishings that had been passed down through generations and works of art that were hundreds of years old, she now was amazed by the fact that the local wives redecorated their homes each year, buying completely new furnishings from top to bottom. According to Isabella, of particular pride to the women of Midland were their collections of crystal ornaments.

Though Neiman Marcus, the famous Dallas department store, valued its key clients in Midland enough to fly merchandise in by private jet, this didn't make the city a style capital. It was still primarily a jeans-and-boots kind of a town. One Texan retailer said, "These are folks who spend their money on land, lots of it. They have always had the resources for couture clothing, but it just does not go with the lifestyle. But diamonds? They always work with denim."

The primary weekend diversion was not lavish hunt balls or even shopping or line dancing, but watching and talking American football—high school football. So committed to local teams were they in this part of Texas that, as depicted in the film *Friday Night Lights*, it was possible for the high school football coach to earn more than the school's principal.

Isabella tried to fill her days as best she could. She enrolled in a course in interior design and took a number of jobs, including travel agent, interior designer, and shop assistant at a Guy Laroche boutique. There, she told friends, she would spend her days reading *War and Peace* while waiting for the odd customer to come in and occasionally glancing up to watch tumbleweeds blow past the open door. "Who wants to live in Texas and drive into a Guy Laroche shop?" she said. "They'd rather fly to Europe and get to Chanel."[1] She also started teaching herself English history, beginning with Henry VIII and reading two books on each monarch. At night she would often go to the home of one of her new American friends, watch *Dallas* on TV, have her nails done, keep everyone in stitches, then report it all to her British friends. "She said she'd tell them the most filthy jokes," said Metcalfe. "They adored her." She would also take in whatever cultural offerings were available in the state. When she went to Dallas to see an exhibition of El Greco she sent postcards from the exhibit back to her friends in London.

Shortly after she arrived in Texas, Isabella phoned Cheshire late one night, waking her father and stepmother with another surprise. She and Taylor had gotten married. Evelyn was upset; he'd met Nick only once. The wedding was a simple service, done by a justice of the peace in a Midland courthouse with little fuss in part because it was a marriage of convenience. Taylor had become a naturalized U.S. citizen and, although they were madly in love, Isabella's need of a U.S. visa and Taylor's American passport were the immediate factors that had led to their engagement. And there were certain tax benefits to be had if she was in the United States legally. Evelyn had been due to inherit a family trust, and he decided to pass it directly to his daughters, thereby helping them save on future inheritance tax. If one of them was a non-domiciled Brit, i.e., not living in the United Kingdom, even more money could be saved on taxes. Isabella had volunteered, but what started out to be good for the family turned out to be bad for her siblings. Thanks to her lavish spending habits, her sisters would not see their share of the money from the trust.

Still, marriage to a man she loved and a substantial private income couldn't hide Isabella's apathy for the place in which she was living. She complained to her friends that she felt cut off from them, and from culture in general. Things got even worse. The oil boom burst in 1982. The price of oil fell to eleven dollars a barrel and drastically altered both the fate of Midland and the likelihood of Taylor's success. Three banks in the city failed in 1983, and the newly constructed homes and office buildings stood empty as businesses and the people who had arrived to work in them left as quickly as they had come.

The decline hit Taylor hard. His dreams of making a fortune in oil were dashed. On top of this, Isabella was having serious health problems, making her even less able than she might have been to boost her husband's spirits. In February 1982, she was diagnosed with Crohn's disease, a serious intestinal disorder. "Just my luck," she told her friend Liza

Campbell. "I look like a hag and now I have this disease that is named after a hag." She had visited doctors in the UK, but the condition had been undiagnosed. Three months after she arrived in Midland, she began to get frequent stomach pain and eventually was unable to keep down a glass of water without being sick. She and Nick flew to Houston to see a doctor who operated immediately. The diagnosis came later. Surgery for the disease called for a portion of her lower intestine to be removed as well as a blockage between her upper and lower intestines. The procedure left her with a seven-inch scar across her middle which she'd complain about for the rest of her life.

Her illness was exacerbated by her father's seeming lack of sympathy. While she was in the hospital in Texas, he was on holiday in Barbados. When she asked why he hadn't rung, he said he didn't have her number. When she suggested that a trip to Barbados might help her recuperate, he told her there was not enough room.

By March 1983, it was time to give up on Midland and on oil. Isabella wrote to Liza Campbell in a letter Anna Wintour read at her memorial service, "We are leaving this den of doom and heading for New York and I am over the moon. Please, please can you send me the Piero de Monzi skirt as I have missed it so much, and insure it for £150,000."

Back in New York things began to look up. Taylor took a job with Salomon Brothers. With the money from the trust, he and Isabella put a deposit on a brownstone apartment at 51 Charles Street in the West Village and while renovations were being done on their new apartment, they took a flat uptown. Isabella described the finished apartment in the book *Home*:

> It was a classic—the first floor of a brownstone. It had a beautiful square drawing room, lovely light. I knocked through the two bedrooms and had a huge four-poster bed and big cupboards for my clothes. That was the first time I really had somewhere. The flat was on the wild side, but very classic. I had a Mary Fox Linton black-and-white sofa. I

cooked—I love cooking—and I had a very modern galley kitchen with a black rubber floor.[2]

Once ensconced inside, Nick and Isabella entered what appeared from the outside to be a state of domestic bliss. Zara Metcalfe said, "It was the most stable they'd been. It was very much about him being responsible and having to make mortgage payments. I remember Nick showing me around the flat and being hugely proud." As before, Isabella's closest friends were English, as was her lifestyle. "I remember throwing dinner parties and being desperate for her to arrive," said Metcalfe. "I knew as soon as she entered everyone would have fun." Isabella's excuse for being late: "I'm so sorry I'm late, I was having sex. He insisted on doing it doggie style," and she'd drop to all fours to demonstrate. "There were no limits to her jokes," said Metcalfe. Taylor would be roaring with laughter. She was still fond of an impromptu striptease. Frequently, at restaurants or dinner parties, she'd simply decide to remove her top. "I don't think she was a sex maniac," said Metcalfe. "It was about being provocative." Another friend, Michael Zilkha, said, "I remember once sitting at the front table at Nicola's and her volunteering to the owner that she would show her breasts in return for a bottle of champagne, and the transaction being duly consummated. Izzy [sic] was incredibly sexy in her *jolie laide* way, and at that time quite confident of her desirability."

On Sunday afternoons, Isabella would cook an old-fashioned English lunch, with all the traditional fare: roast beef with roasted potatoes, vegetables, gravy, and horseradish sauce. "You just didn't get that in New York," said Birley.

The circle of Brits in New York had become more interesting since her first stay in the city. Her close friend Lucy Birley, who had married the pop star Bryan Ferry at the same time Isabella married Taylor, had moved to New York and was living in a brownstone on nearby West Twelfth Street. "There was a whole English group of artists that we hung out with," said Birley. "It wasn't a particularly fashion-y scene."

In 1983, most of the designers making it big in America made nice clothes, but led sedate lives. American fashion at the time was dominated by really ambitious and hardworking professionals, led by Ralph Lauren, who was the sole sponsor of the *Man and the Horse* exhibition at the Met, and followed in importance by Calvin Klein and Donna Karan. Halston had begun to decline due to a series of business mistakes, and Isaac Mizrahi would not appear on the scene until the end of the decade. Isabella said, "It was that whole art scene that really appealed to me; the clothes just sort of followed on."[3] Fashion, as seen on the runways, hadn't played a big part in her life at that point, but art had. She'd grown up surrounded by it, with museum-quality portraits hanging on the walls of her friends' homes. Liza Campbell said, "She was the only person I know who would go to art galleries and you'd see tears coursing down her face. Whether it was pre-Raphaelite or a woman in a tower or anything gothic, she'd be really properly moved."

Anna Wintour, a fellow Brit and part of Isabella's extended circle (Lucy and Bryan Ferry were renting a brownstone owned by Wintour's husband), had recently been made creative director of American *Vogue*, a new position that had been created just for her. According to Wintour, a British restaurateur, Brian McNally, told her "about this fabulously eccentric creature" who worked as the coat check girl at one of entrepreneur Ian Schrager's nightclubs. Isabella recounted the story differently, telling one friend she was working as a waitress in a Hamburger Heaven when Bryan Ferry came in and got her a job with Anna Wintour; to another she said she was selling scones on the street when Ferry found her. Later she wrote in the book *When Philip Met Isabella* that she was selling apricot-studded scones in a food shop, La Manga, until she was introduced to Anna Wintour by Bryan and Lucy Ferry. Whatever the reality, an interview with Wintour was organized.

Wintour had been at *Vogue* since October 1983, but her tenure there was born of conflict. At the time she was brought in, *Vogue* was edited by Grace Mirabella. But Wintour wasn't hired by Mirabella, and she wasn't wanted by Mirabella. It was Alexander Lieberman, Condé Nast's artistic director, who had hired Wintour. He and Si Newhouse, the owner of Condé Nast, had a fondness for pretty English editors (they had already hired Tina Brown away from *Tatler*), and they wanted Wintour in the Condé Nast stable. But they weren't convinced she was ready for the top job at *Vogue*, so they concocted a new title to go with the perilous—but at $125,000 a year, well-paid—post: creative director. Wintour had interviewed with Grace Mirabella earlier, but the two failed to bond after Wintour told her that the job she most wanted at *Vogue* was Grace's. Now Mirabella had to face that she was working with an openly declared rival in her midst. Wintour had one completely loyal friend on the inside, the assistant she had brought with her from *New York* magazine, Laurie Schechter. The stress of the situation led to two key turns of events: by the time Isabella came in for her interview, Wintour had been removed from having anything to do with the fashion pages, and her hardworking assistant, Laurie Schechter, had been promoted to overseeing photographers and the shoots for the front pages of the magazine. Wintour was looking for someone to take over Schechter's more menial tasks, and Isabella was invited to interview for the position.

On February 2, 1984, after meeting Anna, Isabella described the interview process in a letter to Liza Campbell. An edited version was read by Anna at Isabella's memorial service :

> *I am waiting all day for Anna Wintour to take me on at* Vogue. *So far I've seen one of the toughest girls in the dizzy world of fashion, but I'm positive if this job doesn't work out she will have elephantine memories of my superb interview. The fashion world is definitely "me." I lied like the devil on my resume; I said that I'd been to London University, etc.*

Wintour has compared her staffing of *Vogue* to casting a film, praising her employees as much for their individuality as their specific skills. Isabella played her part to perfection. Noticing a biography of the writer Vita

Sackville-West on Anna's desk, she told Wintour, "I've cried each of the three times I've read it," simultaneously (though unintentionally) demonstrating both emotional sensitivity and highly sophisticated cultural taste. "Issie," the ever-rational Wintour replied, "there's nothing to cry about." Then she gave her the job.

But there *were* things in the biography for Isabella to cry about. In some ways Vita Sackville-West's life ran parallel to Isabella's. Vita lost the stately home in which she grew up just as Isabella lost Doddington Hall. Vita spent her life married to a man with whom she felt a closer intellectual bond than a physical one, as Isabella would say of her relationship with Detmar Blow. Both attracted legions of admirers who were drawn to them by their strength, and both exuded an air of belonging to another era. Both had tricky relationships with their mothers, and both enjoyed dressing in outlandish costumes—though, in Vita's case, it was often the clothes of a man.

The job at American *Vogue* was Isabella's first step toward becoming a fashion personality, but that didn't mean she was particularly good at it. When she began work there, she was given a desk outside Wintour's office and directly next to Laurie Schechter. Her tasks were relatively simple ones: taking messages, sending and retrieving items sent by courier, going through the post, having Wintour's shoes reheeled. It was a job that required exponentially more organizational ability than it did creativity, and in that it was the worst job possible for the chaotic Dizzy Issie, as she was known in *Vogue*'s halls. Isabella said she was "very frightened" by Wintour's "organization and steely determination. When someone rang up, Wintour put the message in a folder. Everything would be filed, every conversation would be filed, every single piece of paper," [4] Isabella said. Although she was scared by Wintour's rigor, it was also reassuring to work for someone who knew so clearly what she wanted. "It was just incredible," Isabella said later, in one of her typically altered reflections. "Those were the best years of my life working with Anna. I learned so much. She taught me to be efficient and to have passion, to be responsible and reliable. And to have a great sense of humor. What people don't realize is that Anna has a cracking sense of humor."[5]

The appeal of the job wasn't just working in fashion and it wasn't just working for Anna Wintour; it was working at Condé Nast, a family-owned company known for its generous benefits. (Recently editors attending an event in Washington, D.C., received an e-mail message reminding them that the maximum they could expense for the evening was $1,000 per person.)[6] For a British import, corporate life in America must have seemed like a family unit. The company provided the things that good parents do for children: health care, food, security, a sense of belonging. In exchange, all you had to do was show up and perform reasonably well. Nowhere was this more the case than at Condé Nast. Isabella's salary may have been small, but she was instantly part of a certain set—a class, if you will—of editorial employee. If corporations were titled families, Condé Nast was up there with the Windsors. When Isabella needed to collect Wintour's shoes, she would have done so in a chauffeured-driven town car. If she spent her lunch hour at her desk, Condé Nast would pick up the tab—even if she spent most of that time talking on the phone to her friends. If she had lunch out with a famous friend every once in a while, Condé Nast would have paid for that, too. Wintour's office would have been inundated with invitations to the best cultural offerings and the most exclusive parties New York had to offer. And the city had an army of publicists who would bend over backward to make the top editors—and their representatives—happy. Free meals, chauffeured-driven cars, ample socializing—all in all, it wasn't unlike the life of a rich aristocrat in England. The problem Isabella had was that within the Condé Nast aristocracy was another stratum of society, and she was at the bottom of this one. The creative talents working there had enormous free rein and generous salaries (often including interest-free loans, so they could buy homes fitting their status), but the poorly paid underlings were expected to behave as efficiently as they would at any other major corporation. Although everyone enjoyed better perks than they would at most any other media company, historically at *Vogue* a clear division existed between the worker bees and the social butterflies. And as things worked at *Vogue*, there was no way an assistant was going to be able to make the transformation to butterfly anytime soon.

But neither was Isabella a diligent worker bee. When Wintour wasn't around, Isabella would pick up the phone and chat with her friends. Instead of taking the pressure off Laurie Schechter, Isabella's unorthodox working style was making her colleague work twice as hard, as she now had to cover for Isabella to make sure the office ran as Wintour wanted it. "Instead of it being helpful, I now had to worry about what was going on," Schechter said. And that was made harder because Isabella bristled at being given instructions. She didn't see herself as working for Schechter; she saw herself as working for Wintour. If Schechter asked Isabella to do something, or tried to show her the way something should be done, Issie would snap at her. "It wasn't an easy teamwork situation," Schechter said. "After a time it was like you'd rather do it yourself so you don't have to deal with the rest. She had that Scorpio's sting."

After nine months—and the threat of a lawsuit after a photographer's portfolio went missing when Isabella arranged a courier without taking note of the tracking number—Schechter decided to say something to Wintour. "I finally had to go to her, because she was going to lose me—not so much because I was going to quit, but because I was going to fall over."[7] Wintour herself was an independent spirit who had not risen through the ranks of assistantships, but had succeeded by taking big jobs at smaller titles until her work was recognized. But although she loved Isabella's exotic nature, when it came to the running of her office, she valued Schechter's skills more. She quietly negotiated a move for Isabella to the office of André Leon Talley, *Vogue*'s fashion news director, a protégé of Wintour's and, by now, a good friend of Isabella's.

But despite Leon Talley's whimsical wardrobe, he possesses a focus and a drive that have solidified his reputation as one of the industry's most powerful figures. He may not have been as tightly controlled as Wintour, but he also needed an assistant who could deal with the mundane details that make up a large part of life at a magazine. Within a couple of weeks, the talk of the office was that Isabella and André had suffered a falling-out and were not speaking to each other, though they ultimately made up.

Perhaps Isabella's tenure at *Vogue* might have turned out differently had she worked there later in her career. Although she was friendly with famous people like Jean-Michel Basquiat—she had him autograph one of his books for Schechter—it didn't occur to her to suggest that she could get them to do something for the magazine. Years later, she'd realize the power of her connections and would enlist everyone and anyone—from her beautician to her friend Rupert Everett—to pose for or contribute to the various titles where she would work.

Today what Isabella is remembered and praised for by her colleagues at American *Vogue* is not her work habits but her unorthodoxy in dress. André Leon Talley wrote after her death, "On my first day at work, going in to meet with the creative director, I spied Isabella wearing a beautifully embroidered Chinese cheongsam, pecking at a typewriter in black, three-button, waxed calfskin opera gloves. That vision—Issie with a slight Louise Brooks bob in a red satin dress, attempting to type a memo with gloved hands—remains in my mind's eye. By the time she became my assistant, she had moved on to Jean Paul Gaultier's serious navy blue suit with a chiseled, scissor-cut backless jacket over a pencil skirt. This last uniform, bought off the rack on sale, reminded Blow of her favorite designer, the American-born Mainbocher."[8]

Mainbocher was an American designer (known for well-tailored but fairly conventional suits) who had opened a couture house in Paris in 1929. One of his most famous clients was the Duchess of Windsor, for whom he designed an entire wedding trousseau. Isabella would later describe her own look as "classic with a twist," or, if she was feeling inventive,

"Duchess of Windsor on acid."[9] In her speech at Isabella's memorial service, Anna Wintour said that Isabella brought far more to *Vogue* than simply a fabulous wardrobe, and she covered up her former employee's shortcomings:

> *Of course, the truth is that even when she was wearing her sexy 1940s secretary look, Issie was actually far more efficient and capable than the fancy dress would suggest. She could even type, because she'd been to secretarial school at some point in her checkered career history. Dressing up was about making her job into an event. Issie had the most wonderful ability to elevate even the most basic of tasks and turn it into something memorably thrilling. She had no time for anything humdrum, banal, or mundane—to the extent that the task of cleaning her desk every night had to be done with a bottle of Perrier water and Chanel No 5.*

It was going to take more than Perrier and Chanel No. 5 to mask the problems Isabella was having outside the office. Her relationship with Taylor was beginning to suffer. Nick had begun to waver about his new career as a banker and arranged to leave Salomon Brothers with a payoff that meant he didn't have to work for six months. While she was getting up and going to work, he was spending the mornings relaxing in bed, dreaming of returning to London. Isabella, at last in a job she found interesting, had no interest in returning to London and didn't take Nick's unemployment well. Isabella became afraid that he wasn't going to be able to take care of her after all. "She had a real fear of being poor," said Zara Metcalfe. "She was genuinely frightened of being out on the streets. Nick couldn't deal with his job, and she got totally freaked." Taylor's change of heart about "making a fortune" was a central factor in their relationship breaking down. "She needed money, and lots of it, and only a rich man could provide that," said a friend. "And Nick's values were changing." When an older, uglier, but very rich man started to pursue her, she went to dinner with Metcalfe and said, "Shall I?" Metcalfe was surprised. Isabella backed away from the conversation, but she could not shake her fears. "She was a really sexy woman and she was very flirtatious and she loved to be outrageous and shock people," said Grenfell. "But in her own way she was quite conservative. For people who didn't know her they'd think she was this louche woman, but really she wanted that old-fashioned life." And Isabella was increasingly convinced that Taylor would not be able to provide her with it—and trying to explain this to friends who knew them both was not easy. "Our relationship cooled after that," said Metcalfe. "I think she showed a side of herself that she hadn't wanted to." Isabella's relationship with Taylor also cooled. "They weren't really fighting," said a friend who stayed with them at the time. "But I remember Issie saying, 'Let's just get divorced, there's no point.'" Isabella wrote to Liza Campbell in London and said that Taylor was suffering from a bout of depression. "They were both fragile people," said Campbell. "He coped with her frailties, but when he had a collapse, she just didn't have the strength to do that."

Isabella's desire to be looked after wasn't the only reason she couldn't cope with Taylor's time off. She saw his quitting the rat race as a sign that he was unable to cope with daily life, perhaps because that is what it would have meant for her. She was finding it harder to ignore what she'd been trying to hide for years: that she could find herself inexplicably sad. She may not have diagnosed it as depression, but she knew something was amiss. She could keep the feeling at bay by living to excess and surrounding herself with friends who lavished attention on her, but when she was alone, or when she saw Taylor become disillusioned with the idea of striking it rich, she had to face it. One friend, who remembers turning around in a car filled with friends and loud music one day to see Isabella in the back with tears quietly streaming down her face, said, "She just couldn't stand Nick's depression. I imagine it was very frightening because of what was lurking within her own makeup. She was compensating tremendously and on the run from where she ended up. She knew that big black hole was there."

No one with any ambition then would have willingly left New York for London. New York in the mid-1980s was the center of intellectual, cultural, and financial power in the Western world. Nick got a job working with Morgan Guaranty in London, and the newly ambitious Isabella remained in New York. But ambition finally gave way to a stronger characteristic in her makeup, job or no job. Isabella was intuitive, and after a year her intuition told her it was time to go home—largely because she missed Nick. "My mistake," she said later, "was that I never took a commercial line. I just went with the wind."[10] Although they had formalized their divorce in New York, in London they attempted a reconciliation. But the issue of money would not go away. She and Nick drifted apart, not with anger but with sadness.

In 1988, when Isabella was back in London, Anna Wintour, the woman she thought of as her mentor, would finally get the top job at American *Vogue*. She'd secure her position there not just by tightly controlling every aspect of the magazine, but by wielding her considerable influence within the industry at large. As big corporations and private equity groups bought up brands with the hopes of reviving them, Wintour would serve as chief kingmaker, making it clear which designer she thought should go where with the implication of the magazine's endorsement if her wishes were followed. Meanwhile, England would go from being a quaint land where a prince married a princess in a fairly-tale wedding to the cultural capital of the world where a man who floated a shark in a tank of formaldehyde would become a world-renowned artist and a multimillionaire. Led by the shark-floating artist Damien Hirst in the art world and the pop bands Blur and Oasis in music, London would overtake New York as the Capital of Cool, and Isabella would be at the center of it all.

*La Vie
en Rose*

CHAPTER FIVE

It was raining when Joe McKenna and Isabella left their desks at Tatler. Tim
Willis, her boyfriend, who was also one of Joe's best friends, had arrived at Vogue
House so they could all go for drinks. But because of the rain and the mass exo-
dus of workers from nearby buildings in Mayfair, there wasn't a taxi to be found.
They walked several blocks—she in her black velvet Bill Blass suit, Rigby &
Peller push-up bra, and Manolo Blahnik heels—until they came to Claridge's
Hotel on Brook Street. "We can get a taxi here," she said. Tim and Joe were
suspicious. They weren't guests at the hotel and they weren't headed there either.
Isabella tottered over to the doorman on her stilettos. "There's a quick blow job in
it for you if you can get us a taxi," she said in her throaty upper-class tones, look-
ing up at the doorman from beneath her umbrella. He looked down at her, mouth
agape, and broke into a laugh. Then he stepped out and signaled the next car in
his queue. They got their taxi.

Mosh Gordon Cumming was surprised to see Isabella walking down King's Road in Chelsea carrying a suitcase and crying. Gordon Cumming steered her car to the curb, rolled down the window, and asked what was wrong. Isabella told her she didn't know where she was going to sleep. Back in London without Nick, Isabella fell into the erratic existence she had lived as a teenager. She stayed with Gordon Cumming for a bit and then went to the Chelsea flat of another friend, Natasha Grenfell who'd also moved back to London. "She arrived with her bags and asked if she could stay," said Grenfell. "She had no place else to go." It wasn't that she was broke; Isabella still had money from the family trust, but much of it had been spent on the New York apartment. (The total amount of the trust is unclear, but a friend remembers that it was still providing her an income of £10,000 a year in 1986, and her stepmother said that it would be worth several million today had it not been drawn down.) The larger truth was that Isabella hated to be, much less live, alone.

Back in England again, she had no place to call home. After his leg was removed, Evelyn had decided that he would base himself in London. In 1980, he sold £1.3 million worth of farmland attached to Doddington Hall and several of the industrial buildings with it. (Isabella's stepmother, Rona, would buy it back years later when the man who had bought it fell into financial difficulties.) Rona had sold her house in London after her marriage to Evelyn and had bought a townhouse at 37 Kensington Square, where Evelyn and she were now living. Isabella could have stayed there— her stepmother and father would not have let her sleep on the streets— but they were critical of her, as parents can be, and dismayed by the way she was spending the money in the trust.

Isabella came to visit them at Kensington Square dressed in a green and gold turban and a short skirt. When she entered Rona and Evelyn's palatial bedroom, the central feature of which was a mahogany four-poster bed with traditional English chintz spread, she found her stepmother getting a facial. Eleanor, the beautician, had recently begun visiting special clients in their own homes. She watched as Isabella came and gave Rona a hug, thinking it seemed there was a nice family feeling between them. "What's going on here?" Isabella asked. "I want one!" It seemed, Eleanor thought, to be a normal and loving family.

In Isabella's absence, Rona had become a formidable force in her own right. When she married Evelyn, many of his old friends in Cheshire wrongly assumed she was after his money. It seemed to be a classic case of a rich older man foolishly succumbing to the charms of a much younger woman. But Rona already had her own money and now Rona was working at Lloyd's, the three-hundred-year-old British insurance institution, where Evelyn himself had worked after World War II. Evelyn had taken Rona to Ascot in the late 1970s, and looking out over the rows of Rolls-Royces and Bentleys near the stands, she asked him who owned them. "They're all members of Lloyd's,"[1] he said. If the privileged men of Evelyn's era had to work, then Lloyd's was one of the more acceptable options open to them. Historically it had been a privilege to be able to invest in Lloyd's. The "names," as its investors are called, were invited to become part of the syndicate that required them to risk their entire personal wealth for a slice of the profits to be gained from underwriting the firm's insurance operations. The company's legacy as the safest of places to invest one's money came to an end when asbestos and the attacks of September 11 left many names bankrupt. Rona became a "name"—one of the now seven-hundred-odd rich individuals who put up the money to back policies, and in 1989 ran and won a seat on Lloyd's ruling council, taking the "unusual step" of sending the members an election pamphlet with her photo on it.[2] Rona had to pay out nearly two million pounds following September 11 but remained heavily invested. "I'm a Lloyd's lady," she said.[3] That Rona was not a stereotypical dim-but-beautiful younger wife, but was, in fact, a formidable force in the City, did little to improve her standing in Isabella's eyes. Or at least it didn't improve the way she described Rona to her friends.

Visits to Kensington Square were filled with apprehension for Isabella. "She never knew how Rona was going to be—friendly or unfriendly," said a friend. "I think she felt Rona was rather disapproving of her, and [Isabella] was always trying to keep in her father's good books." To a degree, they were right. "Evelyn didn't understand her way of life," said Rona. "But it did amuse him. She was a bit too exotic for him to deal with. He was very establishment."

Isabella increasingly lived in a world of her own making, inventing stories, dressing up, saying outrageous things to keep the world around her lively. Rona was a reminder that good things come to those who buckle down and work hard, something Rona herself took pains to communicate to her stepdaughter. "I would tell her, 'You can't go on trying to shock,'" said Rona. "'There's a limit.' I told her it would end in tears." Still, Isabella's experience at *Vogue* didn't teach her to value the people with their noses to the grindstone—after all they were the ones doing all the boring, menial work. It was somewhat logical to dismiss this kind of work ethic as beneath her. Just as she could dismiss Rona as "money-grubbing" and ignore the reality that Rona was actually more than happy to work for a living.

I sabella's next stop was a place more welcoming of her fantastical tendencies. She was called to the UK outpost of Condé Nast, Vogue House, on Hanover Square. Condé Nast publishes the global editions of *Vogue*. But *Vogue* wasn't Isabella's immediate destiny; she was headed for another glossy magazine in the Condé Nast stable, *Tatler,* which in 2009 celebrated its three hundredth anniversary. *Tatler* is a sort of *InStyle* magazine for the people whom the world has forgotten—it depicts a land where individuals with titles, not screen credits, still reign supreme. It began life in 1709 as *The Tatler* and had as one of its first contributors satirist Jonathan Swift. But *Tatler* as we know it now really came to life in 1901, when editor Clement Shorter observed that his weekly publication was written "for the moment merely . . . we live in an age of chatty scraps."

In 1982, Condé Nast bought the title after its editor, Tina Brown, had breathed life back into it. Brown, who took the mantle at age twenty-five in 1979, was convinced that the coverage of "British Society" that was *Tatler*'s remit should no longer be limited to the titled aristocracy, but should include the new boldface names like Mick Jagger and Sting. By the time Isabella arrived for her interview, the magazine was in its fifth or sixth revival. (Brown's appointment to the editorship of *Vanity Fair* in New York in

1983 helped make *Tatler,* her launching pad, one of the most watched magazines in the English language.) *Tatler*'s last heyday had been the pre-war years of the late 1930s—when its pages frequently covered the parties of Isabella's grandparents Jock and Vera Delves Broughton. Although *The* had been dropped from the title in the 1960s, Isabella used it when referring to her place of employment, a subtle, if subconscious reference to her knowledge of its history and her family's place in it.

Michael Roberts, now fashion director at *Vanity Fair,* was then *Tatler*'s style director. He summoned Isabella to the *Tatler* offices at Vogue House. "André [Leon Talley] called me and said there's this girl you should see, and I did and I loved her," he remembers. He can't remember what she was wearing the first time they met, but it was likely the Mainbocher-esque Bill Blass suit that she brought from New York. "She wore it every single day," said Joe McKenna, a stylist who worked in the fashion department next door to Roberts. "Black velvet fitted jacket, peplum waist, very tight straight black velvet skirt. That was her uniform." The uniform of the rest of the staff tended to look more like the pages of the 1980s bestseller *Dress for Success*—conservative suits tailored for women featuring big shoulder pads and sensible shoes.

Isabella made an impression. "There were a couple of other girls," Roberts said. "But this was the one that I wanted. What she was wearing, her breeding, the background. She was so perfectly *Tatler.* She wasn't a *Vogue* person, she was a *Tatler* person." Although she hadn't been cut out to juggle all the mundane tasks required of an assistant at Condé Nast, André Leon Talley could see that Isabella's taste and passion were worth cultivating, and he thought she'd be better suited to the Fashion Department, and so he recommended her to Michael Roberts in London.

Within the staff of a fashion magazine, there exists a division between those on the publishing side, whose job it is to sell ads and promote and sell the magazine, and the Editorial Department, where the content is developed. Within Editorial is yet another divide. The Fashion Department that organizes the fashion shoots is run and staffed by a different set of people from those responsible for the words and the photos that accompany the non-fashion pages. During Isabella's time at American *Vogue*, her boss, Anna Wintour, had been kept from working on the fashion pages, as that was seen by many as Grace Mirabella's way of containing her rival whose main interest was fashion. But Michael Roberts's job at *Tatler* was to bring fashion to the feature pages. He would organize the photographs that would accompany the feature stories, but often they were stories based only around photographs of society personalities in designer clothes. Instead of answering phones and tracking portfolios, Isabella would now be responsible for visiting designers and requesting the items Michael wanted to use in his shoots. It was a good fit: given the stature of *Tatler* in the British media landscape, if the odd glove or £1,000 dress went missing because of Isabella's disorganized nature, no one was really going to mind much.

Isabella got the job, which paid about £10,000 a year. In addition to the income from her trust, it was a more than a decent sum for a single girl to live on. But her steady income, the magazine's illustrious history, and even its current corporate ownership didn't impress her father. "It's a magazine for kinky lay-about druggies," a friend of Isabella's remembers him saying.

One couldn't blame Evelyn for his impression. *Tatler* under Tina Brown had gone from revering the aristocracy to skewering them—ever so lightly, of course. Headlines set the new tone: "Oh, Edie, Edie, why so Seedie?" about American heiress Edie Sedgwick, or "Wild It's Rich It's Heady It's Frothy! Look out Hollywood, It's Guinnessty," about the Guinness family. Roberts, as style director, put together the photo shoots that would visually display the world of modern aristos—queue shots such as "Bra Boys," with young men in Kent photographed wearing bras by Rigby & Peller and pajama bottoms from Harrods. "We were crazy enough ourselves," said Roberts. "[Isabella] was just one more crazy person coming through those doors. My shoots were more crazy than her when she came in."

The quirky tone and outrageous photography made the magazine one of the most-read publications of the era, and those running the magazine, became minor celebrities themselves. "People like Michael Roberts of *Tatler* are discussed and psychoanalyzed in absentia for hours on end," wrote Nicholas Coleridge, now the editorial director of Condé Nast UK in his 1988 book *The Fashion Conspiracy*. "Elusive, waspish and black, Roberts is the maverick voice of fashion; his monthly photographs of Etonians wearing body paint and raccoon hats are unlike anything else. Since 1982 he has organized ten shoots at the public school."[4] When Isabella arrived, Roberts understood immediately the power of her connections—something her years in New York hadn't diminished. *Tatler* was more informal than the glossy, professional American *Vogue*. Its tone was that of a young, hip members' club, and Isabella knew all the members. Roberts couldn't care less that Isabella was talking on the phone to her high society friends—in fact, he'd encourage it. Just as long as they showed up on the day of the shoot. Although she was nervous about wanting to please him by picking the perfect items, helping organize Michael's shoots was a job far better suited to her abilities than being Wintour's secretary.

London had changed a lot in the five years she'd been gone. Margaret Thatcher had been elected the year Isabella left, and a by-product of all the union breaking and economic reform was a rush of money into the capital—money it was now cool to show off, even if it was self-made, not inherited. Londoners were playing as hard as they worked. Or, as was the case with junior staffers on *Tatler*, much harder than they worked. The *Tatler* office culture mimicked the irreverence of the magazine's covers. It might have been part of Condé Nast, but its atmosphere was a far cry from the fear-fueled efficiency in the offices of American *Vogue*. There, professionalism and punctuality were the pathways to success. At *Tatler*, it was more a competition of cheek. "Our office was totally chaotic. It was the engine of the whole thing," said Roberts, who, for one cover, famously styled designer Vivienne Westwood to look like Margaret Thatcher. Cheek on the cover, cheek in the offices. "I remember tying a rope to a bathroom stall so one editor couldn't get out," said Joe McKenna.

Keeping regular hours was not mandatory at *Tatler*; in fact, it was likely to be eyed with suspicion. "This was *Tatler* before Health and Safety [legislation]," said Kate Bernard, a writer who worked at *Tatler* at the time. It was a magazine glorifying the posh and mischievous, staffed by people who were, mostly, either posh or mischievous or, like Isabella, both. And, as at Isabella's old school Heathfield, there was a dearth of straight men in the office. Whether he knew it or not, the new editor, Mark Boxer, bore the brunt of the female office-based fantasies. "I remember going to the office with Issie one day and saying to her, 'I had the most extraordinary dream last night,'" said Bernard. "She said, 'Was it sexy? Was it about Mark?' I was really peeved she figured it out, and she said, 'Look, it's obvious. There's a lot of sex there.'" Particularly vexing to Isabella and her colleagues was the question of where Mark Boxer went on his long lunches.

"You never knew who was in the building in those days," Bernard said, referring to *Tatler*'s lax work schedule. And Isabella was no exception. "She was never a 'get-to-work-on-time' girl," said Roberts. "The office functioned well, and it functioned even better when she came in." It was also a far funnier place when she was in attendance. A long list of antics was ascribed to Isabella, often as much for what she was not wearing as for what she was. Overheard:

> "Issie has been banned from the offices of *Vogue* for leaning over the slide table with no knickers on."

> "You missed it—Issie caused a fuss at the tea station by bending over the sandwich tray with no knickers on."

> "Someone just told me that Issie's breasts popped out of her top when she was in the lift with the editor."

"Someone just walked into the ladies' loo and found Issie in there getting a bikini wax."

Isabella's main talent turned out to be getting her friends to participate in the crazy shoots that Michael Roberts conceived. "My aim in life was to show that England was just this hotbed of whoopee-cushion fun," said Roberts. "My stuff was all about making people look like they were doing the funniest thing they'd ever done in their lives. Even if they were standing in the rain. All this naughty public school stuff. I was very into that for years." (*Public* in the UK actually meaning "private." Children of the rich were initially educated at home by tutors. Schools were later established for the education of the public at large and were thus referred to as public schools, even though they were privately funded. They eventually attracted the children of the wealthy.) Isabella's friends, who had lived that naughty "public" school stuff were more than happy to oblige bizarre requests when asked. The shoots were just another form of a party. For one shoot, called "Beatonesque"—done in the glamorous, romantic style of celebrated society photographer Cecil Beaton—Isabella gathered together a few of her best friends (Lucy Ferry, Mosh Gordon Cumming, and Tina Oxenberg) and put them all together on the grounds of the stately homes belonging to friends and distant relatives. "By then I knew Issie's strengths," Roberts said, "which were amazing enthusiasm, and that she knew or was related to every single eccentric aristo in England." And when Isabella would inevitably forget a critical prop for a shoot, she'd simply pack one of her gang into a taxi with a twenty-pound note and ask them to retrieve it.

"Land Girls," a feature about women of Isabella's age who lived in stately homes, included intriguing tidbits, such as Charlotte Morrison being the only person apart from the queen with the right to keep and eat . . . swans. "The Gang Bang" featured four beautiful women who could shoot as well as the boys.

Isabella was happy not only to enlist her friends and their stately homes but also to donate her own childhood home and even her own money. For one shoot, the entire crew decamped north to Cheshire to stay at Doddington Hall. "She went way over budget and had to pay for the food and wine herself. She just went through the trust," said her friend Celia Lyttelton. For a story on posh people's pets, Isabella, not convinced that the real pets her friends owned were exotic enough, used her own money to hire an animal trainer to bring in some rare species. All well and good, until Michael Roberts decided that a reshoot was required. Suddenly, panic. Even if she spent the money to hire the animal again, could she be guaranteed that the same trainer pets would be available? Would Michael Roberts and Mark Boxer recognize that the heiress who at the last shoot owned a pet tarantula was now being photographed with a spider monkey? Would they care?

The first Contributor's Page item on Isabella, in 1988, read, "When asked at dinner parties what she does at *Tatler*, she is apt to reply through a veil of ostrich feathers and a lipstick slick: 'I do historical research, I find unbalanced people, I choose photographers and places to shoot them.'"

As Isabella got more and more confident of her styling abilities, she began to push for her own pages. "She started off as my assistant and then she got impatient; she wanted her own pages and she started to outgrow her job," said Roberts. "She was great when she was a full-time fashion assistant, but she felt it wasn't enough for her. I know she longed to do her own thing . . . but of course I couldn't understand why she'd ever want to leave the wonderland that I'd created. This Garden of Eden." Isabella's impatience paid off: she was promoted and given four pages of her own every other month. "She did these stories that I thought were very interesting but were not things that I would ever do," he said. "Like a whole four pages on people with scars. Facial scars. Scars, armor, bugs, Gothic. They were all very Gothic. They were completely the opposite of what I was doing."

Fashion shoots, at their best, create a fantasy world. Roberts's fantasy was of the world that Isabella grew up in. One where the posh veneer could only barely mask the mischief at hand. But that was Isabella's reality, so her fantasies were found elsewhere. She mined her family's history and the history of Britain for inspiration. While shooting "Posh Pets," she must have thought more than once of the unusual companions her grandmother Vera had brought back from her travels. Knowing Issie's upbringing, it's unlikely that she created "Rags to Witches"—haute couture clothing shot on scarecrows—without thinking about her days scaring the other schoolgirls while playing at Gigi Callander's abbey. British history is bloody and dark, and that appealed enormously to Isabella, whose own family name was born in battle. Although she was fond of her work, she was also dismissive of its importance. "The whole point of my job is to make bad clothes look good," she said.[5]

But that didn't mean she wasn't having fun. Even outside of shoots, Isabella took pleasure in costuming her friends. When her pal Liza Campbell's father remarried, he and his wife began dressing like beatniks in matching black turtlenecks. "Issie . . . noted the recurrence of this low-key uniform and one day came over for tea with twelve friends in tow, having instructed each of them to dress in a black polo neck as a silent joke," Liza Campbell wrote in her memoir. "To their delight, Angelika and Hugh did not disappoint. Fifteen people stood sipping champagne in the Tower Room looking like a guild of jazz critics, their hosts appearing to notice nothing strange at all."[6]

Nick Taylor introduced Isabella to one of her subjects. Selina Blow had grown up in a house that Taylor told Isabella she would just love—filled as it was with suits of armor, shields, and incredible costumes. Selina was tall ("from our French blood"), dark (the Sri Lankan mother), and beautiful. Isabella went to meet Selina at the townhouse on Elizabeth Street on the fringes of Belgravia. "She arrived wearing a Katharine Hamnett jacket, black tights, and Manolos," said Selina. Although Selina was dating Isabella's ex-husband, Nick, the two women quickly bonded. "I was taken by her charm, humor, wit, and gentle concern for others," said Selina. "All my barriers melted down and I almost felt bereft when she left." But when Isabella asked Selina to emerge from a tribal hut wrapped only in a bit of gold lamé for a shoot, she said no. Instead, she posed in "Under the Arches"—an Isabella story if ever there was one, based on the so-called Gothic revival in the world of design. The jewelry got credit; it all came from S. J. Phillips, Isabella's favorite vintage jeweler. When the shoot was finished, the gems were returned and Isabella and Selina went to a pub. "It was a real worker's place, with people playing darts," Selina said. She was astounded to see Isabella beating the locals at arm wrestling. "The men were watching saying, 'Oi, blimey!'"

Isabella soon took the exotic twenty-one-year-old under her wing. She brought Selina, wearing a pair of rubber boots and "pretty grim" socks, to see the designer Anouska Hempel in her studio, and when Isabella discovered that Selina was fascinated by the French Revolution, she brought her to meet John Galliano, who had based his 1984 design school graduation collection, *Les Incroyables*, on that historical upheaval, with giant frock coats and frilly blouses. She also brought her to meet shoe designer Manolo Blahnik' and his sister, Evangeline. And when she got a job working with the Sex Pistols' former manager Malcolm McLaren and Lisa Marie Presley on a video, she put Selina in charge of the styling. "Issie said, 'It will be fun for you; you do it.' Even if you had never done something before, Issie would say you were just as good as someone who had been at it for twenty years," Selina said. "I think anyone can be a stylist," Isabella said. "I think you can learn in thirty-five minutes."[7]

Working on a British magazine meant that for the first time Isabella was making the acquaintance of a new species of friend: office mates. Whereas in New York she primarily hung out with the girls she knew from London, in London she now spent increasing amounts of free time with people she got to know through work.

"She seemed to be really excited to be in London," said McKenna. "She was instantly likable, eccentric, and very self-deprecating. She had a great sense of humor about everything, particularly herself." McKenna worked in the Fashion Department at *Tatler*—technically Isabella and Roberts were not fashion—they were in features. But the three shared a love of clothes. And both McKenna and Isabella had an added love of misadventure. They became best office friends. Through work and through Roberts, Isabella was starting to meet more and more of the fashion crowd. And the more designers she got to know, the more power she had with them, and the more adventurous she became in her dress. Forget about just making interesting choices. Now that she was close with Roberts, she could make interesting *requests*.

During a visit to the design studio of Rifat Ozbek, the Turkish fashion designer who was close friends with her boss, she spotted a suit he'd designed with a Mongolian fur collar on the coat and skinny black trousers. She asked, "Can I have one, but with fur trim on the cuffs of the jacket, on the hem of the jacket, and on the hem of the trousers?" Ozbek replied, "Issie, you will look like a poodle who just came out of the barbershop." Issie replied, "And? That sounds nice! Who wouldn't want to look like a poodle that had just been groomed?" The suit quickly joined the Blass as a favorite in her wardrobe.

At the time, the choices Isabella was making in her wardrobe stood out more for their inappropriateness to the occasion than for their exceptional individuality. Roberts described Isabella arriving at the office one morning: "She came off the bus in the Manolos and a cocktail dress and a hat with a veil and things with black lace. Everyone assumed she'd been out at a club all night." A lot of it was by the designers of the day— Christian Lacroix, Rifat Ozbek—in the fashions of the late 1980s, such as, say, the poof skirt she adored for its ability to show off her legs.

But Isabella was never interested in new for the sake of new. So it seems fitting that her first real fashion discovery was neither a dress designer nor a hat designer—not Ozbek, nor Bill Blass, nor even the Gothic allure of chain mail—but a conservative lingerie maker called Rigby & Peller. New among established British brands—it was founded in 1939—Rigby & Peller had been making bespoke underwear for the queen since 1960. Throughout the autumn and winter of 1985, Isabella wore her black satin push-up bra—and only her black satin push-up bra—under her jackets, having decided that no shirt was necessary. When spring and summer arrived, she decided that the jacket wasn't necessary either. Joe McKenna found the spectacle of Isabella buying lunch dressed thusly was worthy of a write-up in the *Times*. "This girl has done more for Rigby & Peller (bespoke corsetiere to her Majesty the Queen) than anyone else. She praises their satin bustier above everything else in her wardrobe and has been known to wear it as an outer garment. Often. She praises the fabric, the cut, and the fact that they cover all the little whalebones in velvet plush, and she takes all her friends, small-bosomed and large, up the South Molton Street stairs to convert them," he wrote.[8]

Just as her enthusiasm for their artistry would promote the dress designs of Alexander McQueen and the hats of Philip Treacy, her love of Rigby & Peller was infectious. "I remember her taking me to Rigby & Peller, saying, 'You really have to sort your tits out,'" said Celia Lyttelton. "We both took to wearing jackets with nothing else under them."

Isabella's other great discovery came in one of the famous London clubs of the 1980s. From 1986 to 1989 there was only one place to be in London on Wednesday nights: the ballroom that is Café de Paris off Leicester Square. That was the night the DJ Fat Tony was in residence and would open and close every set with the same song "La Vie en Rose," sung by Grace Jones. "And you would stay from beginning to end," said McKenna. (Isabella and Grace Jones would later compete over Philip Treacy. Not for his favor, but for the most fabulous of his hats.) One night in the summer of 1986, peering down from the club's balcony, Isabella spotted Tim Willis on the dance floor. Willis did not fit the typical mold of Isabella's boyfriends. He hadn't been to Eton, or Oxford, or Cambridge; he hadn't come from an old family; and he wasn't rich. A Catholic boy who had gone to a Jesuit boarding school in Lincolnshire (a county in the north of England) and Edinburgh University, where, thanks to his charismatic nature and a serious intellect, he had gotten his own newspaper column by the age of twenty-eight. He did have one thing in common with Isabella's previous boyfriends; he was strikingly good-looking, with a strong jaw and wavy blond hair.

As part of the media set, the two also had a few friends in common, starting with Isabella's new office buddy Joe McKenna. "I was always saying I needed a girlfriend," said Willis. "So Joe organized that I would go around to his place and we would go out with Issie and Lucy [Ferry], which we did." A second meeting was organized with the help of another industry friend, Gabe Doppelt, who threw a dinner party at her apartment in South Kensington. Afterward, Isabella offered Tim a ride home in her "bashed-up" red Citroën 2CV, although his Notting Hill flat was not remotely on her way home. When they arrived at his place, he said, "It's too corny to invite you in for a coffee." But up she went. "She was extraordinary looking," said Willis. "She had the teeth and the bags under her eyes, but all that was lost when she smiled or laughed. It just disappeared." Willis was the first, but not the last, self-made middle-class boy Isabella would draw into her intoxicating sphere.

Joe McKenna, Isabella, and Tim Willis began to hang out regularly during the week. Isabella would arrive at McKenna's house in Notting Hill with a bunch of flowers, a box of chocolates, or a bottle of wine ("She never, ever came empty-handed," he said.) and then Willis would arrive. Then the three would go out or stay in. "She was so engaging that she'd make everything fun." She didn't drop any of her usual antics; in restaurants she continued to make sexual innuendos to the waiters, but in such a manner that even Willis would laugh. When the night was over she'd go with Willis to his flat, and the next day at work she'd recount to McKenna all of the details he had missed. "She would tell you every single detail about what happened in the bed and out of the bed," he said. "It was a great period for Issie. She had a sense of abandon that you don't find in many people."

Tim had a similar sense of abandon. "It was a very fun time. She was becoming a bit of a character, and I was doing well. We had no responsibility, and there was plenty of money. We were out every night. In those days there were dinner parties." On occasion he behaved badly. Late one evening early in the relationship, when they were still seeing other people, Willis rang one woman in Clapham and asked to see her. She insisted it was too far to come at that hour. "I have a car," he said, and "borrowed" Isabella's Citroën to make the trip. Unfortunately the girl in question was best friends with an assistant at *Tatler* and reported the incident to her. When she found out, Isabella, still besotted, kept her cool, rang Willis, and said, "I hear you have a car." Later Isabella would abandon the little red Citroën by the side of a road and spend £6,000 on a silver BMW. "It was very Bond," Willis said of the new car. "But she couldn't afford it."

The money from her trust meant she could buy nicer and nicer things, but that didn't mean she treated them any better. Her clothes, no matter how expensive, would frequently end up on the floor, ripped and covered in stains. Casual disregard for precious things was another historical trait of the aristocratic class. When money abounded, new things could always be bought. But in Isabella's case, it was extreme. It seemed nothing was so precious that it could not be discarded once possessed. The power she got from these things came not from possessing them but from desiring them. Once they were hers, these things immediately began to decline in value.

Isabella's pet name for Willis was Rep, for "reptile," because he was a journalist. According to Toby Young, a magazine industry friend, Isabella claimed the nickname from Vere Harmsworth (also known as Viscount Rothermere). *Reptile* was his term for all journalists. Harmsworth was the father of her old chum Geraldine, and as owner of the *Daily Mail, Mail on*

Sunday, and the *Evening Standard*, he was known as "the last of the English press barons." Owning a publication, or three, was an appropriate role for an aristocrat, but journalists didn't fit into the class system. Historically, theirs was a vocation for the working class, but over time the power of the papers has led to increasing numbers of aristocrats taking up the call. Still, they have to tread a delicate balance between covering the people they have known for years and making sure they don't alienate themselves in doing so. Talking about treading that line while at *Tatler*, Tina Brown said, "I always saw society as a story. I mean, I had to get in there, to cover the story, but it wasn't where I wanted to be."[9]

Thanks to Isabella, Willis now found himself in the middle of society. As she'd later do for numerous designers and photographers, she helped pave the way for him to make a name for himself. In July 1986, when Jerry Hall turned thirty, Isabella brought Willis to the party. Later, when she was invited to a reception at St. James's Palace, she naturally invited Willis. When Andy Warhol came to London and a dinner was thrown for him at a Chinese restaurant in Earl's Court, Isabella arranged it so that Willis would sit next to Warhol, in the seat of honor. So far, normal for a besotted girl-friend in her twenties—except that all of these events made the pages of Willis's "People" column in the Sunday edition of a recently launched newspaper called *Today*, which was meant to rival the UK tabloids, in part by using color print as *USA Today* was doing in the States. The celebrity- and royalty-studded parties to which Isabella was invited made perfect fodder for Willis's page. And she didn't mind at all. "She was very sweet to me," Willis said. "I was a journalist, so people were suspicious if you're not part of the fraternity. Particularly toffs. She used to put herself out to set stuff up for me. And she got herself in a lot of trouble with all of her friends when I'd write these things up. She just laughed."

Weekends were also spent in the company of Isabella's friends and family. They would usually drive to the countryside to stay at Wilbury, the Palladian home of Natasha Grenfell's mother, or in a cottage nearby they decided to rent. Or they'd go to Cheshire, where Isabella's father was often alone. "She was a really good daughter . . . She'd cook him roast chicken and fuss over him," said Willis. She even took Willis to meet her beloved aunt Rosamund and her husband, the war hero Lord Lovat, bringing with her on the sleeper train a rare breed of hen as a gift. In typical Isabella fashion, she dressed Willis for the occasion in a Fraser family kilt. Lord Lovat was less than enthused. "We went to see him, and he had to go for a walk up and down the garden, he was so horrified," Willis said.

Although it was her promotion of fashion designers that would make her famous, it had long been in Isabella's nature to help anyone she was close to. In 1984, Hugh Fraser (the brother of her uncle Lord Lovat) a conservative MP, and also the ex-husband of the writer Lady Antonia Fraser, died. The Frasers' eldest son Benjie inherited Eilean Aigas, the house on an island in the River Beauly in the Scottish Highlands, where he and his brothers and sisters had grown up. The house was in disrepair, suffering from dry rot, and Benjie had been urged to sell it, but had refused. To earn money for the repairs, Isabella decided he should rent it out and signed on to be his first tenant, insisting that he and his cousins come back to the house to stay with her and her friends. "It is absolutely beautiful, the most romantic place you can imagine in Scotland," said Geraldine Harmsworth. Guests would play football or enjoy the massive picnics planned by Isabella. "The cheeses and wines that were imported via Inverness railway station had never been seen outside Jermyn Street," said Fraser. "No expense or delicacy was spared for our rainy days sitting on tartan rugs up some hilly peak of Glen Strathfarrar." Days were spent walking the Scottish hills—Isabella as often as not wearing Manolos for the hikes, and insisting that the others wear traditional dress. She managed to get Bryan Ferry into Benjie's Fraser kilt—a look he wore onstage at a subsequent show. At night the expected, the unexpected, and the occasional adulterous liaison took place. "Issie loved that it was all going on," said a guest. "She totally encouraged it." When she and her friends vacated Eilean Aigas, Isabella encouraged a string of her fashion friends to rent the house, including the stylist Grace Coddington and supermodel Linda Evangelista.

Although Tim and Isabella were in love, they were still—at least emotionally—too young to consider marriage. Willis got caught cheating twice. After the first occasion, he took Isabella to visit St. George's Hanover Square church, near her office, and bought her a book on Byron, with whom she had a fascination at the time. "She was very touched."

Willis, like many of Isabella's childhood friends, suffered demons and he coped by a hedonistic round of pleasure featuring copious amounts of alcohol—thereby blending in with the crowd at the time. "I have my own trouble with depression," he said. "I used to drink way too much, and she was on my case about it, quite rightly. Both she and a previous girlfriend drank half a bottle of vodka to see what it was like. I came home and found Isabella drunk, and she said, 'This is ghastly! Why do you do this?'"

Although she would sometimes be wracked with insecurity about her finances, her looks, and her job, Willis didn't notice signs of depression in her. "Issie would get very upset, but very seldom," he said. She was "much, much, much more up than down. She did drink; she smoked dope. There was plenty of coke around, but she didn't do it. She didn't need it."

After two years, Willis decided to call it off. "At first I was very pleased with myself," he said. "And then I was absolutely heartbroken."

In the wake of the breakup, Isabella decided she needed a place of her own and bought a flat on Holland Road in Holland Park. She stayed there only once, with Willis, and subsequently sold it. Then she moved into the Gerard Road, Belgravia, home to Maria St. Just, Natasha Grenfell's mother. Willis, desperate to get her attention, flooded the house with daily deliveries of her favorite flower, the white lily. He ran into Maria St. Just at a party of interior designer Nicky Haslam's in September of 1988, and St. Just said, "We love the lilies; they make the house smell delightful. Do keep sending them. You haven't a hope of getting her back, but do keep sending the lilies."

Despondent, he would ring friends and talk for hours about the mistake he'd made, moving the calls westward as the hour got later, to find people who were still awake. "I phoned Gabe [Doppelt] in New York and said, 'I'll never meet anyone like her.' Gabe said, 'You're right, you won't.'"

Willis was at the house of their mutual friend Celia Lyttelton when he learned that Isabella had gone to spend a country weekend with a new suitor. "Celia was encouraging me to drive out there. I rang Issie and said, 'I'm coming out.' She said, 'Please don't.'"

For Isabella's thirtieth birthday, in November 1988, she threw a party in a friend's flat, which Willis attended. "She looked so pretty," he said. "She had a rose garland on and a little virginal white puff ball mini." Unfortunately for him, she also now had a fiancé.

True Loves: Detmar and Hilles, Philip and Hats

Philip Treacy and Isabella arrived at Orly airport outside of Paris in 1991 to find there was a train strike. They followed the other passengers who had been on the flight from London toward an eighty-seat coach bearing a destination sign that read, "Paris." They sat and waited, and talked and waited, and waited some more for the driver to appear. He didn't. Isabella, dressed in a vintage green velvet Paul Poiret cocoon coat and a hat of mesh and black tubing she and Treacy called the Hoover, looked at Philip, then looked at the empty driver's seat, and then looked at Philip and said, "Shall I?" "Isabella, you can't do that!" Treacy replied. It was, he'd quickly learn, the wrong thing to say to her. She took the driver's seat, put her foot to the gas, and began revving the engine. Periodically she'd turn to look at the passengers, who were aghast, and at Treacy, who was in hysterics. Finally, the driver appeared and asked what she thought she was doing. "We are waiting!" she said.

O n a gray morning in late September 1988, Isabella and her cousin Benjie Fraser left central London and drove due west to attend the wedding of Emma Elizabeth Roper Curzon and Robert Murphy in Salisbury Cathedral. In lieu of a boyfriend, Isabella had drafted Benjie as her date, promising it would be an ideal place for him to meet a girlfriend. In the back of his car was Selina Blow, the now ex-girlfriend of Isabella's ex-husband, Nick. Although Isabella was suffering from the breakup with Willis, she hadn't lost her sense of humor. Periodically throughout the journey, she would look over her shoulder and coo, "How is the little Sri Lanki in the back?"

Isabella had dressed for the occasion in an ostrich feather hat by Hamptons-based designer Anne Moore and a tight coat by Katharine Hamnett. Upon leaving the Gothic cathedral, which boasts, among other things, the tallest spire in England, Isabella caught the eye and the ear of a dark-skinned man in a hot pink coat. It was Selina's brother Detmar, wearing a coat his grandfather had worn when he was an ambassador from Sri Lanka. Detmar was, he said later, entranced by the birdlike sound of Isabella's voice and her unusual outfit. When she, Selina, and Benjie walked out the North Door, he made his move. "I love your hat" was his mating call. "I love your coat" was Isabella's return call. "And I wish I was wearing my violet shoes for you, but it's muddy." At the reception afterward, Isabella was surrounded by friends, and Detmar had to bide his time until he could get a moment alone with her. "Come to Hilles!" he spouted when he had a chance. And then: "Can I have your phone number?" She gave him her number at work and the two talked, he said later, of "being the court jesters, being kicked to death ourselves with our suffering."[1]

Detmar had grown up fifty miles away to the north, in Gloucestershire, on his family's estate, Hilles. Like Isabella, he was part aristocrat, part "commoner." But in his case it was his grandmother Winifred who had the breeding.

Winifred Tollemache came from a family with a history dating back to the Norman conquest and had grown up in Helmingham Hall, a stately home in Suffolk. At the time she met Detmar Jellings Blow, an architect, he was traveling in a camper with his own band of stonemasons. The union shocked her family. "You are marrying a commoner with no land," her cousin Lord Dysart told her.[2] It was true, but he was already a success. In 1913, he began work on Hilles, that year having earned more than £250,000 (or £1.1 billion today) as an architect. The marriage helped cement his career as the architect of choice for grand families. He was eventually given the job of running the Duke of Westminster's estates, the largest in the country. Detmar J. began to build Hilles in 1913, in part so that Winifred could again reside in, and preside over, a stately home. "He wanted the house to be romantic, dreamlike, more than grand," said Simon Blow, his grandson and Detmar's cousin. "Hilles was designed to be a place of Arcadian and socialistically minded entertaining." Detmar Jellings was part of a group of high-minded socialists and he based Hilles on the philosophies of his friend William Morris, who believed in a return to medieval England, where everyone had a craft and was happy with it. "There were parties for the tenant farmers and parties for my grandparents' artistic circle, often mingling as one," said Simon.[3] Rudyard Kipling, Eric Gill, and pre-Raphaelite muse Lady Plymouth were some of the guests at the time.

Winifred and Detmar J. had three children: Purcell, Jonathan (Detmar's father), and Lucilla. As his reputation and income grew, Detmar J. bought the surrounding farms of Gloucestershire until Hilles the house sat in the midst of an estate of nine hundred acres. But the land, the house, and the children didn't bring happiness. In 1933, Detmar J. was accused by the Duchess of Westminster of embezzling rent money earned from the properties in the Westminster estate and managed to convince her husband, by now Detmar J.'s best friend, of his guilt. Although he was subsequently cleared of the accusations, in the wake of the scandal Detmar J. was shunned from society and fell into such a dark depression that his eldest son, Purcell, was made to sleep in his bed in order to prevent him from throwing himself out the window. Detmar J. died at Hilles of natural causes in 1939.

By this time, Purcell had married, moved to London, and was working as an architect himself. Jonathan had stayed behind to help their mother at Hilles. Purcell's son Simon wrote of his grandmother Winifred,

"She feeds him with admiring words that make him scared when away from her. He follows her around the house and he is devoured by envy of any who take the spotlight for a second off him."[4]

When Winifred died in 1954 it emerged that she'd left the vast bulk of the estate not to Purcell, the eldest, and of course not to her daughter Lucilla, but to Jonathan, her favorite. In May 2009, Simon Blow wrote an article in *Tatler* accusing Jonathan of murdering Winifred in order to gain control of Hilles. As evidence, he cites a letter written by his aunt Lucilla that says she saw Jonathan putting something under her mother's chicken lunch. Later that evening, when Winifred fell ill, Jonathan refused to call a doctor. "It is our belief that Uncle Jonathan had placed pieces of hemlock plant under the chicken," wrote Simon.[5]

Jonathan was obsessed with his mother's lineage. He once said to Simon, "Don't you think we have better blood than most of the dukes in England?" That might have been part of the reason he had an affair with his brother Purcell's wife Diana, who also came from an aristocratic family, the Tennants. Simon says Jonathan was eager to see Diana divorce his father, who was suffering from Huntington's disease and was frequently drunk and violent. Then, according to Simon, he had hopes to marry her, but ultimately realized he couldn't. "He read in the Bible that you cannot marry your brother's wife. And he got quite upset. And very drunk," said Simon.

In 1966, at the age of forty-two, Jonathan Blow did find someone he could marry. Helga de Silva was seventeen and modeling in a fashion show at Berkeley Castle in Gloucestershire when Jonathan, who was there with his cousin, spotted her and said, "I rather like the dusky one." Simon wrote in his memoir, "She's skinny as can be, but beautiful, with full lips."[6] Helga was from Sri Lanka, and her family was an important one there. Her mother had attended the Slade School of Art in London and had worked with Corbusier. Her father had been a Member of Parliament and ambassador to France and Switzerland and had been instrumental in the Sri Lankan movement for independence.

Shortly after they married, Jonathan put the house at Hilles into Helga's name. "Hilles was given to me as a twenty-first birthday present," Helga said. "I would have far preferred a party," she told Jonathan. "You have me, you don't need a party," Jonathan replied. The move was in part for tax reasons and in part because he feared his young, beautiful bride might leave him. Instead, it was he who left her. In 1977, after fathering three children, Detmar, Amaury, and Selina, Jonathan Blow committed suicide by drinking the weed killer Paraquat at Hilles. His youngest son, Amaury, age nine, found him collapsed at the door of his bedroom.

Jonathan had been suffering from depression for years, frequently locking himself in the library at Hilles and drinking until he passed out. Helga said that only three of their fifteen and a half years of marriage "were magical." For the remainder, she was stuck, she said, on a "merry-go-round," trying to keep Jonathan's condition secret from their family and friends. Over the years, he had tried various treatments for his depression, including electroshock therapy, but none of them worked. Trying to protect his reputation by keeping the illness hidden didn't work either. Detmar told a friend that the headmistress at the local school in Edge took him outside and said, "Your father is a pig." People would find Jonathan drunk in ditches and return him to Hilles. The illness took its toll in countless ways. Not only was he unpredictable, but Helga was consumed with the task of taking care of him, to the detriment of their children. "The saddest of all is that in order to keep Jonathan alive and trying to give him the will to do so, others were sacrificed," said Helga.

Detmar lived in the Upper Holcombe farmhouse on Hilles for some of his young life. "My father farmed me out with a nanny," he said. "My mother had three babies in three years, but my parents were the sort who didn't really like young children."[7] At eight, he was sent away to boarding school. When it came time for him to go to secondary school, he didn't go to Eton, as his father had done, but went instead to Harrow, a public school known for having students that are more likely to succeed on the football pitch than in the halls of Westminster. In the United Kingdom, Harrow is known as "the other place," because it isn't Eton.

When Jonathan died, Detmar, the oldest son, was suddenly thrust into the role of man of the house, although he was only fourteen. "After my dad died, everything died," said Selina. "The house went silent. My mother was traumatized—she still is." Selina continued, "Detmar looked after her; he took on a father-figure role. My mother would stay up all night playing my father's Edith Piaf and Marlene Dietrich records. Her life stopped. My father's ashes were kept in the house for twenty-five years."[8]

Just as with his father and grandmother, Detmar formed a close attachment to his mother, and she to him. "My poor brother, Detmar, had a difficult role," said Amaury. "My mother used him to take charge of us, and I think as a surrogate husband for a time."[9] While Selina and Amaury disappeared into a world of fantasy games, Detmar would attend to their mother, even carrying her handbag from place to place. "He's obsessed with his mother," Isabella said later. "Basically, he was married to her for years. She has a huge influence on him. He's been surrounded by glamour since he was tiny. Trotting down the road carrying her Hermès bag— sorting out the lipsticks and mascara."[10] Shortly after, Helga remarried, and after divorcing her second husband, she began to spend most of her time in Sri Lanka.

After graduating from Harrow, Detmar again broke with tradition by not going to Oxford as his father had, but enrolling at the London School of Economics, to study history. When he graduated, he set out to follow in the footsteps of his mother's family and practice as a barrister. His mother's brother, Sir Desmond de Silva, was one of only four chief prosecutors appointed by the United Nations to oversee prosecutions for war crimes before international criminal courts. He is is one of the most respected human rights attorneys in the world. He is also the sixth-generation barrister (with only one break) in the family line of barristers since 1828. He would have liked for Detmar to be the seventh generation. Upon graduation, Detmar did a pupilage at the office of Raymond Lewis, who shared chambers with de Silva. It was a set of chambers known worldwide for fighting for and upholding human rights. However, Detmar didn't stay for long, saying he wasn't fond of criminal law and wanted to go into a field that was more lucrative. He then turned his hand to the solicitors branch of the legal profession in England by working at the offices of Raymond Tooth, a divorce lawyer, known for getting big settlements for rich clients, including the ex-wives of Jude Law, Eric Clapton, and Russian billionaire Roman Abramovich, but stayed for only a year. Eventually he was hired by a firm of solicitors called Withers, which had a history of representing rich and aristocratic clients in a variety of areas. When he met Isabella he was dividing his time between Hilles and Helga's London residence on Elizabeth Street.

B ack in London after the Salisbury wedding weekend, Isabella was walking down the street with her host, Maria St. Just, telling her about Detmar and declaring, "I'm madly in love with him," when Detmar suddenly appeared on the opposite side of Gerald Road. Isabella, uncharacteristically startled, said to Maria, "Oh, my god. That's him." But he kept walking blindly past. The opportunity was not lost on Maria, who told Isabella, "If you're really serious about this person, you have to go back and not let him out of your sight."

That was all the encouragement Detmar needed to take up pursuit. The following Thursday he rang, told her he was preparing lamb with an apricot marinade, and invited her to a dinner at his place that evening. She came, wearing a short silver skirt. "The Pam Hogg look!" said Detmar, referring to a 1970s designer famous for short, tight metallic looks. "Amazing body. I thought 'phwoar!'" When Isabella went upstairs to make a phone call, Detmar followed her and jumped on her. She said, "Get off me, you silly Sri Lanki."[11] Downstairs, his fifty-something girlfriend was not amused. After dinner at Detmar's, the three decamped to another dinner, this one at Geraldine Harmsworth's house in Fulham. After requesting a glass of milk, Detmar took advantage of a shortage of chairs to pull Isabella onto his lap. That was enough for the girlfriend, who broke up with him on the spot.

Detmar was not Isabella's usual physical type. Both Willis and Taylor had been, as her friends put it, manly men. Detmar was not. Her friends found him a comical character. He had a nervous air about him and spoke with a giggle—much like a tipsy old lady. Although not unattractive, his rounded features led one more toward feelings of sympathy than sexual excitement and passion. But he had an ace up his sleeve: Hilles.

Hilles couldn't compare with Doddington Hall in terms of grandeur—it had "only" nine hundred acres—compared with the Delves Broughton's initial 40,000—but its setting, décor, and sordid history gave it an allure all its own. The estate sits in the middle of Gloucestershire, in a relatively uninhabited part of England favored by artists. It's a five-minute drive from the nearest paved road until you see the imposing stone walls of the house. From the house one can see views over the Severn Valley to the Malvern Hills and Wales. Inside, exposed oak beams support the ceiling and the unusual rectangular protruding bay windows let light into alcoves off the main hall. Friends and family enter through the square kitchen, in which a large wooden table takes up most of the space. On the walls are the antique coal heaters, which were used before central heating, surrounded by pieces of blue-and-white Spode china. Following a fire in the 1950s, the rest of the ground floor became one big room. Its walls are paneled with dark wood, and a massive floral William Morris rug covers the dark wood floor. Above the fireplace is a plaster coat of arms of the Stuarts, a unicorn on one side and a lion on the other, in gold and silver. On another wall is Detmar's pride and joy, a portrait of his grandfather, Detmar Jellings, by Augustus John, the famous Welsh artist who had been a friend of his.

Though comparatively a "new build" in this part of the world, the house is filled with portraits of Stuart monarchs. Tapestries by Burne-Jones were hung by Detmar Jellings to enhance the medieval air. The walls leading to the main stairwell are decorated with guns, swords, and other miscellaneous kinds of weaponry. Here and there stand suits of armor. There is little in the way of soft furniture, and the whole place has a rather dark, medieval, and slightly cold air. It is a life-size theatrical set. The ashes of Jonathan Blow remain in a box on a desk by the dining table, in front of an eighteenth-century French clock, which has not been wound since his death.

Just as Hilles was built to give Winifred a place to reign, and gave Helga a place to call home in a country that was not her own, it won over another aristocratic woman for the younger Detmar Blow: Isabella. "I felt that Isabella fell in love with Hilles and the romance of Hilles," said her old friend Lucy Birley. And it was love at first sight. "Her obsession was not fashion," said Philip Treacy. "It was with Hilles. She talked about the house's past inhabitants as if she'd known them—but she didn't. They were Detmar's people. It seemed clear it was a replacement for Doddington Hall."

Isabella came back from the first weekend at Hilles completely enthralled. Detmar was equally enthralled by her boundless energy and enthusiasm for the kind of life the estate could provide. "When he met Issie, she absolutely transformed him. With her very distinctive style and captivating conversation I think he felt she was the answer. He could bask in her glow," said de Silva, Detmar's uncle. Detmar rang her on the following Monday, told her he was coming to London to get his hair cut, and asked to see her. When she arrived, he said to her, "I don't want to have an affair with you. I want to marry you."[12] Isabella said yes. They had known each other for sixteen days.

When Isabella told her friends that she was in love and engaged, many were less than enthusiastic. For one thing, she was nearly thirty and Detmar was still only twenty-four years old and divided his time between two houses, both owned by his mother. Although they could see the idealistic appeal of Hilles, they could also see that the reality of it was somewhat different. Detmar's siblings, Selina and Amaury, were still living there, while Helga was in the country only infrequently. "We were slightly concerned because it wasn't like she was just marrying Detmar," said Natasha Grenfell. "She was marrying the whole family. The mother wasn't around, and they were like these lost children. Lucy and I were concerned that she was taking on a handful." Selina agreed with their assessment. "We were three urchins living in this rambling dark house." Isabella called them "Les Enfants Terribles," after the novel by Jean Cocteau. When it became increasingly clear that both she and Detmar were fantasists, happy to live in a parallel reality of their own making, people were unsure whether it was a match made in heaven or the makings of a disaster.

Isabella took some time to get used to Detmar's siblings. "At first I couldn't understand a word they were saying," she said. "They'd suddenly be boxing in the middle of lunch."[13] Once, when Selina and Detmar got in a fight and Selina had him pinned to the ground, Isabella had to pull her off him. "She was incredibly strong," Selina said. "She could pick Detmar up and run with him." Still, Isabella jumped into the role of surrogate-mother-cum-chatelaine wholeheartedly. She began to visit the farmers who lived in the cottages on the estate, to make sure they were okay. When her sister Julia came for a visit, she sent her to the estate shop, called North-western Farms, and told her to put a pair of boots on Detmar's account. And she stepped in to look after Amaury and Selina. "Isabella brought things we'd never seen before," said Selina. "Harrods vans coming down the drive; boxes from Asprey. It was all very rock and roll." And she did it all with style. "It's often so cold [at Hilles] that I have to wear my thirties Schiaparelli monkey fur coat to cook Detmar's breakfast,"[14] Isabella once said. Her conversation often turned to box hedges, dry walls, and government grants. "It was going to be the Garden of Eden in her eyes," said Philip Treacy. And one she didn't think she could be thrown out of. She thought she could get back part of the life left behind at Doddington Hall. The night before her wedding, she got a phone call from an old friend of hers and Tim Willis's, Duncan Roy. He rang to ask why she was marrying Detmar. She said, "I'm not marrying a man, I'm marrying a house." But although the estate—the nine hundred acres—belonged to Detmar, the house didn't. It still belonged to Helga. When Helga had arrived at Hilles, it was a ruin, she said. She and Jonathan had enjoyed doing it up together. So, when Isabella got there, Helga's stamp was on the place. "I was lucky in that I had an empty shell to play with," Helga said. Isabella soon discovered she would have to work around the wishes of a mother-in-law who had lived in the house all of her early adult life.

If Isabella was a slightly unusual daughter-in-law (in one photo, she and Detmar donned suits of armor to pose at Hilles), she met her match in Helga, who was living in Sri Lanka running a hotel from the childhood home her mother had designed. Helga's Folly, is a place of renown near Kandy. In the day of Helga's mother, it had hosted revolutionaries, including Mahatma Gandhi; it was the place where actress Vivien Leigh had her affair with Peter Finch in 1951; and, more recently, it was the inspiration for a song by the Stereophonics, "Madam Helga."

Helga is every bit as colorful as her hotel's history. Even in her advancing age, she was not one to walk into a room unnoticed. "It's not every mother-in-law who wanted what Isabella was wearing," said Philip Treacy. "And empathized and loved it and was right there with her in the gold thigh-high boots looking great." When Detmar took Isabella to meet Helga at her house in Elizabeth Street, Isabella wore a black veil and, said Helga, was "tottering on the highest heels I have ever seen." Isabella told Helga that her grandfather had owned tea estates and she had a great desire to visit Sri Lanka. "We bonded," said Helga. "I could see that not only Detmar and I but everyone would love her. It would have been difficult not to." She was, Helga thought, a "kindred spirit."

But similarities can also lead to conflict, even implicitly. Isabella told friends that on the eve of her wedding, Helga told her that she was lucky Detmar was marrying her. "Oh, you like toy boys?" Helga asked. "Yes, I do," responded Isabella tartly. She explained later: "They're faithful because they are still under their mother's armpits . . . Detmar was so in love with his mother that I knew he'd love me. She gave him a respect for women."[15]

But it was in the planning of her wedding that Isabella met the man who truly would become her soul mate. Philip Treacy was born in Ahascragh, a small village in the western part of Ireland, in 1967. He was one of nine children—seven brothers and a sister. His father was a baker, and his mother a housewife. At the age of five he began sewing dresses and hats for his sister's dolls, stealing time with his mother's sewing machine when she left the house. "My mother had chickens, geese, pheasants and ducks, so all the ingredients of the hat were in my house," he said.[16] Despite the size of the village—it boasts five pubs and one supermarket—his parents were enlightened. Philip was more concerned that his mother would catch him using her sewing machine than catch him making dresses. He remembers a neighbor asking his father, "Don't you think it weird that this boy is making dresses for dolls?" and his father responding, "Whatever makes him happy."[17] After high school, Treacy went to Dublin to study fashion, and after an internship in London with Stephen Jones, then Britain's most famous hat maker, he decided to focus solely on hats. When he applied to the Royal College of Art to do a master's degree, there wasn't a millinery course, but the school was thinking of setting one up. Treacy became the first student.

As much as he learned from his tutors, Treacy learned much more about the world of fashion from his participation in Isabella's wedding. The day before the event, she phoned him and asked if he'd like to come to Hilles by helicopter. One of her old boyfriends had one and would happily give him a lift. Treacy, by now fairly overwhelmed by Isabella, said he'd prefer to take the train.

The day itself was marred by the absence of Lavinia, Isabella's youngest sister. She'd married young, at age twenty, and had been living in the countryside with her husband, Doug, and their two children. Dougie, whom everyone remembers as a kind and gentle soul, had gotten in trouble as a young adult. It was enough to alienate Isabella's mother, who'd never approved of the union. In the week before the wedding, Dougie's car broke down on the highway. As he waited for help to come, he was hit by another car and killed. The blow was too much for Lavinia to bear. The wedding went on as planned, with Lavinia's children in attendance, but Lavinia stayed home.

"I was totally bewildered by this whole world that I discovered on a Saturday afternoon in Gloucestershire," said Treacy. "I'd never been there before; I was totally on my own." Although he came alone, by now he knew several of the other guests. Manolo Blahnik, who'd made Isabella's pointy shoes, carried her through the mud from the house to the waiting car, with the help of designer Rifat Ozbek, dressed in all white. Isabella looked at him and remarked, "I'm the one who is supposed to be wearing white." Treacy was stitching Isabella into her headpiece in one of the cottages on the estate when her father walked in. "I remember her looking quite unusual for a bride," Treacy said. But Evelyn didn't think so. "He said, 'You look marvelous darling!' He didn't look shocked or surprised in the slightest. *Marvelous* isn't something that would come into everyone's minds." It certainly didn't come into the mind of Isabella's mother. As Isabella came down the aisle escorted by Evelyn, dressed in her purple gown with her Philip Treacy headdress, Helen was heard to hiss to Julia, "It's absolutely ridiculous."

For the ceremony, Philip had made knights' helmets for Lucy's boys, Otis and Issac, the pageboys, and issued them strict instructions to keep their face guards down, "as if they were going into battle." It was too much excitement for one of them, who peed on the floor, and an unknowing Isabella dragged her train through the puddle. Geraldine Harmsworth's daughters were the flower girls, and the bridesmaids were wearing Treacy-designed floor-length jesters' caps.

Treacy was surprised to see that even the groom's side held their own on the dressing-up front. Helga wore a towering gold turban he'd made for her, Amaury wore flowing Arabian robes, and Selina, a tall *Cat-in-the-Hat* green velvet hat that, Treacy thought, was fantastic with her nose.

Isabella's old Oxford friends might not have looked wild, but during the long service, whenever the vicar said, "Let us pray," what sounded like a sigh of relief could be heard from the harder-partying of the crowd, who would take the opportunity to bend their heads and do a line of cocaine.

Not many pictures survived the day. The wedding photographer had been recruited during one of Isabella's dinner parties at Elizabeth Street. "I was a little drunk, so I agreed," said Julian Broad, a photographer she'd met at *Tatler*. The following morning, Broad realized it was far too big a job for him to do alone and he asked Isabella and Detmar to hire a professional. He'd also bring his own camera, he said, to take some extra shots. They said they would, but when Julian arrived at the church and asked Detmar if they'd hired someone else, Detmar said, "No. You're it." Another friend was supposed to be making a video and had set up eight video cameras in the vaults of the cathedral. Seven malfunctioned, along with two of the cameras Broad had brought. "It was awful," said Broad. When Isabella found out, she was so angry she didn't speak to him for three years.

Following the ceremony at Gloucester Cathedral, the party decamped to another cottage on Hilles for a few hours of finger food, champagne, and conversation—everyone felt bonded by the theatricality of it all. Hilles the house was off-limits due to Helga's fear that the celebrations would ruin the William Morris carpet. On Isabella's finger was her grandmother's wedding ring, inscribed "From Jock to Vera with eternal love July 11, 1913." "People say it's bad luck to wear it," Isabella said, "because they divorced and my grandfather Jock was accused of murder . . . but I think it's fine."[18] For a wedding present, Isabella and Detmar were given one hundred rare Soay sheep, the ones with curly horns. The couple departed in a blue helicopter—the same shade as Isabella's Alain Mikli eyeglasses. And lest the not-so-observant not notice this, she ran to board shouting, "Look, look, it matches my glasses!" Watching it all, Treacy thought, "It was one of the best days of my life."

After the wedding, Treacy became dejected at the thought of not seeing Isabella again and of having to return to a world where one wasn't commissioned to make knights' helmets for weddings every day. But then his phone rang. It was Isabella calling from her honeymoon. She had one thing on her mind, and that was the next hat he would make for her head. It was to be a mortar board, similar to what students wear when they graduate, in dark purple damask, to wear to a charity party she was attending with Lucy Ferry. She and Treacy went together to Watts of Westminster, suppliers to the clergy, to pick out the ecclesiastical fabric. When she came for a fitting, she told Treacy that she wanted the hat to be wide, really wide. He tried to point out that there were certain practical issues involved in wearing a hat that was three feet wide, but she wouldn't listen. When she got to the party, she found she couldn't get through the door without turning sideways. The hat met its demise at a dinner with the photographer Lord Snowdon when Isabella leaned too close to a candle. The whole thing went "*Whoosh!* It went up in flames like a zeppelin that had been shot down in World War I," said Treacy. Snowdon watched aghast, saying with typical British reserve, "Darling, your hat's on fire." All that was left was the metal frame.

At the end of 1989, Isabella got a phone call from Liz Tilberis at *Vogue*. She was looking for a new staffer for British *Vogue*, and Alexandra Schulman, one of the subeditors at *Tatler*, had recommended Isabella. It seemed the perfect move for someone obsessed with fashion. But *Vogue* is a very different proposition from *Tatler*. At *Tatler*, which was focused on skewering society, Isabella had the freedom to dress her friends as she saw fit. At *Vogue*, the focus was on selling clothes, something that really didn't interest her at all. Michael Roberts, her boss at *Tatler*, said, "I remember one minute she was my assistant, the next minute she wasn't my assistant but she was telling me what she was working on because she had her own pages and the next minute she was upstairs [at *Vogue*] but calling downstairs to tell me how dreadful upstairs was. That it was so boring and they were so commercially led."

Uninspired by the reality of working at *Vogue*, she focused her energies on her new friend Philip Treacy. When it came time for his graduation show in June 1990, she and Lucy Ferry donned Philip Treacy hats and walked the catwalk. When he was looking for someplace to set up a workshop, she insisted that he come and live and work at Helga's house on Elizabeth Street. When he needed connections, she introduced him to everyone she possibly could. At one *Vogue* party she grabbed him by the arm and frogmarched him toward Karl Lagerfeld, introducing the terrified twenty-something to one of the world's most famous designers as if she were doing the designer a favor. "Karl," she said. "This is Philip and he makes great hats." Lagerfeld sent someone to see the hats, and within weeks Isabella had arranged a trip to Paris so Treacy could meet the designer again at Chanel.

For that visit, Isabella had arranged a stay at the flat of Lord Rothermere, Harmsworth's father, on the banks of the Seine. The next day the two crossed from the Left Bank to the Right, Isabella in her green velvet coat and wearing on her head a metal frame wrapped in black silk tulle. Treacy had made the hat for the accessories designer Judy Blame, to wear to singer Neneh Cherry's wedding, but when Isabella saw it, she'd claimed it as her own. Treacy made another for Blame. "[Issie] could just about cope that someone else would have one, because she wasn't going to bump into Judy," Treacy said. "Let's give her a good day out in Paris," Isabella said speaking of the hat.

They arrived at the Chanel studio to meet with Gilles Dufour, the studio director and the rest of his team, none of whom really knew who Isabella was. French design might be progressive, but the attitudes of those working in the hallowed halls of an institution like Chanel are not. "They just sort of looked at her like "Who the fuck are you?" Treacy said. Isabella stared right back and said, "We'd like some tea, please," as if they should be waiting on her. They said, confused, "Tea? There is no tea." Isabella was not backing down. She'd come from London to introduce them to Philip Treacy—not the other way around—and she wanted some tea. "There was a bit of a standoff about tea," Treacy said. "To a person interested in fashion, to be in Coco Chanel's studio is a Holy Grail. It is a bit intimidating." But not to Isabella. "She never kowtowed to anyone."

Treacy got on with the job of opening the hat boxes, and when they looked at what he'd created, pointing out that they, too, were using tulle in their next collection, it was agreed that they'd collaborate. Treacy got the job. (When Isabella later said in the book *When Philip Met Isabella* that the Chanel collection that season was based on the tulle hat she was wearing, Karl Lagerfeld took umbrage.)

But Philip managed to design hats for the house for ten years. His first, a twisted birdcage, appeared on the supermodel Linda Evangelista, then at the height of her fame, on the cover of British *Vogue*. For Isabella, seeing that cover was a transcendent moment. Although she'd spent her life helping her friends—it was her way of showing affection—her efforts had now been recognized by the greater world.

In July 1992, Treacy was working in the basement of 67 Elizabeth Street when he heard a massive bang from the house under construction next door and watched as a layer of dust rose up and settled on everything in his workshop. Two days before Ascot Ladies Day, his biggest day of the year, a man arrived at the door and said, "You have to get out, now." The building next door had collapsed and theirs had been condemned. "There'd been some dust coming through before," Treacy said. "But then a whole lot of dust came in, and we were going to complain when we found out [the place was condemned]." Isabella and Detmar were moved by the Grovesnor Estate, owner of most all of the property in Belgravia, to temporary lodgings in Ranelagh Grove, in nearby Pimlico. The council that governs the neighborhood found Treacy a vacant space on nearby Ebury Street for his workshop.

Not only was he now separated from his best friend and muse, but his new space was much less atmospheric than Helga's basement had been. There was industrial gray carpet throughout, and the house looked as though it, too, were on the verge of collapse. "The hats were looking good, but that was about it," he said. "It was beyond shabby chic. It was pretty grim." And he still needed a place to sleep. Elizabeth Street, condemned or not, was still standing, so he continued to spend his nights there. "We got used to the condemned aspect of it," he said.

Treacy's work for Chanel soon caught the eye of Valentino, one of the last of the previous generation of designers still working for his own label. Valentino's clients—or Val's Gals, as they were known—included all of the world's major socialites and most of the royals. Val was now as rich as many of his clients, with his own château outside Paris, homes in New York and Rome, and a yacht in the Mediterranean. The thought of his paying a visit to Ebury Street, with its threadbare carpet and pockmarked walls, was terrifying. To bridge the gap between them, Treacy rang Isabella and begged her to join the meeting. Isabella loved the old-school elegance of both Valentino the man and his clothes. So she dressed for the occasion, in a full-length monkey coat and a black satin tricorn hat with chicken feathers. It was not a sight Valentino and his business partner, Giancarlo Giammetti, expected to see descending the rickety stairs to Treacy's studio. "They hadn't come across her before," said Treacy. "They just thought she was great." Before long, Philip and Isabella were having tea at the Ritz in Paris with Valentino and Joan Collins. "Quite possibly Valentino was showing Joan Collins Isabella," Treacy said. "It was a little odd, looking back. But it was fun."

In late July 1992, Isabella turned up at Ebury Street to see Treacy. "She said, 'I found this incredible designer and I bought all his clothes,'" Treacy recalled. "That was totally Issie. She didn't just say, 'Oh, I saw some nice clothes today.' She'd say, 'I saw the most incredible clothes today and I bought everything.'" Before long, she brought Alexander McQueen around to meet Treacy. "There was tension," Treacy said. "When Isabella met someone she loved, she wanted you to be their best friend immediately as well." But aside from being talented and gay, the two had very little in common. Treacy had grown up in a large, loving, stable Irish family. McQueen had grown up under the shadow of a father who hated the idea that his son was designing dresses. Philip and Lee, as McQueen was born, did not become the best of friends. "He was very different to me," said Treacy. "He was a little angrier then." While Treacy, who had now been working steadily for almost three years, had a solid clientele, many of whom were fairly famous, all that the newly graduated McQueen had was bravado—but lots of it. "His confidence was impressive because if he just thought such-and-such designer was rubbish, he would say so," Treacy said. Of course, by now Treacy was working for many of those designers. "I thought, 'It's amazing that he feels that that legend of fashiondom is crap in his words.' It was funny." Not so funny was the realization that suddenly Treacy had a rival for Isabella's attentions. "It was like Isabella had found another lover," he said. "And I was going to have to get used to it."

The Making
of a
Queen

On Julien Macdonald's first visit to Hilles, Isabella announced, "We'll go walking in the morning." Macdonald awoke and came to the kitchen to find Isabella in a kilt, a threadbare Victorian beaded jacket, Doc Martens, tartan socks, and a Philip Treacy hat with red plumes that fanned out around her head. She had a rifle over her arm and a bag of bullets hanging by her side. He asked why she was carrying the gun. "In case I want to shoot something," she replied, looking at him as if he were an idiot. Midway through their walk, happily talking about the exhibition of photographs of women in mermaid-like dresses they'd been working on, Isabella screamed, "Don't move!" And she pointed. In the field they'd just jumped a fence to get into was a massive red bull. "Issie," Macdonald said, "you're in a red hat." In an instant she considered: Bull. Hat. Red. Spain. Matador. Bullfight. Gored! "RUN," she yelled. The bull was pawing the ground as they threw themselves back over the fence.

Lee Alexander McQueen's first fashion show was one of many graduation collections premiered at the end of the spring term at the famous London fashion college Central Saint Martins in July 1992. McQueen was only twenty-three when he finished the course, but already he had been working for seven years. He hadn't intended to take the course in the first place. When he crossed the threshold of the school that boasted such illustrious alumni as John Galliano, Rifat Ozbek, and Katharine Hamnett, it was to apply to teach a class in pattern cutting. The creativity evident in his portfolio led to an offer to take a place as a student, rather than as a teacher of a technical but fairly boring subject. Central Saint Martins is famous in the fashion world for pushing students to their creative limits. It is also infamous for leaving them lacking in some practical skills that employers would like them to have. As a result, most of the students who've gone through the school have been sought more for the strength of their ideas and their attitudes than their sewing skills. Thanks to his time on Savile Row, McQueen had both—in spades. Bobbie Hillson, a former *Vogue* editor who founded the Central Saint Martins postgraduate fashion course said, "He clearly had terrific talent . . . He was also technically brilliant, even though he'd never actually studied design. And still only twenty-one or twenty-two."[1]

At the time he was studying at Central Saint Martins, London Fashion Week was seen as a week off in the international fashion calendar. The army of journalists and retailers who trekked from New York to Milan to Paris several times a year for the catwalk collections would skip London. It was regarded as a place where, at best, fantastical but usually unwearable ideas were further dragged down by an inability to meet the delivery schedules required by retailers. The most fashionable women in Britain tended to wear the designs of foreigners—be they Japanese, French, or Italian. In his book *The Fashion Conspiracy*, author Nicholas Coleridge wrote:

> *The British have always been a peculiar race, willing to die for their country but equally willing to die for another country's merchandise; a love affair that spawned an empire through our passion for Chinese and Indian silk, and later embraced first Florentine, then Parisian couture. To walk the length of upper Sloane Street in the mid-eighties is to see the old love affair transmitted into a passion for Italian, French, German and Japanese designer clothes. It seems somehow typical of England's per-*

versity that only a handful of British-made garments are for sale from one end of the designer Strip to the other."[2]

Suzy Menkes, then the fashion critic for the *Independent* and now at the *International Herald Tribune*, thought the problem with English fashion lay in the making: "the tragedy of English street fashion is that we have no tailoring. The tailoring in England looks like it was put together with a knife and fork, and a blunt one at that."[3]

Lee McQueen arrived on the scene as if especially conjured to answer Menkes's plea. Isabella, like most journalists and stylists working in fashion in London, watched the graduate shows from Central Saint Martins with a hungry eye. Spotting talent early brought kudos to journalists and exclusive deals to retailers. It was the finale shows that had gotten the conceptual designs of Hussein Chalayan and John Galliano into the windows of Brown's, the London retailer known for launching new talent. Chalayan had buried his graduate collection in dirt to see the effect it would have on the clothes, and Galliano's 1984 graduate show, *Les Incroyables*, of voluminous shirts and coats, had been based on the French Revolution.

In 1992, Isabella arrived at the Central Saint Martins show unfashionably late and took the only seat she could find, on the steps. Collection after collection went by, most with the usual student failings of trying too hard, until she saw the clothes of McQueen, based on Jack the Ripper. For the show, McQueen had cut impeccably tailored jackets reminiscent of the Victorian era and then covered them with fake blood. "The tailoring was excellent," Isabella said of that first show. "No one spotted it: They kept thinking it was just blood and paint, they weren't looking at the cut!"[4] Particularly arresting were the jackets with protruding waists that stood away from the body thanks to wires in the seams and a transparent wedding dress lined with human hair. It was a cohesive collection of only ten garments, but Isabella knew from the second she saw them that she had to own them. She began to make calls—to the school, to McQueen's tutor, and to his mother, who repeatedly told her that

McQueen was not at home. To her son she said, "Who is this loony lady calling?"[5]

At the time, McQueen was living with his parents in a townhouse in Stratford, a grim part of London's East End comprising largely state-funded apartment buildings. His father, Ronald, was a taxi driver and his mum, Joyce, was a genealogist. He was the youngest of six children, three boys and three girls. His first fashion sketch was done on the wall of his sisters' bedroom when he was three. It was Cinderella with a tiny waist and a huge gown. (After he became famous, he asked his father if he could pull back the wallpaper that had been added to see the drawing. "He said, 'If you peel off the wallpaper, you can paper the whole fucking room again.' ")[6] McQueen soon moved from doodling on walls to making dresses for his sisters, when he wasn't watching kestrels, the small falcon-like birds that circled in the sky from the roof of a high-rise building across the street from his house, or participating in synchronized swimming. "I'm not the typical gay man," McQueen said. "I come from a very straight background. But I've never denied being gay either. I just don't see that as a focal point in designing clothes."[7] He spent much of his school days drawing dresses and defending himself as necessary from boys who called him McQueer. "It takes a lot for me to get going," he said. "But there's a breaking point in everyone, and if they don't shut up you've gotta shut 'em up."[8] Lee was the darling of his older sisters. "They would call me up to their room and I'd help them pick out clothes for work. Just, you know, what skirt with what cardigan, but I was always trying to make them look strong and sheltered."[9]

When he turned sixteen, he left high school and did a night course in art. In 1986, he and his mother saw a documentary about Savile Row that said the tailors there were a dying breed and were in desperate need of apprentices. They decided that Lee should try to get a job there. He turned up at Anderson & Sheppard, tailors to Prince Charles, and was hired on the spot. He spent two years on the Row, learning how to make jackets, a process so boring that he said he took to scrawling obscenities on the canvases. (John Hitchcock, the managing director of Anderson & Sheppard, says that a jacket in question was recalled and no obscenities were found.) This was followed by a stint at Gieves & Hawkes, to learn how to make trousers. His last stop on the Row was the theatrical costumiers Angels & Bermans, where he learned pattern cutting. "I was interested in the technical side," he said. "Learning all these old techniques, 16th-century pattern cutting and stuff like that."[10] At twenty he went to work for Koji Tatsuno, a trendy Japanese designer who impressed McQueen because "he made these fantastic clothes using antique fabrics, tailored jackets with beautiful linings,"[11] and then to Milan, where, again, he turned up on the doorstep of the place he wanted to work and asked for a job. Romeo Gigli, then at the peak of his fame for his feminine and romantic styles, looked at McQueen's résumé and hired him as a pattern cutter. In 1990, Gigli separated from his friends and business partners Donato Maiano and Carla Sozzani, and temporarily went out of business. After only nine months, McQueen decided to go back to London.

London is home to far fewer big designer companies than either Milan or Paris, and finding a job in one of the few design houses there is tricky, even for the most talented of young designers, not to mention one who has never studied formally. With his training on Savile Row and subsequent work experience, McQueen sought gainful employment at Central Saint Martins. When they offered him a spot as a graduate student, he borrowed the tuition money from his aunt and enrolled.

When Isabella finally met McQueen she began effusing about his clothes, announcing her desire to own them. "She asked how much this jacket was, and I just thought I'd try it on, didn't I?" McQueen said. "So I said £450. And she bought it!"[12] They settled on a price of £5,000 for the entire collection. Each week Isabella would arrive with an installment of cash, and McQueen would take a piece out of a bin bag and give it to her. If she arrived without cash, he would walk her to the nearest cash point and wait while she withdrew the money. It took nearly a year, but she bought the entire collection.

Her commitment didn't stop with shopping for herself. She took McQueen on as her protégé number two. And one of the first things she did was introduce him to protégé number one, Philip Treacy. The problem was that by now Treacy was working for many of the designers McQueen criticized, including Karl Lagerfeld at Chanel. While Treacy saw himself as part of the evolution of fashion—and respected those who had come before—McQueen saw himself as standing apart. The only living designer he respected, he said, was the avant-garde Japanese Rei Kawakubo, who was behind the conceptual Comme des Garçons line. Kawakubo's forte is rethinking the very idea of clothes. Her Paris show in 1981 featured a collection of mannish coats with unfinished seams—confusing to critics who were used to seeing polished collections on the Paris runways. Asked if he had respect for Chanel and Versace, McQueen said, "No, no respect at all. What, putting a bit of chain mail in a load of different bright colors! No, no, no. I've seen these people in the flesh now at a *Vogue* party in New York and it's like Michael Jackson's *Thriller*. These old and decrepit people who've lived it up and didn't know when to stop. All these zombies dancing around."[13] While walking one editor through his collection, he defined it in opposition to one of the legends of modern British fashion: "I mean it's not just great swathes of tartan wrapped round a body like Vivienne Westwood does."[14]

The zombies fired back. Yves Saint Laurent called McQueen a "talentless upstart," and Vivienne Westwood said that "his only usefulness is a measure of zero talent."[15] Yet Isabella loved that McQueen was so outspoken, and she stood by him regardless. "Some were sniffy about his talent," said Treacy. "It's easy now for people to say he's brilliant, but this was when he hadn't got going at all and she was talking about him being the next Saint Laurent—which at that moment sounded pretty wild. But she was right. She was like a bulldozer. She would tell everyone about him in such an effusive way. She thought he was just the bee's knees."

Even McQueen wasn't quite sure what to do with Isabella's enthusiasm. "I've been called 'the new Saint Laurent' by some woman at *Vogue*," he said. "But what the fuck does that mean? It just sounds poncey. At the end of the day, clothes are clothes and I'm making really good ones."[16] He also took objection to Isabella's telling people that it was her idea that he call himself Alexander instead of Lee. "I dropped my first name when I started working for myself because I was signing on [to receive unemployment benefits] at the time," he said.[17]

That Alexander (as Isabella always called him) did not fit in with the rest of Isabella's friends did not concern her at all. "Normally, all I'm interested in is what the person has created," she said. "Hopefully they're not a mass murderer or a mass rapist, but their personality is not important to me at that stage. They've got to be pretty extraordinary to make things like that anyway."[18] When Lucy Ferry lost a maroon alpaca Dior coat at a pie-throwing party thrown by her future husband, Robin Birley, Isabella suggested that she have Alexander McQueen make her another. Ferry agreed, and McQueen came to her house to discuss the coat. They decided it should be alpaca, like the one she lost, and he asked for a deposit so that he could buy the fabric. McQueen asked, "Would you like to see what I'm into?" She said okay. "He gave me this book and it was full of pictures of deformed children and people who had been Napalmed. I was completely fazed." Nevertheless, Ferry gave him a check for £300. When the Elizabeth Street house where McQueen had been working was evacuated, the coat was lost in the confusion. Years later, whenever Ferry saw McQueen at a party they would greet each other with a secret code salutation, "Alpaca!"

In November 1992, *Vogue* ran a six-page story on Isabella, Detmar, and their life at Hilles. It was a proud moment for Isabella: in it, she could show off not only her new husband and his stately home, but also the work of her two disciples. In the pictures of their bedroom, which had been the top-floor nursery at Hilles, one can see on the walls, behind the Timorous Beasties canopy bed with its giant insect motif, black hats made by Philip

Treacy. But in the main picture Isabella is hatless, and throughout the spread she is dressed completely in McQueen's graduate collection: a black trouser suit with flared jacket, a long purple frock coat with black stripes, and, unusually, a white dress made of layers of sheer organza with flower petals between the layers. It was the first piece she commissioned from McQueen, and its ethereal and delicate femininity made it stand out from the rest of his clothes. The price for a six-page ad in *Vogue* would easily have run into the tens of thousands of pounds, but in that issue, young Alexander McQueen got the publicity for free.

During the Christmas holidays that year, Isabella and Detmar went to Sri Lanka to see Helga. On January 5, 1993, Isabella got the news that her father had died. She returned home immediately. Once home, the news got even worse. Evelyn had left her and her sisters only £5,000 each. The bulk of his estate—finally tallied to be near £4 million—went to Rona, her stepmother. Isabella was distraught. She phoned Treacy early one Saturday morning. "I didn't realize how traumatic [the will] was for her," he said. It shouldn't have been. According to Rona, Isabella, Julia, and Lavinia had been told by their father not to expect an inheritance. "He took care of them when he was alive," Rona said. "It was the sensible thing to do because there's no tax between husband and wife. I insisted that he discuss it with the children, so there were no surprises. But she chose not to take it in." (Although Lavinia and Julia expected that their stepmother would inherit the bulk of the estate, they thought it would specify that his estate would be divided equally among the sisters upon Rona's death.)

In tears, Isabella rang friends she had not seen in years, unable to see her father's bequest as anything but another parental rejection, and she considered taking legal action against Rona. "The only thing I found in my father's safe was my gold ballroom dancing medal," she said. "My stepmother gave it to me and said, 'Here's the medal.' I said, 'Thank you. Is there anything else?' "[19] There was, of course. There was the trust that Isabella had been given at twenty-one, but much of it had been spent by Isabella in the last ten years. Because of Isabella's spending habits, and the fact that the trust had been put in her name to save on taxes, Julia and Lavinia had never seen any money from it, although, says Rona, "they should have done." Evelyn's will was a blow for Detmar, too. He had been led to believe by Isabella that there would be more money on the way. Now he had to come to grips with the fact that he'd have no help supporting his wife's flagrant spending habits. "Five grand is fuck all money, man," Detmar said. "People talk about the upper classes, but they are fucking tough. Callous, you know."[20]

Isabella fit the slight into the Cinderella fantasy she had created about her childhood. She and Treacy undertook massive preparations for her father's funeral. She had her hair and makeup done, and took preview Polaroids with Treacy, who was doing everything he could to help. "It was a very big deal, going to her father's funeral. She said, 'I'm not going to go looking poor.'" The trauma unearthed latent fears. Like her grandfather, she developed a pathological fear of being short of money, a fear that would only get worse as time went on. That the vast sum of money that had trickled down through hundreds of generations of Delves Broughton blood had run out meant, for Isabella, facing up to the inescapable notion that she was not working because she wanted to, but because she had to. Although Detmar had land, he didn't have the cash to support her lavish lifestyle.

Meanwhile, thanks to her relentless promotion, by the time Alexander McQueen had his first professional show in February 1993, he was already the talk of London. This was the first occasion on which the British Fashion Council backed a new designer, and his show, *Nihilism*, was one of the most eagerly anticipated of the season. This was helped by the fact that four of the UK's best-known designers—Vivienne Westwood, John Galliano, Katharine Hamnett, and Rifat Ozbek—had decided, for commercial reasons, to show in either Milan or Paris. International buyers simply weren't making the trip to London. If the designers had to go abroad to sell their collections, why not show there, too? Those who made the trip to see Alexander McQueen's show at the Bluebird Garage on King's Road that day would not soon forget what they saw. "It was one of those nineties happenings where no one quite knew what we were going to see, but there was a huge amount of curiosity about it," said Katie Grand, the fashion director of *Dazed and Confused*, the newly launched youth culture magazine that had set out to rival the *Face* magazine. "There was no seating, and it was all incredibly cool. The girls came out covered in terracotta makeup and that weird proportion with the bumster [the ultra-low-cut trouser] which is now so famous. There were so many beautiful things in that show—it was just relentless."[21] The bumster got him more attention than anything else, but it was designed not to show off the buttocks but to lengthen the torso, for a look he found empowering. McQueen used materials in that show never before used in fashion to create new textures—things like shellac, beetle blood, and human hair. The result was as he intended. "There was so much repression in London fashion," he said. "It had to be livened up . . . My job was to produce ideas."[22]

After the show, Grand photographed Isabella in McQueen's clothes at his studio in Covent Garden for *Dazed and Confused* magazine. When they were finished, Isabella decided that they should go visit McQueen in his flat in Essex. The drive from London, which should have taken forty minutes, took three hours, due to the fact that—this being 1993—they had no mobile phones and no GPS. They also had no maps and no directions. Grand, manning the wheel of her Fiat Panda, had begun to question the wisdom of trying to find the flat in the first place. McQueen didn't even know they were coming, and with only an address to go on, it was looking less and less likely they'd ever get there. At a set of traffic lights in one of the county's less savory parts, Isabella hopped out of the car and starting flagging down strangers. "Whoo hoo! Whoo hoo!" "Oh, darling!" she said when she captured one, "Where is this?" she asked, pointing to the scribbled address. Eventually they arrived, and McQueen disappeared into his bedroom. He came back with a garbage bag and began rummaging around in it. Out came the pieces from his second collection. After the impromptu show, he gave Grand a rust-colored coat.

Soon Isabella suggested to McQueen that he move into Philip's old space in Elizabeth Street, which he did, bringing with him only a pattern-cutting table. With the assistance of the Grovesnor Estate, Treacy had moved into a new townhouse, also on Elizabeth Street. A week later, Isabella's assistant, Stefan, moved in to live with Treacy as his boyfriend. The two still live together. "There was a joke that she sold me for a Gilbert and George hat," Stefan said of his passing from Isabella's employ to Philip's live-in lover. Beneath a tiny shop at 69 Elizabeth Street, next door to Helga's house, he had a workshop with ten people assembling and packing his hats. Isabella stopped by one day after a trip to the Victoria and Albert Museum. She had with her an image of a ship hat from the Marie Antoinette period. She raved to him, "Isn't it incredible?" Treacy liked it, but thought that it was merely an artist's fantasy of the great lengths to which French women of that era went in their dress. It wasn't. Isabella gave him a copy of *Pleasure and Privilege*, by Oliver Bernier, a book describing lavish French lifestyle before the Revolution. She'd left a bookmark in chapter 5, "The Rule of Fashion." There he read, "You could not be in fashion unless you wore towers of hair piled up nearly three feet high and generously supplemented with cushions and hair pieces . . . To be really modish you had to wear a headdress *de circonstance*. Thus, when Admiral d'Estaing won his battle over the English fleet, ladies wore an entire ship, almost a foot high and dangling with a jeweled anchor in the back."[23] In other words, wearing a ship on your head was as cool as owning the latest pair of Gucci sneakers, and Isabella wanted in. Treacy worked on the hat for weeks, toiling on the weekends and late at night, when he was alone and had the space to spread out all the materials he needed. At the same time, Alexander

McQueen was putting together his next collection next door. Treacy had hoped to keep the ship a secret until his show, but Isabella, like an excited child, had told McQueen about it. He used this knowledge to tease the girls who worked for Treacy: "I hear you're building a ship in there."

While her protégés were busy on Elizabeth Street, Isabella had been working at *Vogue*. Though she had been there over a year, she was still struggling to find her place. "She was just pretty wild for British *Vogue*," said Treacy. Instead of doing full features, as she had at *Tatler*, she was given only the odd assignment for pictures that would run at less than half a page. Her credits were for styling the singers from Shakespears Sister (holding pigs and wearing Philip Treacy hats), or the members of the group Right Said Fred (in colorful suits by Thierry Mugler and Claude Montana, and without shirts and wearing platform brogues). "She was always looking for an idea, trying to find a way [for her work] to fit in," Treacy said.

When British *Vogue*'s editor, Alexandra Schulman, called Isabella and said that she was to help Steven Meisel with his first shoot for the magazine, it would have seemed to be that moment. Here was a project right up her alley. Subsequently known as the "London Babes" shoot, it was the first—and last—time that the illustrious and expensive American photographer Meisel would shoot for British *Vogue*. He brought Joe McKenna with him from New York to do the styling. On arriving in London, Schulman told McKenna that Isabella would help him with the casting. "She was fantastic. The girls she brought me were Plum Sykes, Honor Fraser, Stella Tennant, and Louise Campbell"—in other words, a host of her aristocratic friends and cousins. Many of these girls had never modeled before and would go on to have long and successful careers, initiating the bluebloods-on-the-runway trend that would last for years. Stella Tennant arrived for the shoot "smelling of goat," Isabella said.[24] And she had an enormous ring through her nostril. Steven Meisel and Isabella thought it looked wonderful, but *Vogue*'s more conservative editor, Alex Schulman, wanted it removed. Isabella later said that removing it would have required a trip to the hospital—at least that's likely the excuse she gave Schulman—and the nose ring stayed. Stella was an instant success. Although this was her first modeling job, her second was the cover of Italian *Vogue*, also organized and styled by Isabella and shot by Meisel. Meisel took some of the most famous photographs of Isabella at the same time.

When it came to choosing the clothes, however, things with Joe McKenna got complicated. Although he thought she was in charge of the models, Isabella insisted that McKenna take a look at McQueen's clothes, but day after day, the designer didn't appear. Finally Isabella told McKenna it was because McQueen didn't have the money to get to Vogue House. McKenna told her to have him take a taxi and pay for it out of petty cash. McQueen came to see McKenna with a plastic supermarket bag full of clothes. "I'd come from New York, where fashion was very slick. I was expecting a rack of clothes—or at least a garment bag." In McQueen's bag were two pieces of wool lace with rough edges and uneven hems. Isabella began raving about them. "I just didn't get it," McKenna said. "Until we put them on Stella Tennant and then you could see that there was something going on." The McQueen pieces made the *Vogue* shoot—again, a remarkable achievement for a designer so early in his career—but other items that Isabella wanted, such as a dress from Hyper Hyper, a hip street brand, did not. McKenna and Isabella began to bicker over which one of them had ultimate control.

Later the shoot would be seen as the trigger of a seminal movement in fashion—the arrival of the aristocrat as model—and Isabella would be seen as the key force behind it. Six years later, in an April 1999 article, Jeremy Langmead credited the shoot with kicking off the current vogue for unusual piercing among teens. But at the time, the production caused a rift between the two old friends and was the last straw in Isabella's working relationship with *Vogue*. Whether it was the politics of the shoot, the anarchy of Tennant's nose ring, or just that her time had come is unclear.

But shortly thereafter it was decided that Isabella should leave *Vogue*. In a compromise possibly meant to keep the peace with her and her famous coterie of friends, she was moved in September 1994 to the Contributing Editors line on the *Vogue* masthead.

Despite the soaring careers of her two protégés, at the end of 1994, Isabella was still casting about to find what she should do with her life. Work would come in—she would style an album cover here or there—but without a full-time job, she felt constantly on edge. "She would come to visit me and say, 'You can make hats and I can't do anything,'" Treacy said.

What Isabella could do, and did continually, was talk up Alexander McQueen to anyone who would listen—and even more to those who wouldn't. "She was the first to tell me about McQueen," said Michael Roberts, her old boss from *Tatler*. "I have to admit I didn't get it." She phoned Roberts in Paris and told him that McQueen was "the only hope for British fashion." She got him to come to McQueen's second show, called *Banshee*, at Café de Paris on Piccadilly. "The whole affair was chaotic, damp, and smelly," Roberts said.[25] And in the middle of it all was Isabella with the word *McQueen* stenciled onto her hair in silver. As she had done for Philip Treacy when he graduated, Isabella walked the runway for Alexander, wearing the lace dress Stella Tennant had worn in the "London Babes" shoot and then a high-collared purple shirt. Isabella showed Roberts the clothes that he later said were "as different, new and difficult to understand as those shown by the Japanese designers when they first took Paris by storm."[26] McQueen said a brief hello to Roberts, but left Isabella to do the talking. ("Tongue-tied and chubby" was Roberts's opinion of McQueen.) Isabella brought critical attention to McQueen's show in other ways. Modeling alongside her was her assistant at *Vogue*, Plum Sykes, who had also starred in "London Babes." "I did have the elongated, spiderlike proportions he loves, and the clothes fit me perfectly," Sykes said.[27]

Isabella's position with McQueen was still that of patron or mentor, not collaborator. While she and Philip Treacy would on occasion concoct ideas for hats together, McQueen came up with his ideas alone and he had never asked Isabella to work on his shows in an official capacity. For the first two shows, a friend he knew from Central Saint Martins did the styling. And in 1995 he replaced her with Katy England, a girl he met outside a bead shop in East London. The first show she worked on was called *Highland Rape*, and she found herself in the middle of a media firestorm afterward. The show was based on the aftermath of the final battle of the Jacobite Rebellion, in which the revolutionary Jacobite Highland Scots were defeated by the British troops and the survivors were put to death or, in the case of the women, raped. McQueen called it "total genocide."[28] The quality of the clothes nevertheless stood out amid accusations of misogyny at the sight of women in torn clothing and with bloodstained faces. McQueen said, "They [the critics] completely misunderstood *Highland Rape*. It wasn't anti-woman. It was actually anti the fake history of Vivienne Westwood. She makes tartan lovely and romantic and tries to pretend that's how it was. Well, eighteenth-century Scotland was not about beautiful women drifting across the moors in swathes of unmanageable chiffon."[29] Although Katy England styled the show, the models were pure Isabella: Honor Fraser and Stella Tennant both made an appearance.

Isabella's influence in McQueen's collections could be seen in less direct ways, by people close to them both. She frequently invited him to Hilles and would quiet the other guests so he could work. When she learned of his love of birds, she introduced him to the sport of falconry. Surely that was in his mind when he would present his *Icarus* collection on the haute couture runway for Givenchy in 1997. And in the last collection he worked on before his death in 2010, his fabrics were printed with Renaissance-style artworks—were these not the characters from the miniature Primavera tapestry he'd stolen from the Blue Room at Hilles? When asked about his inspiration for the spring 2010 *Neptune* collection, McQueen told an interviewer that he had looked up "Neptune" on Wikipedia. But before there was Wikipedia, there was Isabella. "My role is to pass intellectual information on to the designer," she said. "Anything that inspires me I pass on, be it a book, a film, an image, a piece of music, things from flea markets."[30] McQueen would march her to the ATM so she could get the money to pay for his clothes, but Isabella would march him to museums. And in the hands of McQueen, a single vase could become an entire collection. Asked if Isabella influenced him, he said, "Course. She's like a disease. A terminal disease. Everything she does rubs off on you."[31] Her role in his life would, at times, frustrate the loyal group of workers he kept close to him. "Everyone gets frustrated and annoyed with me in the office," Isabella said. "I'm sure they find me a complete pain."[32] And at times, they did. Although she wasn't involved in a show's preparations, Isabella would take liberties, like coming backstage beforehand and expecting the busy team do her hair and makeup, too, or borrowing clothes from the press office that she would then give to her assistants.

Though the McQueen collections didn't land Isabella a job on his team, it did provide her with her next project. She was taken by the innovative knits featured in the collection, and when she asked who had made them, she was told it was a young gay boy from the rural Welsh Valley who had been taught to knit by his mother in a knitting circle. Julien Macdonald was still a student in Brighton when he came to Elizabeth Street to find McQueen working in the basement with nothing but a table to cut patterns on. Annabelle Neilson, a fun-loving socialite who had married banking heir Nathaniel Rothschild in 1995, or some of his other new fans might be around to listen as McQueen issued Macdonald the strangest of instructions. "Can you knit a sweater with hair from my grandmother's dog?" Julien gave it a go and came back with a sample. In this case anyway, they decided not to proceed, but Julien's talent and willingness to try the bizarre made him the perfect addition to McQueen's team. Isabella called Macdonald "Brother Julien," because he had an angelic look and he once wanted to be a priest—he'd written his dissertation on stigmata—and he called her Blow Job. Soon Isabella began to ask Macdonald to make things for her, often via handwritten notes. "She'd write, 'Look at Cézanne and make me a sweater like that,' " he said. "It could be about a color or a poem, but there was always some literature or art reference—some mad reference. Often, I didn't have a clue what she was talking about." Isabella would follow up by sending color photocopies in the mail.

The creative commune spirit of Elizabeth Street during the week was transplanted to Gloucestershire on the weekends, when Isabella took all of her new disciples to Hilles. Her other guests would range from fashion editors to the guy from down the meadow who was fixing the fence—just as Detmar the architect had intended. "Life at Hilles, it was the talk of the village," said Macdonald. On one memorable occasion Isabella was arrested while shopping in town. A lamb had gone missing from the local butcher, and the police said someone fitting her description had been seen taking it. "It was a scandal," said Macdonald. "But, please, someone fitting her description?" Detmar had to go and get her released.

On one of the trips to Hilles, Isabella made another discovery. Iris Palmer was a girl who lived nearby in Gloucestershire, and one of the artists who lived in a cottage on the Hilles estate told Isabella that she might make a good model. Isabella went to visit Iris at her parents' house and liked what she saw. She promptly put her in the Philip Treacy show, as well as the Alexander McQueen show, and introduced her to Sarah Doukas, founder of the modeling agency Storm. "With Issie, it was straight to the top," Palmer said. When the young model got a job in New York, Isabella arranged for her to stay in the apartment of her friend Sarah St. George. "I forgot to shut the blinds and when I woke at six I was gobsmacked. I had all of New York beneath me."

When Macdonald finished his master's in knitwear at the Royal College of Art in 1996, Isabella styled his graduate collection. And, as she had done with Philip Treacy, she then introduced him to Karl Lagerfeld—who made him the head of knitwear for Chanel.

In early 1996, despite having a new talent to promote, without magazine pages to style, Isabella's self-esteem began to plummet. It also didn't help that she and Detmar had begun to try to have a baby and weren't having any luck conceiving. Treacy invited her to style his catwalk show, hoping it would give her a boost. He was surprised by her response: "I can't do that," she said. He was stunned. Isabella hadn't yet started talking about being depressed and he didn't understand what was at the root of this sudden insecurity. He convinced her that she could, and they enlisted the corset maker Mr. Pearl and also called in pieces from their friends. Isabella matched the corsets with trousers and the lace Antonio Berardi dresses with sparkling knickers.

The show was one of the highlights of the season. After the shows, that March, fashion critic Amy Spindler wrote in the *New York Times* that Isabella was "the key to the two strongest shows in London this season."[33] At the British Fashion Awards, both Alexander McQueen, who was named Designer of the Year, and Philip Treacy, who had won Accessories Designer of the Year, gave speeches full of praise for Isabella. Lucinda Chambers, the fashion director of British *Vogue*, said of Isabella, "her talent is really taking up designers and supporting them verbally—and I'm sure financially—and creating a buzz about them. She's a character herself, so it rubs off on the designers and they also get publicity as a result of it."[34] Isabella was beginning to get a fair amount of publicity in her own right.

In the summer of 1996, a British journalist named Toby Young was in New York trying to save his job. He had been hired on a whim by Graydon Carter, the editor of *Vanity Fair*, and so far had failed to impress. On August 18, 1996, Young suggested the magazine do a story on London's uncharacteristically upbeat mood. He was summoned to a meeting in Carter's office to make his case, and to do so he decided to test a John Maynard Keynes theory that the key to convincing someone of the rightness of your point of view lay in asserting it as emphatically as possible, and described the results in a book about his life in New York.

> *"London's hot right now," I said, trying to inject a note of definitiveness into my voice. "It's buzzing. You can almost feel the electricity as soon as you land at Heathrow."*

"Really?" asked David Harris [the art director].

"Absolutely," I replied.

"You think this Swinging London Mark II thing is totally for real?" asked Aimée [an editor].

"No question," I said looking pointedly at each person in turn. "Make no mistake: this phenomenon is very, very real" . . . A silence descended on the group. A consensus had emerged. London was on fire.[35]

Toby's pitch had worked. *Vanity Fair* began to plan a twenty-five-page cover story devoted to Cool Britannia. In addition to putting up various staffers, the magazine set up a mobile office in a suite at the Dorchester, one of London's most expensive hotels. Young estimated that the hotel bill was over £100,000 for a month's time. Featured were artist Damien Hirst, film director Richard Curtis, the pop band Blur's bass player Alex James, actor Keith Allen, model Sophie Dahl, *Loaded* magazine editor James Brown, actress Patsy Kensit, pop band Oasis's lead singer Liam Gallagher, and Prime Minister Tony Blair. The world of fashion was represented by Stella McCartney, the daughter of Beatle Paul McCartney, and Alexander McQueen. Young arranged for Isabella to be hired as a consultant on the massive project. He knew her from her days with Tim Willis, her ex-boyfriend, and he understood the nature of her connections and her persuasive powers.

For the "Cool Britannia" piece, McQueen told photographer David LaChapelle when they met that he insisted he take the portrait of him and Isabella because "we heard you were the most expensive photographer in the world." Isabella jumped in and started raving about LaChapelle's work. "What I remember most is the laughter," the photographer said. "They were both so optimistic about the future. When I think about that shoot I think about how much fun it was. How much laughter and how much joy." McQueen had suggested posing as Queen Victoria, but instead he wore a corset, a long skirt, and red leather gloves, and he clutched in his hand a flaming torch. Isabella wore a McQueen dress with a tall collar over her lower face and a Philip Treacy hat, and she held the train of McQueen's skirt. In the background Hedingham Castle, in Essex, burns and a horse rears up over a fallen knight. It is the most famous portrait of the two ever taken. The setting and pose show not just their shared love of English history, but also that Isabella was content being perceived as Alexander's handmaiden. In portraits with Philip Treacy, she appears more as a wife, usually standing beside him as his equal.

For McQueen's interview for that issue of *Vanity Fair*, Isabella escorted interviewer David Kamp to the meeting. Kamp had been in London for a month and was suffering from a cold. "I found myself speeding toward the gentrifying neighborhood of Hoxton while Issie Blow, who was wearing some kind of black netting over her face, cradled my head, stroked it, and repeatedly cooed, 'Oh, Day-vid! Poor, poor Day-vid!'"[36] In the interview, Kamp mentions that John Major, a previous prime minister, had said in a speech that "our country has taken over the fashion catwalks of Paris." McQueen's reaction shows how he feels about people taking credit for his work. "Ah, fucking plank! I'm not one of his own! He didn't get me there, the fucker! Fuck him! So fucking typical of government! They do nothing to help you when you're trying to do something, then take credit when you're a success! Fuck off!"[37]

Just as Isabella was getting tired that people such as Lucinda Chambers were assuming she was rich and didn't need to work, McQueen was getting tired of seeing his accomplishments diminished. Although he appreciated Isabella's enthusiasm and was grateful for her support, hearing her say she'd discovered him was beginning to grate. "I fucking discovered Alexander McQueen,"[38] he'd say. "He worked hard himself, really fucking hard," said LaChapelle. "And he also wanted people to know it was him. He needed his autonomy. He needed people to know that. She was so in love and so heavily promoting that, at times, it could be overwhelming. It was like she birthed him, but if the goods weren't there, he never would have made it."

In fashion circles, the talk of the summer of 1996 was the search for someone to replace Gianfranco Ferré at Christian Dior. The Italian designer had produced collections that were elegant and wearable and in keeping with the house's esteemed history, but he had failed to reignite the imagination of the press. His presence at Dior simply wasn't the new breath of life that Bernard Arnault, owner of LVMH (Moët Hennesy–Louis Vuitton), had been hoping would attract a new generation of customers. Asked whom she thought should have the job, Isabella did not hesitate: Alexander McQueen. The job was given instead to John Galliano, but his hiring opened up an empty seat in the game of musical chairs—that of designer for Givenchy, a more recent acquisition of Arnault's.

When McQueen was asked if he wanted one of the most prestigious posts in fashion, he said . . . *maybe*. With his line just coming into its own, he was not at all sure he needed the added pressure of designing for another label. Plus, Givenchy had both a haute couture collection and a men's collection, which meant he would be responsible for six major collections a year for the house, in addition to four of his own. "I can't imagine anyone doing that," he said. "My first concern has to be McQueen. Givenchy would be a lot of money, but I'm not really into that. Plus, Paris does nothing for me . . . Basically all these big companies don't care about you as a person. You're only a commodity and a product to them and only as good as your last collection."[39]

In the end, despite his reservations, he decided to take the job, encouraged by both his mother and Isabella not to let the opportunity slip through his fingers. For Isabella, the posting seems to have been the answer to her own career dilemma. She anticipated going to Paris and working with McQueen at Givenchy, in much the same way her friend Amanda Harlech had worked for John Galliano and would soon be working with Karl Lagerfeld at Chanel. The role of a paid muse like Harlech is a difficult one to define, and varies from case to case, but generally it comes down to telling an often gay designer what real women actually want to wear. Isabella encouraged designers in the other direction—pushing them to make the most inventive things possible, not the most practical. It worked for Philip Treacy: the attention he got for the outrageous designs she wore led to commissions for more watered-down versions that could be worn by the rest of the world. But Alexander McQueen wasn't looking for that from his staff. He was looking for creative yet practical people who could bring his ideas to life.

But he still relied on Isabella for advice and support. She went with him to Paris for the signing of his contract. In the room were Bernard Arnault, the very picture of a reserved, dignified, impeccably dressed French executive, and his key managers, all with impressive résumés and all similarly attired in suits in shades of gray and shining black shoes. In the middle of the meeting, McQueen excused himself, explaining in graphic terms that he needed to use the toilet, and left the room. When he came back, he signed. After the signing, McQueen was given a huge pot of Beluga caviar. But he and Isabella had a train to catch. "We couldn't wait, so we shoveled it into our mouths with our hands," he said.[40]

Although the money was exciting for Alexander—with his first payment he repaid his aunt for his Central Saint Martins tuition and bought himself a house in Islington—the job turned out to be a nightmare. Givenchy had been showing haute couture for over forty years. Preparing these collections required the upkeep of a full atelier of seamstresses in Paris—many of whom had worked at the company for decades, under the direction of Herbert Givenchy himself. The suave Givenchy could not have been more different from the young, brash, troubled boy from London's East End. And the fact that McQueen spoke no French didn't help to endear him to the women he was now meant to supervise. Neither did his demands. "When I sent the designs to the atelier staff they freaked out and said it was too complicated," McQueen said of his first collection. "I said, 'This is couture, darling, you've got to be able to do it.' "[41]

Despite Isabella's support, no job offer for her was forthcoming. When he went to Paris, McQueen took Katy England and several of the key members of his own team, saying he would pay them out of his own salary if he had to. "He could have taken [Isabella]," said Julien Macdonald, who was the next designer hired by Givenchy. "Perhaps he was keeping her for himself. Givenchy had its own structure; there were people already there." McQueen never explained why she was excluded, and Isabella never asked him outright, but the snub was a turning point. "It really upset her and made her see her future in a much bleaker way," said Michael Roberts. "I think that she felt that somehow maybe the situation would be rectified, and if she talked out of turn that she would lose that opportunity. She always held on to the possibility that it would be made right in the end." Could she, who was well practiced in navigating social hierarchies and in dealing with the elite from a previous generation, have helped bridge the gap between McQueen and his new staff? Possibly not. The French elite are very different from the English: they don't really understand or appreciate the individuality of the English eccentric.

When she went to visit McQueen's studio at Givenchy, she was even more dismayed to see that he was working with Joe McKenna, whom she hadn't made up with since the "London Babes" shoot. It was awkward for both of them. "I didn't feel good, because I felt she should be there and not me," said McKenna. So, in January 1997, while her cousin Honor Fraser debuted on the runway as the new face for the brand "McQueen for Givenchy"—its new Audrey Hepburn—Isabella was sitting in the front row of the audience whooping and hollering and cheering them on, but wishing, perhaps, that she were backstage instead with Team McQueen.

*Sniffing
for
Truffles*

CHAPTER EIGHT

Sean Ellis wanted to do a fashion shoot based on a battle scene from the 1981 film Excalibur. *The only problem was that* Excalibur *was a film about King Arthur. Suits of armor predominated in the battle scenes and there was no way that* The Face *magazine, cool as it was, was going to let him do a fashion shoot without any clothes in it. Isabella knew just what to do. "Don't worry," she said. "I'll just start talking to all the designers about chain mail and how it's going to be the next big thing." Six months later there was a new trend on the catwalks of the world: chain mail. Isabella called in pieces from the likes of Alexander Mc-Queen and Jeremy Scott and mixed them with suits of armor Sean had borrowed from the film. They had their shoot.*

I sabella was at home on Elizabeth Street flipping through *Dazed and Confused* magazine when something caught her eye. It was a lingerie shoot, shot unusually, and provocatively, from the ground up. Although she hadn't been working much, she was always looking out for new talent. "I feel like a pig that is looking for truffles," she would regularly say. "I'm looking everywhere. No matter where they are, I'll find them. When she saw the lingerie shots that day, she suspected she was on to such a talent. After carrying the magazine around in her bag for a month, and showing the photos to everyone she knew, she set about tracking down the photographer who'd taken them. When she phoned Sean Ellis, she found he knew of her from British *Vogue*, and in return for her gushing praise, he told her that he was a big fan of her work—in particular the "London Babes" shoot.

Sean Ellis had only recently stopped living out of his car when he got the phone call from Isabella. He'd moved to London four months earlier, in 1994, to take a job assisting photographer Nick Knight, one of the generation of innovative photographers whose digitally manipulated work came to the forefront in the 1980s. Although he lived in Brighton, Ellis had told Knight that he lived in London, because he was sure that, otherwise, he wouldn't be offered the job. Nobody wanted an assistant who lived two hours away—particularly not a fashion photographer who needed his assistants to be on set before him to assemble the equipment and stay afterward to put it all away again. Once Ellis got the job, he found he was working around the clock six days a week, and had little time left to look for a place to live. Rather than wear out his welcome with the few friends he had in the city, he started parking his Saab by a health club near Knight's studio each evening, putting the front seat all the way down, covering himself with a duvet, and going to sleep for the night. Since it was winter, he'd often have to leave the engine running to stay warm. Then, in the morning, he'd use the gym's facilities to shower and change clothes.

Ellis was also working to establish himself as a photographer in his own right, and, at the time, one of the quickest ways to do that was to have one's work published in *The Face*. Since its launch in 1980, the magazine had made its name as the most important youth culture magazine in the United Kingdom. Everyone from fashion designers to advertising executives regarded its pages as a barometer of what was happening and who was hip. Having one's work in the magazine was a surefire way to get the kind of lucrative advertising jobs that photographers, stylists, and makeup artists working in fashion needed to survive. Although the magazine didn't pay its photographers—often not even covering their costs—Ellis was keen to shoot for them. In exchange for working gratis, photographers were given more freedom to shoot the way they wanted than they would have at a glossy magazine like *Vogue*, where the editors or, increasingly, the advertisers typically dictated what they wanted in the images.

When Ellis arrived on the scene, creative pairs were the talk of the day: Photographer Juergen Teller and stylist Venetia Scott, a romantic couple as well as a professional one, championed the look of young innocent girls during an age when glamazon supermodels reigned. Mario Testino and Carine Roitfeld specialized in surprising and sexy juxtapositions—a man and woman in matching thongs, say. When Sean Ellis called *The Face*'s creative director, Lee Swillingham, to say he'd like to shoot for them, Swillingham's first question was, whom did Sean want as stylist? Ellis suggested Isabella Blow. The mixture of an older stylist (Isabella was nearly forty) from a conventional magazine like *Vogue* with a young photographer like Ellis was just quirky enough to get the attention of *The Face*'s creative director.

Swillingham knew of Isabella, but he hadn't seen any work by her in a while. He asked, "Is she still working?" Although she was styling a few fashion shows, major shoots with her byline hadn't been seen since she left British *Vogue*. Ellis said he'd ring her and ask. When he laid out the proposition, Isabella didn't get it. "I don't know what I'd be able to do for *The Face*," she said. "It's young and cool. What do you want with an old fuddy-duddy like me?" Ellis explained that the mix—she with him—was the point. "She hadn't worked for one-and-a-half years. She was very delicate about work when we met," he said. "But I was confident that I could get good images out of her."

Isabella said he should come and see her. When he arrived at Elizabeth Street he found two young, pretty, distant relations of Isabella's at her house. Edwina and Laura Belmont had a look that he thought was both young and old at the same time—not unlike the team of him and Isabella. Together he and Isabella concocted the idea of a post-apocalyptic world where these two children are left to fend—and dress—for themselves, using photos they find from the Victorian era as inspiration. "I wanted to give young kids back some identity and some strength and make them look like they're very strong," Ellis said. "I wanted a way out of heroin chic," he said, referring to the look that had emerged as a reaction to the healthy supermodels of the 1980s. Instead of strong, powerful women like Claudia Schiffer and Linda Evangelista, skinny models such as Kate Moss were being photographed with dark circles under vacant eyes, looking as if they were severely malnourished.

Isabella and Ellis's first story, called "Taste of Arsenic," featuring the white-faced little girls in corsets holding dolls and wearing bits of metal they could have found in a dump, struck a chord with the magazine's readers. It also added to a new revenue stream for Isabella.

Isabella had been friends with Sarah Doukas, the founder of Storm models, since the mid-1980s, and while not all the models who credit Isabella with giving them their start came to be represented by Storm—Stella Tennant signed with the Select agency, and although Isabella encouraged her cousin Honor Fraser to model, she wasn't the one to introduce Honor to Doukas—she brought enough business their way to make for an official kind of agreement. "We gave Issie money for everybody," said Doukas. "She knew our Accounts Department so well!" In addition to the Belmont sisters, Isabella would bring Iris Palmer, Augusta Ogilvy (her friend Geraldine Harmworth's daughter), and Laura Ashcroft to Doukas's door. But the most famous and lucrative of her finds was Sophie Dahl.

One day in 1997, Isabella, laden with shopping bags, dressed in see-through trousers and a bustier, and struggling to keep a hat on her head, was failing to emerge elegantly from a taxi on Motcomb Street in Knightsbridge when Dahl, who'd stormed out of a restaurant crying after a fight with her mother, came over to help. Isabella later said of Dahl, "I saw this great big blowup doll with enormous bosoms. I just could not believe the size of her bosoms. . . . I had this overwhelming desire to touch her."[1] At the time, Dahl, eighteen, was, at her mother's insistence, at secretarial school in Kensington, and miserable. Isabella dried Sophie's tears and asked her if she'd like to be a model. Dahl said she would, so Isabella took her back into the restaurant and said to her mother, "I'm going to make your daughter into a model." She then phoned Stefan, her former assistant who was now Philip Treacy's boyfriend. He picked the two up in Isabella's VW Passat station wagon and drove them to Elizabeth Street, where they toasted their meeting with a glass of champagne.

Despite her bravado, when Isabella took Dahl to Storm, she wasn't certain that Sarah Doukas would be able to use her. Sophie was almost 6 feet tall, a size 12, and wore a 38DD bra—far too large for a model at the time. "Will you please take a look at this girl?" Isabella asked Doukas nonetheless. She knew the limitations of the industry, though, and clarified her request: "But I don't think you'll take her." Doukas met Dahl with her public relations officer, Paula. "What she saw, we saw. But the rest of the [people around the] booking table were like, 'What are you smoking?'" said Doukas. Storm signed Dahl up in January 1997, and from then on she worked every day.

Dahl's career was helped by the fact that she was the granddaughter of Roald Dahl, author of *Charlie and the Chocolate Factory*, *James and the Giant Peach*, and *The Fantastic Mr Fox*. Born Sophie Holloway, she was the daughter of a famous British actor, Julian Holloway, and writer Tessa Dowell. But even being the inspiration for the character Sophie in her grandfather's work *The BFG* (Big Friendly Giant) couldn't make up for the fact that the samples produced by the fashion designers simply didn't fit her. When present at a shoot, Isabella would simply insist that Dahl be shot naked. Isabella promptly introduced Sophie to Alexander McQueen at a cheap café in Hoxton. He was art-directing an issue of *ID* magazine and brought Dahl to Sean Ellis's old boss, Nick Knight, to shoot. When Knight saw her, he said he thought she'd be much larger—that she wasn't big enough. He shot her naked and enlarged her digitally so that, although she was lying on her back, her breasts appeared to defy gravity. Having a plus-size model photographed by one of the coolest fashion photographers working attracted attention around the world. Dahl landed lucrative contracts with brands such as Versace and Yves Saint Laurent, and Storm would pay Isabella a percentage of all the money made. "I was never told that she was getting money," Dahl said. "But she did say to me once, 'You didn't make very much this year.' I thought, 'How weird.' I didn't know that was how it worked. I think they don't tell you because it makes people feel icky."

The problem with urging sophisticated girls from aristocratic or famous families to model was that they weren't as willing to put up with the abuse models usually suffer in the fashion world. Iris Palmer left after only a year, fed up with the unrealistic pressures placed on her. "I was not pleased by the treatment of the girls," she said. "I was very outspoken in an eighteen-year-old way. I stopped modeling to regain my anonymity—which I got back very quickly." And Isabella may have been friends with these girls' mothers, but that wasn't going to cloud her judgment about what happened in a shoot. "You think you're going to wear a bra?" she said to one. "No, no, no, no way. We're not working for Marks & Spencer. No way, baby girl. You're going to be naked at the end of the day—didn't you hear?"[2] Plus, these girls could be expensive. When Isabella asked Lady Alexandra Spencer-Churchill to China to pose for portraits by Donald McPherson that would appear in *Tatler*, she told the girl she would personally cover the costs of her €800 fee and the €750 upgrade to business class.

Ultimately, not many of the girls Isabella brought to Storm made big money for the agency, and Sophie Dahl left after a number of years to write books and do a cooking show on television.

Meanwhile, Isabella and Sean's work for *The Face* may have been less than directly lucrative, but it was receiving accolades. After "Taste of Arsenic," the two did "The Clinic," a shoot so dark and so different—Ellis's reference was Italian lesbian vampire movies, and it was shot in an operating theater—that it caught the attention of even the world outside fashion. Ten years before Gunther von Hagens's *Body Worlds*, an exhibition of real cadavers, became a global success, Ellis shot models before a plastic model of a human body he'd borrowed from the London School of Biology. Afterward, he received calls from the video director of Nine Inch Nails, who wanted to look at the photos for reference, and from Anna Wintour, who wanted Ellis to shoot for American *Vogue*. But each success made the next project more daunting. "We wanted to show we could do something more amazing than what was in our last shoot, but it got harder and harder," he said. "I was spending six thousand pounds per shoot."

For their next project, a fashion shoot based on a battle scene from the 1981 film *Excalibur*, Isabella mixed a minidress by Alexander McQueen, a pair of chain mail trousers by Jeremy Scott, a chain mail one-shoulder dress by Christian Dior, a headdress by Paco Rabanne, and a knitted chain mail top by Lainey Keogh with suits of armor borrowed from the film. Ellis rented horses, and an enormous set was built. Jeremy Scott and Alexander McQueen starred alongside the models as war-weary fighters on the battlefield. "It's not about fashion, it's about what fashion is like, about the battle of working in the industry," Ellis said. "Alexander, Jeremy [Scott], Issie and me, we're under enormous pressure to perform in certain ways. To me, the knights fighting Alexander McQueen are his critics."[3] The pictures ran in August 1998, and were a critical success, but by then the team of Isabella Blow and Sean Ellis had begun to disintegrate.

As their profile grew, the kind of work Ellis was hoping for started rolling in. Big-paying clients, including Pepsi and Wolfgang Joop, came calling. But although Isabella complained constantly about not having money, she was not inclined to do the boring jobs that would have paid the bills. "With us it was always, 'We'll show them,'" said Ellis. "But she didn't know how to channel that anti-authority attitude. Issie had more of a problem with the division between art and commerce than me. With her it was always war. The last stand. Do or die."

One day, Ellis called Isabella from the set of a cosmetics ad campaign and told her that the shot had been widened and they were in need of a dress. The client had already authorized a £2,000 payment for the item and £4,000 for the stylist. But Isabella was at a fashion show and said she was too busy. "I said to her, 'This is the easiest 4K you are ever going to make!'" Ellis said. "That was one of the times that sort of broke things between us." It was also one of the reasons that she'd never have the same financial success as her old assistant Katie Grand, who became one of the best-paid stylists in the business.

On a shoot with another photographer for a cell phone ad, Isabella, the photographer, and the client were reviewing all the items Isabella had gathered to use in the shoot when she spotted something on the table that didn't fit in. "What is that hideous thing?" she asked. It was the product they were meant to be shooting.

P art of the reason many of the designers she worked with adored her so much was precisely because she was so anti-authoritarian. Frequently the reverse was also true—she had a fondness for those willing to stand up to the establishment. Yes, Isabella had heard about a young American designer called Jeremy Scott. But who hadn't? He was an unusual and much-talked-about arrival on the European fashion scene. Born in Kansas, he studied in Brooklyn and promptly moved to Paris. Like Alexander McQueen, he didn't let his youth and inexperience stop him from saying exactly what he thought of the fashion status quo. He had a penchant for shouting, "Vive l'avant-garde!" after his shows, and lest that didn't get him noticed, his unconventional looks—gold-capped teeth that spelled out "Jeremy," shaved eyebrows, and an asymmetrical haircut—certainly did. When Isabella first came to his studio, he had his most recent collection in a garbage bag. "I always think that's a sign of someone who's going to be good, who is struggling and determined to make it work," she said. Out of the bag Isabella pulled a dress with a fur tail, and thought, "That's interesting." "Where are you from?" she asked Scott. "Kansas City," he replied. "God," she thought. "You've come a long way."[4]

In October 1997, Jeremy Scott showed *Rich White Women*, a collection of luxurious pieces all in white that could be worn in a multitude of ways.

The collection attracted the attention of not only Isabella, but also André Leon Tally and the fashion director of Saks Fifth Avenue. The clothes, combined with Scott's brashness, led to at least one British paper titling their review, "Move Over McQueen—Here Comes the Kansas Ranger."[5]

Once again, Isabella launched another unofficial promotion campaign and phoned her former boss Michael Roberts, now working for *The New Yorker* but based in Paris, and began raving about Scott. Roberts did an illustration of her dressed in one of Scott's hunchback furs for *The New Yorker*. "I went to see him because of her," said Roberts. "I was dragged to this ghastly studio, looking at this stuff, mostly made out of ugly fabrics, but when she justified it, or slipped something on, it looked kind of right." As she had done with Alexander McQueen, Isabella began talking Scott up to everyone and anyone, wearing his clothes, and defending him in the press. In 1998, the legions of supporters for *Rich White Women* turned their backs on him. In March of that year, Scott showed his *Gold* collection at the Trianon in Paris. It was ravaged by critics. *Women's Wear Daily* called the "gold lamé concoctions unworthy of 14th street . . . your worst fashion nightmare."[6] It featured such deviations from the norm as shoes with different heel heights (causing models to walk with a limp) and a mink jacket with a handle that went over the head from shoulder to shoulder and a skirt with an inexplicable extra pant leg. According to the *New York Times,* one journalist, Sally Brampton, vowed that she was going to make sure that Scott never showed again. "Can you imagine such a venomous reaction? To a fashion show?"[7] Isabella said. Isabella had introduced Scott to several companies that became his sponsors, providing him with the luxurious materials in the show including Swarovski and Saga Furs, and to people he could partner with, such as shoemaker Christian Louboutin and Fogal, the stocking company. Of the collaborations, *Women's Wear Daily* said, "What a waste." When Jeremy came out on the runway, instead of shouting "Vive l'avante-garde," he shouted, "Isabella! Isabella!"[8]

But Isabella would not be swayed by the opinions of others. Detmar took a position in Jeremy's business, to allow him to trade in France, and the French office of Detmar's firm set up the company. "I adored her and Detmar," Scott said. "I'd do anything for her." Although his aesthetic was different from McQueen's—Scott was infatuated with pop Americana, and McQueen, with old English history—the arrival of a new designer upset McQueen. As did the openness with which Scott criticized McQueen's efforts at Givenchy, saying he hadn't paid the house's heritage enough respect. "Isabella told me he threw an ashtray at her and said he wanted to kill me," said Scott. "But I don't know that I believe it. She was always talking about other people and how they did her wrong." Scott had a feeling that one day it could happen to him.

As documented in the *Vanity Fair* "Cool Britannia" feature, as London fashion was becoming cool again, thanks to the likes of Alexander McQueen, a similar thing was happening in the art world. The reputations of the so-called YBAs—Young British Artists, such as Damien Hirst and Tracey Emin, who launched their careers in the early 1990s—had been solidified. Their works were now selling at prices only serious collectors could afford and were shown in the world's most respected galleries, including Britain's national museum of art, the Tate. Two of the most shocking of the YBAs were the Chapman brothers, Jake and Dinos, who came to national attention when they exhibited models of children with genitalia where their facial features should have been. The sexually explicit and disturbing work appealed to both Isabella and McQueen. Isabella decided that McQueen should do a project with the Chapmans, and she got in touch with Stuart Shave, a recent art school graduate who was working with them. She left word that although she was in the south of France on holiday, he must call her immediately. She must have forgotten this message, because when Shave returned her call, she said, "How dare you ring me on holiday!" He reminded her of her previous message. "Oh," she said, and after a pause, "What star sign are you?"

"I couldn't believe the person I got on the other end of the phone," Shave said, "with such humor and audacity and transparency. She started phoning all the time and asking intimate questions before we'd ever met." The collaboration—McQueen made a denim zip-front jumpsuit for a Chapman mannequin—came to fruition. But when Shave and the Chapman brothers decided the photos should run in American *Vogue*, Isabella, who had commissioned the work for the *Times* of London, wasn't at all pleased that her publication had been overlooked. In fact, she was livid. When she calmed down, Shave invited her to the East End home-cum-studio of Sue Webster and Tim Noble, another pair of artists he was helping to promote.

In the wake of the YBAs came the next generation of artists—many trained by the same tutors as the YBAs, but not yet ready to show in the same West End galleries. They were making their reputations in London's more affordable East End—often in spaces run by other artists or in their own homes. To earn one's stripes in this landscape one needed to look and act the part. That meant living a life that revolved only around art and art happenings—drinking in local pubs such as the Golden Heart and dressing in clothes that looked like one had spent the day working in them. Jeans, running shoes, and jackets that didn't just looked distressed but actually *were* distressed.

Isabella arrived at Sue Webster and Tim Noble's house at 20 Rivington Street in 1997 to see *Home Chance*, an exhibition of light sculptures of working-class luxuries such as a heart tattoo pierced by a dagger, called *Toxic Schizophrenia*, and a carnival fountain called *Excessive Sensual Indulgence*. She was wearing a McQueen corset and a hat of many layers that descended over her eyes. As she climbed the stairs of the house to view the works on each level, she removed a layer from the hat and left it behind. At the time, Stuart Shave was working out of his one-bedroom flat in a high-rise on Columbia Road, not far away. He told Isabella that he wanted to open an art gallery. "Oh!" she said. "You must meet my husband. He's rich and he wants to open a gallery." Although he qualified as a barrister, Detmar hadn't been one of the elite to be offered space in one of the Inns of Court. Instead, he worked for a firm of solicitors, the general practitioners of the legal world. But it wasn't his job that had made him "rich"; it was the value of the land at Hilles—worth, depending on the state of the property market, somewhere in the region of £8 million. Just as she had done with the designers who struck her fancy, Isabella was working to try to make things happen for Detmar. "Without Issie, he would have been lost," said de Silva, Detmar's uncle. "Issie gave him a purpose."

Detmar and Shave met in 1998, and within three months their gallery, called Modern Art, opened its doors. Although he didn't put in any cash, Detmar arranged for a bank loan using his property in Gloucestershire as collateral. Shave owned 49 percent, and Detmar and Isabella owned 51 percent. In its earliest days, the gallery was four rooms of increasing chaos. In the front was the show space itself; behind it, a tiny office; behind that, a kitchen; and in the back, a bedroom where Shave now lived with his boyfriend and a dog, a Weinheimer—each room messier than the one before. Isabella said that Shave "was living like *Trainspotting*. You can't imagine. Baked beans stuck to the ceiling. Four hundred plates."[9] The roles in the three-way partnership should have been pretty clear-cut. Shave would recruit artists and be responsible for the gallery's positioning; Detmar would handle the accounts with the help of John Bush, the accountant from Hilles; and Isabella would talk up the gallery to her friends. "I add something because I'm establishment," she said. "I can ring up Elton John and say, 'Come down in ten minutes,' and he'll be there."[10]

At the gallery's launch party, Detmar wore an outfit by Dutch designers KEUPR/van BENTM. It consisted of a pair of trousers with one leg stopping at the knee, an embroidered stocking underneath, and a black glitter tail hanging from his waist. "He received compliments all evening," Isabella said.[11] But not from his gallery partner. "When you're running a gallery, it's really about the artist," Shave said. "And you have to let them take center stage." Which is hard when there's a man with a black glitter tail running amok. Shave had begged him not to wear it. "We were going to kill him," said Sue Webster. "He was supposed to be the silent partner." For later events, Detmar toned it down, though he still retained airs that set him apart: wearing colorful suits with full-length trousers and smoking cigars instead of cigarettes. Outside of the gallery, he continued to match his style with Isabella's—with less than successful results. A frilly chiffon blouse might have worked on her, but on him it seemed affected. So did arriving at a lunch with a Lord in matching his/hers turbans. "Driving through the streets of Gloucester they would draw an extreme amount of attention to themselves," said de Silva, who had accompanied them to the lunch. "But Detmar liked this." Isabella wasn't so sure. "It's rather frightening," she said. "I don't know if he's turning into a girl or what."[12]

"When Issie and Detmar came into the art world, there was nothing like it," said Webster. "Immediately people were like, 'No, this isn't allowed. This is too glamorous to be attached to art.' But they got over it. It became enormously successful." In its early days, Isabella brought people to the gallery whom the art world had never met before: Anna Wintour, Tim Burton, Wolfgang Joop, and Alexander McQueen. They were from "a different world," said Caragh Thuring, a friend of Shave's from art school who had been hired to help run the gallery. They were not the serious collectors that Shave would ultimately end up selling to, but boldface names nevertheless, who helped bring attention to the gallery. While a few of Isabella's friends did buy artwork, their role was really more to make an impression. "The artists really enjoyed people like Tim Burton buying their work," said Shave.

Isabella herself found it difficult to understand the art world's nuances, and how that world worked. "There's a lot of subtlety that she didn't understand," said Shave. "She'd sit there and say, 'Why don't you just buy it?' She was quite a bombastic salesperson." But art isn't an impulse buy, like a dress. To people who didn't know her—and there were plenty of them in the art world—Isabella was just a strange yet enthusiastic woman in a hat. She got her first Noble and Webster piece, *Excessive Sensual Indulgence*, in a trade for a one-off pair of red snakeskin flares by McQueen that Webster admired. For the five years that Isabella owned the piece—she later sold it back to Shave for £40,000 to pay off her taxi account—she called it, "Excessive Sexual Pleasures."

While the gallery was creating a buzz in the art world, behind the scenes the combination of Isabella, Detmar, and Stuart Shave was chaos. "All of us were winging it," said Shave. "But at least I'd worked at a gallery before." At one point a check for £10,000 was thrown away, and the three had to go through the trash to find it. Still, Modern Art developed a reputation as a place to see exciting new work. Jake and Dinos Chapman were represented by the Victoria Miro Gallery (then based on Cork Street, in Mayfair), but they did a collaborative project with Modern Art. This helped the gallery became a mecca for a very hard-partying crowd. Isabella would arrive in the mornings to find Shave still asleep in the back, and would threaten to pull her support. "She was not going to get involved in inspiring you if you were just going to let her down," said Thuring. "In a way that was one of her strengths. She would not suffer fools; she could just find someone else. She was very straightforward in that way." At the end of the day, that Shave was able to run the gallery despite the partying kept Isabella on board.

The gallery helped further propel Isabella and Detmar as an "it" couple whose presence was desired at not just fashion events but art events, too. Every evening the social possibilities were endless, and since Detmar relished promoting the gallery, he was keen to go to as many of these as possible. And, of course, he wanted Isabella, always the life of the party, in tow. But now that she'd become such a well-known figure—one whom the paparazzi followed—going out was never simple. Every time she exited her home, she felt she had to be dressed. Really dressed. And she was finding it increasingly difficult to keep up the pace. "She was always exhausted," Shave said.

Isabella may not have been partaking in the illegal drugs that were prevalent in the art world, but by now she was well into another kind of pharmaceutical: antidepressants. Shave said that from the time he met her, she had been talking about them. "She was extremely candid about her medication when we met," he said. "She was always talking about how disorientated the pills made her." Detmar, too, was quickly showing signs of wear. He'd arrive each morning looking as if he'd already done a day's work. But the problem, he said, was Isabella. She was suffering far more than many of the people around her noticed. He had taken to cutting up her credit cards to keep her from spending money, and he couldn't extricate himself from the morning ritual of getting her dressed.

Isabella worked hard to keep her problems contained. Not many of the people closest to her realized she was suffering, because when she did talk about it, she'd make it so funny. Frequently she'd begun to ruminate on her death—not in the way she would later, not in an "I'm going to kill myself" way, but in a way that was unusual. Once, on a train ride to Manchester, she began telling Shave what she'd like done with her body after she died. "My head will be severed and sent to my father's estate," she said. "To cut off my life the way he cut me out of his will." The carriage of mostly homosexual men on their way to the city's gay pride parade went quiet. "My heart will be ripped out," she continued, "and put in a box to be buried with Detmar." She paused. "Quite where I'm going to bury my snatch I haven't decided." The carriage exploded in laughter. No one listening would ever have guessed just how serious she was.

The Tragedy
of Success

CHAPTER NINE

*David LaChapelle was feeling cranky. The flight from Los Angeles had been
more than five hours late. He'd been traveling for months and hadn't wanted to
take the job in the first place. Not for an advertising shoot. But it was for Isabella. She needed the work, and he needed her—so here he was. No sooner had
the bellboy who had brought his bags up to his room departed when there was a
knock on the door. He opened it and found a young Greek boy, Isabella's latest
assistant, standing with a tray, and on it, a martini. David took the martini, but
the boy didn't go. He'd been sent with specific instructions, and he'd only fulfilled
half the job. "David's in a foul mood," Isabella had told the boy. "Go upstairs,
bring him a martini, and give him a blow job."*

Isabella had first come to the attention of magazine editor Jeremy
Langmead when he was an intern at British *Vogue* and she was
working at *Tatler*. Back then, he found himself in an elevator with
her at Vogue House and couldn't help but notice that there was
food all over her clothes. Then Isabella let out a loud burp. "I
didn't know what to do," he said. "So I stared at my shoes." She broke out
laughing and left the elevator. Now, more than ten years later, he had
become one the editors of one of the most visible magazines, the *Sunday
Times*'s style supplement. At the time, magazine-style supplements were
known for being snore-inducing rather than thought-provoking—at
least as far as fashion was concerned. But Langmead, who'd begun his

career at *Vogue* and the short-lived British edition of *Mirabella*, was eager to change that. He wanted to make a statement with his magazine, and the fashion pages were one of the easiest places to do that, thanks to the fact that his bosses at the *Times* were far more concerned with words than images and less likely to question his judgment. For the position of fashion director, he'd interviewed both John Galliano's muse Amanda Harlech and Isabella's old assistant Plum Sykes, but neither could do it. Both, however, suggested he talk to Isabella. She arrived for the interview in a Jeremy Scott cape with antlers on the shoulder. Here was the walking, talking statement he was looking for.

On her first day at work in July 1997, Isabella arrived wearing a full-length gold chinchilla coat and a hat of what appeared to be porcupine spikes. Langmead asked her to come in through an entrance door on the far side of the open-plan newsroom, so she'd have to navigate the entire floor. "The place went completely silent," he said. "She was oblivious to the reaction."

The offices of the *Sunday Times* looked more like those of a bank than a media company. The other journalists sat face-to-face and side by side, hunched over their computers and phones. Isabella brought in a hot pink armchair to keep next to her desk, from which she worked. Her idiosyncrasies didn't stop there. She once told her fashion editors she wanted to do "porcelain," leaving them wondering what, exactly, she had in mind. Was it the pattern? The color? Nothing could be ruled out. Eventually they discerned that Martin Margiela had done a vest made of bits of porcelain, and Isabella wanted to shoot it with other objects from the same material. She had an Old World way of managing, insisting that thank-you notes be written for absolutely everything, to pretty much everyone. And they all had to be done on Smythson note cards, with a Montblanc fountain pen in her signature pink ink. When the pen broke one day, it was a drama that didn't escape the notice of the others on the floor. Still, in other ways, she fit right in. She'd eat lunch in the canteen, sitting between the jour-

Doddington Hall was the historic centerpiece of the Delves Broughton estate in Cheshire, but Isabella never lived in it.

Lady Vera Delves Broughton, Isabella's grandmother, and Mr. Winks, the pet monkey she brought back from her travels.

Isabella and her mother, Lady Helen Delves Broughton, left, and her godmother, Lady Lavinia Cholmondeley, right, in hat. *Courtesy Lady Lavinia Cholmondeley*

Isabella in her vestments in the kitchen of her mother-in-law's house on Elizabeth Street in London. *Courtesy Philip Treacy*

Philip and Isabella in Elizabeth Street. *Courtesy Philip Treacy*

Isabella and Lady Liza Campbell in the early 1980s. Ironically, for a woman who became famous for her clothes, she was equally famous among her friends for her fondness for taking them off. *Photo by Nick Ashley*

Isabella and Julia at the wedding of Richard and Jennifer Neville-Rolfe, June 4, 1988. *Courtesy Richard Neville–Rolfe*

Isabella manning the phones at Philip's Elizabeth Street store. *Courtesy Philip Treacy*

Isabella and Detmar with Otis Ferry, one of the pages at their wedding,
November 19, 1989. *Courtesy Lucy Birley*

Amaury Blow (back left),
Isabella, and Detmar at Robin
Birley's pie-throwing party.
Courtesy Lucy Birley

Isabella dressed for her father's funeral in 1993. She told Philip that she didn't want to go "looking poor." *Courtesy Philip Treacy*

Isabella and Detmar at Hilles with Issac Ferry and her godson, Otis Ferry. *Courtesy Lucy Birley*

Isabella, Donald McPherson, and Hen Yanni on a shoot in Paris for *V* magazine in 2001. *Photo by Donald McPherson*

LIBERTY. THE ART OF THE IDIOSYNCRATIC.

ISABELLA BLOW, FASHION GURU AT THE FACE, SUNDAY TIMES AND VOGUE, FLAUNTS THE SPOILS OF A LIBERTY SHOPPING EXPEDITION. HAT BY
PHILIP TREACY. DRESS BY TRISTAN WEBBER AND ORIENTAL FOUR POSTER BED BY THE WINDOW. LIBERTY. REGENT STREET. TEL. 0171 734 1234.

Isabella in a 1998 advertisement for the Liberty store. Caption reads: "Isabella Blow. Fashion guru at *The Face, Sunday Times,* and *Vogue* flaunts the spoils of a Liberty shopping expedition. Hat by Philip Treacy, dress by Tristan Webber, and oriental four poster bed by the window." Isabella also consulted with the company on which designers they should be stocking. *Courtesy Zanna.tv*

Isabella photographed in a Mr. Pearl corset for Russian *Vogue* in 2000. The corset brought her waist down to only eighteen inches and was so painful she could only wear it for fifteen minutes at a time. Mr. Pearl was also on the shoot and he was wearing a fifteen-inch corset. *Courtesy Zanna.tv*

Isabella in the Kuwaiti desert near the border with Iraq just days before the Iraq War began in 2003.

Photo by Donald McPherson

Hen Yanni on Pom Pom's horse on the William Morris carpet at Hilles. *Photo by Donald McPherson*

Clockwise from back left: Isabella, Philip Treacy, his nephew, and her niece in a 2002 family portrait pose for *Vanity Fair*. Photo by Donald McPherson

Isabella and artist Tim Noble
outside the Modern Art
gallery before the opening
of their show, "British
Wildlife," September 9, 2000.

Photo by Sue Webster

Isabella with Kamel Belkacemi. He is now working with Daphne Guinness on creating an archive of Isabella's clothes, shoes, and hats. *Courtesy Kamel Belkacemi*

Isabella at her desk at *Tatler* holding her prized Fendi "Mellon bag," which she began carrying when she was having her affair with Matthew Mellon, the heir to the Mellon Bank fortune.
Courtesy Kamel Belkacemi

Isabella and Tim Noble at Amanda Eliasch's house in the South of France, 2004.
Courtesy Amanda Eliasch

Isabella in the coat Alexander
McQueen chose for her to wear
in her casket. *Courtesy Lucy Birley*

Isabella and Majed al-Sabah. She made the sheikh a contributing editor at *Tatler* and he created projects for her to manage. *Photo by Donald McPherson*

**The Cathedral Church of
The Holy and Indivisible Trinity
Gloucester**

ISABELLA BLOW

**Tuesday 15th May 2007
3.00 pm**

The program for Isabella's funeral at Gloucester Cathedral. Although Detmar said that he wanted it to be only close friends and family, about three hundred people attended.

Courtesy Stephen Brüggemann

The Head of Isabella Blow, 2002, by Tim Noble and Sue Webster. This light sculpture was the first portrait the two did of anyone other than themselves. 15 taxidermy animals (1 rattlesnake, 1 raven, 1 robin, 6 magpies, 2 hooded crows, 1 carrion crow, 2 rooks, 1 black rat), wood, fake moss, light projector. Dimensions: 50 x 50 x 155 cm (19 5/8 x 19 5/8 x 61 in). *Courtesy the National Portrait Gallery, London*

nalists and the printers, and would amuse everyone on the floor by discussing, at top volume, whom she fancied and why.

But, largely, Isabella preferred to work at her new home. Helga had sold the Elizabeth Street house in the wake of an unpleasant divorce from her second husband, and after two years of living with Detmar's uncle Desmond in Chelsea, Isabella and Detmar decided it was time for them to have a place of their own. In 1997, they bought a decrepit 1826 workman's cottage on Theed Street, a cobblestone street in the shadow of Waterloo Station, only a five-minute taxi ride away from the *Times*. When they arrived, the house, where a milliner once worked, had a flooded basement and windows that rattled in their frames. The £85,000 renovation took almost two years to complete. The results were covered in both the pages of *Royal Institute of British Architects Journal* and the *New York Times*. Isabella hired a calligrapher to stencil the number five above the front door, and found it greatly amusing that, when finished, the script looked like a "fiver," slang for the five-pound note commonly used in tipping. Isabella called the house the NCP car park, after the chain of London parking garages, because it was small and on three floors. They added a two-story glass extension to the rear, and, thanks to a glass floor, one could see clear through to the basement. One of Isabella's assistants had the cellar made into an office, but the sight through the glass panels installed in the floor above of a computer, printer, and checkbooks was hideous to Isabella, who rarely used the area, preferring to sit on the ground floor in front of the Noble and Webster sculpture *Excessive Sensual Indulgence*, which rested on a cardboard coffee table surrounded by packages of Benson & Hedges cigarettes, cups of tea, and cell phones.

What the house lacked in privacy it made up for in light. The bathroom had no shade; the window was blocked only by a metal grill. Even the tub was made of glass. The view of Detmar when in it, Isabella said, was "like having a little Botero in the bath."[1] For the first time since she left Nick Taylor and her brownstone in New York, Isabella called home a place that, at least in part, belonged to her.

The move to the southeast of London was more than just a physical one. Neighborhoods in London descended from villages; they still retain old airs, and the people who live in them fit into distinct stereotypes. All of Isabella's friends and the entirety of her London life had been spent in the west—in the boroughs of Kensington and Chelsea and in the nearby neighborhoods of Knightsbridge and Belgravia. These were affluent places filled with the genteel upper class. East London, where Modern Art was based, had become the center of the mostly working-class art and fashion set. Waterloo, where she now dwelled, was neither here nor there. It was remarkable mostly for its proximity to other places. Isabella told the *New York Times*, "It's five minutes from the Savoy and 10 minutes away from communion at Westminster Abbey," her office being only "four quid away by taxi."[2] Although it wasn't far from her old haunts, its character was vastly different.

Visitors said the house was a constant hive of activity—much like in Elizabeth Street, Isabella had people calling all hours of the night and day. In the mornings, Isabella's assistant would arrive at Theed Street to get directions for the day. If Isabella had been out the night before, she'd open the door in the vintage lingerie she slept in and offer porridge. In the evenings they'd be offered champagne and cigarettes. But before long, she decided that the house was a mistake. It was too far from the area of London she knew best, and though the design was arresting, she found it uncomfortable, with too many stairs and too few places to relax. The problem might not have been the house but the increasing amount of discomfort she was finding within herself.

From the outside, everything looked grand. At the *Sunday Times*, as she had at *Tatler*, Isabella opened her address book and persuaded her friends to pose for its pages—starting with members of the royal family with whom she was friendly. "You don't discover a member of the royal family," Isabella said. "They've been on balconies all their lives. I just find royalty so fascinating, like any endangered species."[3] Freddie Windsor, the son of Prince and Princess Michael of Kent, Isabella's neighbors in Gloucestershire, was photographed by Mario Testino in makeup and a cobweb top, looking a bit like a punk, and a bit like a druggie—which was unfortunate, because the day the piece ran, the news pages of the paper ran an article on young Freddie's drug use. After the shoot Windsor said, "Mario made it sound quite fun. If it looks silly—heigh ho! It might be one of those things that you do in the summer that then comes out in the autumn and all your friends say, 'Ooh! What an idiot!' "[4] Isabella was horrified to open the paper to find that she had played a hand in making his prediction come true. Far more important for her career, she was now able to call upon top-notch photographers, who were more than happy to pay for the shoots themselves, so long as they could work with Isabella and have free rein with the images. The most important of these was David LaChapelle.

LaChapelle, the photographer she'd met on the "Cool Britannia" *Vanity Fair* shoot, had in the 1990s established himself as one of the most watched photographers in the business. His pictures weren't so much fashion photographs as comments on popular culture. He would stop at nothing to get the picture he wanted, and was only encouraged in this by Isabella. Together LaChapelle and Isabella put together numerous shoots: they photographed one of Jeremy Scott's discoveries, the exotic half-Japanese model Devon Aoki spanking a fish, Sophie Dahl covered in spaghetti, a crumbling building in New York filled with naked and scantily clad women, a naked Sophie Dahl in front of the Noble and Webster *Excessive Sensual Indulgence* sculpture holding a red ball over her nipple. (The biggest restriction at the *Times* was known as Nipplegate—no erect nipples should appear in the pictures. Isabella would joke on set that she was on patrol, looking for nipples.)

On Valentine's Day 1999, LaChapelle and Isabella set a building alight in New York. At the time, the media was filled with stories about Y2K and how the world would come to an end because computer systems wouldn't be able to cope. LaChapelle and Isabella thought the image of a burning building would capture the apocalyptic mood, so they set it alight themselves. "We didn't have any permits," LaChapelle said. "We just poured gasoline over the thing." When the shoot was finished, Isabella burned the Givenchy shoes that had been featured in the shoot, demonstrating her remaining fury that she'd been passed over for a job at the house. The crumbling building was, she said, nicer than the apartment the *Times* had arranged for her to stay at in New York. "It turned out to be a seedy bedsit that obviously hadn't been lived in for years," she said of the flat. "To cap it all, we returned one evening to discover that it had been broken into."[5] The perpetrators made off with a fax machine and a coat. Unfortunately the coat was a chinchilla fur by Galliano worth £14,000.

Isabella would go to any length in the name of artistic vision, but she had no time for celebrity pandering. While shopping at Manolo Blahnik's tiny store on Church Street in Chelsea, she and her assistant were alarmed to see the store suddenly surrounded by paparazzi. The American actresses Courteney Cox and Jennifer Aniston had come in to do some shopping. "What is going on?" Isabella asked. "It's the 'Friends,'" said her assistant Daniela. "The friends of whom?" Isabella said. On another occasion, when the Spice Girls, then at the peak of their fame, were to be photographed for the *Times*, Isabella picked out the clothes for them from her desk and, instead of dressing them personally, sent her assistant to transport them to the shoot and do the job.

At the time, the magazine supplements didn't attract much fashion advertising, so for a newspaper supplement to have shoots that rivaled the coolest fashion magazines was unprecedented. For Isabella this was a blessing. With a sympathetic boss and no clients to coddle with flattering editorials, she had free rein. The only thing restricting her, aside from Nipplegate, was the size of the budgets. The average cost for a shoot was £1,500 to £2,000. As it was a weekly magazine, Isabella was responsible for seventy-five shoots a season, and every week, fashion's most devoted practitioners and fans would pick up the newspaper in eager anticipation to see what Isabella Blow would come up with next. Given that the *Times* had a readership of two million and British *Vogue* had two hundred thousand, Isabella was instantly vaulted to the most powerful position in London fashion. And London fashion was now the central creative force in the industry. By 1997, it wasn't just a stop on the fashion schedule—it had become *the* stop thanks to the strength of the design talent showing there. From her pink chair at the *Times*, Isabella was in the middle of it all. "She loved being the Queen of English fashion," said Michael Roberts. "And she absolutely was. There was a whole period where you came to London and the show would not start unless Issie Blow was there. Even if Suzy Menkes, [the long-standing critic from the *International Herald Tribune*] was sitting there, the show would not start until Issie arrived. And Issie always arrived late."

But what she was wearing was usually worth waiting for. In February 1998, she arrived at the Julien Macdonald show with a crystal-studded lobster on her head—a real lobster. She'd put such pressure on the designer of it, Erik Halley, to get it ready in time for the collections that he hadn't time to clean it properly. She arrived stinking, which she told David LaChapelle she didn't mind: it would keep people away from her. The sight of Isabella in her rancid lobster that evening was outdone only by the appearance of Michael Jackson, who arrived with a little girl and took a front-row seat next to Isabella. It turned out that Macdonald had hired a Jackson impersonator, but hadn't bothered to let Isabella in on the joke. In fact, since he had told her that he'd once knitted Jackson a glove, she was sure it was the real Michael Jackson, declaring as much to the press after the show.

In addition to going to the London shows, it was also part of her job to go to the collections in Paris. Rather than stay in the kind of hotel that the *Times* could afford, she rented the apartment in the Marais that Alexander McQueen had first used when he was at Givenchy. "She only went to the shows she liked," said Jeremy Langmead. "And those were few and far between." Instead she spent much of her time deciding what she would wear. It had to be something original, never seen before. She spent hours and hours visiting all the designers. Preparing Isabella for the shows became a major part of her assistants' work. In addition to those the *Times* paid for, she had her own personal assistants. "Because she was going to be photographed wherever she went, the sort of effort that went into presenting herself got more pressurized," said Lucy Birley. She didn't need just one outfit a day; she needed three or four. And she'd change anywhere: in the back of a car, in a McDonald's. When she appeared on Bill Cunningham's page of style setters in *The New York Times*, the shot was captioned not just with the day, but also with the hour. "March 10, 3:30: a dress of chain mail. March 12, 6 p.m.: an octopus hat and rhinestone-encrusted lobster necklace. March 13, 7:30: A mink cape with a swashbuckling bow on the shoulder, a gold lamé pants suit and a hat of quills."[6] When a Jeremy Scott fur bustier was delivered late, the father of one of her assistants drove Isabella in it to the Christian Dior show in Paris at over two hundred miles an hour with Isabella in the backseat saying, "It's only fashion — not quite worth dying for!"

Although she said later that the *Times* of London "defined her career,"[7] she found preparing for weeks of constantly being on show exhausting. "I absolutely hate going to the shows because it is so much effort to dress up and look good. That's when I get anxiety—before the shows. I go right down because I'm so frightened."[8] But she hid it from the general fashion show–going public. When her assistants complimented her on how good she looked, she'd say, "I was depressed the entire time." So convincing was her performance that one of her young assistants persuaded her to stop taking her medication during the shows, arguing that she didn't need them to control her moods. Every night, Isabella would show the young woman that she was not taking the pills. Right up until the night she became hysterical over a minor slight and threw the assistant out onto the streets of Paris at 1:00 a.m.

Although it was stressful, the position had it perks. Isabella found ways to leverage the job into interesting trips to other parts of the world. "She *had* to go to Moscow," said Jeremy Langmead. One year, there was a launch party being held for Russian *Vogue*, so Isabella planned a shoot featuring the work of some Russian designers. The *Times* gave her a bodyguard named Ivan, a gay former Soviet military officer, and a bagful of rubles. But the day she arrived, the Russian economy collapsed. The Central Bank of the Russian Federation had decided to let the ruble float freely, and it began a steep plummet. The *Vogue* party was cancelled, Isabella's dress—red Givenchy couture based on Catherine the Great's armor—was repacked, and the wad of money in her bag was rendered pretty much worthless. Isabella was broke. The bodyguard and her driver abandoned her, so she hitchhiked. Or at least that's the story she told when she got back to London. "Muscovite motorists are happy to supplement their small incomes by picking up people on the street," she wrote. "They were surprised, however, to see me flag them down wearing a Galliano yellow fox military-cut coat with an enormous Otto Dix collar. 'You deserve limousine,' commented one man."[9]

In April 2000, Isabella was invited to Brazil for Fashion Week. "I admit I was dreading it," she said. "I thought it would be as tacky as a Carnival transvestite. But I was astonished to see how stylish Brazilians are.... Their Portuguese, African, German, and Dutch heritage, mixed with a multitude of other nationalities, makes the Brazilians among the most beautiful people I have ever seen. Even those who are ugly still look amazing."[10] When another trip to Brazil came up—this time paid for in part by the designer Carlos Miele, for whom she was to style a campaign—she insisted that Michael Roberts come with her. "We were flouncing around changing hotels every five minutes because she didn't like this one; or that one was too far; this one was too near the sea; this one, the lighting was bad; this one, she got so depressed when she walked in she just walked back out again," he said. It was a side of Isabella that he hadn't seen before. The next day they hit the cobblestone streets to look at churches, with Isabella wearing suede Manolos. "She's breaking her legs and I tell her it's just ridiculous and that she has to get some proper shoes." She bought and put on a pair of espadrilles and promptly broke into tears. "I can't. I can't," she said. "Every time I look down at my feet I feel so depressed." Roberts said, "Well, are you going to be depressed or are you going to have a broken ankle?" "I am going to have a broken ankle," she said, and she threw the shoes away.

It was a dramatic change from the carefree traveler she'd been in her youth. When she and Natasha Grenfell decided to go on a trip around parts of India in the mid 1980s, they had flown to Rajasthan in western India and journeyed by train between Jaipur and Udaipur, where they then decided to take the night train to Jaisalmer, a desert fort city. Although they were traveling by train, they weren't average twenty-something backpackers. They stayed in five-star hotels (in Suite 16 at the Leela Palace Kempinski, on the banks of Lake Pichola, where they both decided they'd return for their honeymoons), and on trains, they traveled first class. "Although it was a poncey train, we found to our horror that there were four beds in the first-class compartment," said Grenfell. "We got there first, so we claimed the top two." She and Isabella were reading and listening to their walkmans when the other two passengers, Indian men, came and got into the bottom bunks. "We'd both get fits of giggles," Grenfell remembered. "And the man under Issie took a shine to her. Suddenly I'd hear a slap, because he was reaching into the top bunk. Issie would say, 'You're a naughty, naughty Indian. You are not to do that.' Ten minutes later there would be another slap."

Now being booked into any hotel that was beneath her exacting standards could send her into fits of tears, never mind being groped by a strange man in a shared sleeper car. Unfortunately, she no longer had the means to stay in five-star hotels on her own dime. She was plagued by money problems. She'd use up her monthly budget from the *Times* within the first week of the month on indulgences like taxis to and from the office and tea at the Ritz and then spend the rest of the month traveling by tube and bus. Detmar tried to keep her to a budget, without much success, and periodically would phone Langmead to ask that Isabella be given a raise.

Around this time, Isabella was asked to star in an ad campaign. It was the perfect opportunity, so naturally she said yes. In some industries, getting paid by the companies you are supposed to be covering could get you fired from a newspaper. Not so with fashion. Liberty, one of the UK's earliest luxury stores, established in 1825, had hired its first marketing executive, Julia Bowe. She conducted a study to determine, specifically, the place the Liberty brand had in the consciousness of modern Brits. The public came back and said they saw it as a place for Christmas scarves, stuffed print frogs, and products suited to "batty vicars' wives." The store's long history of working with the best designers of the day had been forgotten. The new team at Liberty wanted to give the brand a new image. Their campaign featured Isabella, climbing into a four-poster bed in a tight satin dress. The tagline was "The Art of the Idiosyncratic." She also worked behind the scenes, recommending to the store buyers which new designers they should be stocking. Bowe was pleased with the fruits of the collaboration, and Isabella was pleased to find a way of supplementing her income without doing work that didn't interest her.

There were more, and better paying, opportunities to come. At a lunch in Gloucestershire, at the house of Prince and Princess Michael of Kent, Isabella sat next to an older, Austrian man. When Isabella asked him what he did, he pulled dozens of gem-like stones out of his pocket. "Those are crystals," she said. "I'm impressed," Helmut Swarovski replied. Most people at the time were referring to them as "rhinestones" or "diamanté" or "paste." Not only could Isabella recognize crystals when she saw them, but she also knew the illustrious history of Swarovski. How, in the 1950s, the company had gone from making chandelier components to supplying crystals for the costumes in Hollywood films. Swarovski phoned his daughter, Nadja, who was working for the company in New York, and said, "You have got to meet this woman." Nadja Swarovski hadn't heard of Isabella, but she had seen one of the David LaChapelle pictures that

Isabella had styled for the *Times*. In it, the exotic model Devon stands with her bottom thrust out holding a three-foot fish and a fishing rod. The pose was loaded with sadomasochistic innuendoes. Swarovski had also seen the Liberty ad featuring Isabella climbing into bed in a Philip Treacy hat and a tight white satin dress. Swarovski had a mission: she wanted to make her family's product cool again. And in Isabella she saw an ally. "People in couture were using our stones just as another ingredient. We needed young designers who could use the stones in a completely different way."

Within weeks Nadja, her father, and Isabella were having a meeting at the Lanesborough Hotel in Hyde Park Corner. In anticipation, Isabella had sent Nadja a Julien Macdonald neon yellow nylon knit dress with sequins. "Don't you think it would look better with crystals?" she asked. Nadja and Helmut agreed wholeheartedly. When Nadja came to London again, Isabella took her around the collections to show her who was who and which designers she would entice to work with Swarovski. "Doors opened," Nadja remembers. She hadn't been invited to any of the shows, but when one was with Isabella Blow, that was of little consequence. "The point was, they didn't know anybody," Isabella said. "They're out in Toblerone country. They were sponsoring the wrong events with the wrong people."[11]

Swarovski gave Isabella a contract that read, in exchange for a fee, she'd attend a monthly meeting, brief them on who was hot, who was not, and what was happening on and off the runways. It was the perfect job for Isabella. Before she could really begin work, however, it was essential that she visit "Toblerone country," otherwise known as the company headquarters, in Wattens, Austria. She arrived during the annual carnival—on a day that was known as "Crazy Thursday," when all the employees were encouraged to come to the office in costume. This, however, was not explained to Isabella beforehand. When she and Mr. Pearl, the corset maker who himself boasted an eighteen-inch waist, arrived, no one gave the pair a second look. "Well," Isabella thought, regarding the costumed employees, "these Austrians are not as boring as they're supposed to be." The collaboration was a good one—Isabella's name became closely associated with Swarovski and Swarovski became closely associated with the most hip designers. The result was a barrage of articles on the new trendiness of crystals and a substantial increase in wholesale sales of crystals to designers and fabric makers. "They used to call me an extreme eccentric," Isabella said of the more conservative members of the Swarovski hierarchy. "But then the cash started rolling in."[12]

Meanwhile, Michael Roberts had been doing illustrations of Isabella in her various guises, and showing them to the editors at *The New Yorker*, suggesting that the magazine do a profile of her. Now that she had the job with Swarovski, it was easier for people outside the world of fashion to understand the impact she was making. In March 2001, the magazine ran an eight-page feature on her. It was a major coup for a fashion figure to be given such treatment by the intellectual publication. The few fashion stories it did almost always featured designers or photographers.

One of the key changes brought by the increasing amount of professional investment in fashion companies was that suddenly designers with little experience could be given big jobs at brands that needed a lift. Although frequently it was Anna Wintour, from her power seat at American *Vogue*, guiding the brands, the *New Yorker* article cast Isabella as the one in the trenches discovering the new talent. The article brought her to the attention to a number of brands that might otherwise never have considered using a fashion personality to promote their products, from the makers of industrial plastics such as Corian to the maker of synthetic fabrics, DuPont. But for some of her old friends with whom she'd lost touch, the descriptions of her life contained in its pages were a sure sign that Isabella had left them for a strange world they didn't care to be a part of.

The attention and the new jobs did not make her feel any less betrayed by the designers she'd been helping. She'd complain constantly to each about the others, and to the photographers about them all. Although she felt she'd had a hand in creating them, she couldn't control the designers or, more important, her access to their wares. They were understandably cautious with their products. It took weeks of sewing to create one of Philip's elaborate hats and only seconds for Isabella to shut it in a car door, lose it, get lipstick all over it, or set it alight. She burned two rare feathers off a hat while leaning over a candle during dinner at the Hotel Costes in Paris and spent the next day searching the city for replacements, which she finally found at Lemairé, the supplier to the haute couture. Isabella begged them not to tell Philip, but when she came back to London she confessed. "She came in and said, 'I have to tell you something,'" Philip recalls. "It was like someone had died." McQueen, too, had to be careful about lending things to Isabella as he never knew in what state they'd come back—or if they would come back at all. But from Isabella's point of view, the reluctance to lend was a unique form of torture. "He likes to use the clothes as power over me," Isabella said of Alexander McQueen. "The thing is, I wish he'd just get on with it and give them to me . . . It's a constant battle and I think he likes it to be that way, and it's always been that way."[13]

There was a much bigger battle being waged in the industry's midst. By the time Alexander McQueen arrived at Givenchy in 1996, the art and commerce debate in fashion had been decided firmly in favor of commerce. McQueen himself bristled at the notion that he was an artist, insisting again and again that he just "made clothes" or that he was a businessman. Still, for such a creative mind, the reality of working for a company where the bottom line was truly the bottom line was somewhat disturbing.

In fashion's earliest history, the men who made luxury goods ran the companies themselves. Guccio Gucci, the company's founder, started by making leather saddlebags. The real Louis Vuitton was a man who made trunks. In the next, and possibly the happiest, stage, the people who loved the designers took over running the companies, leaving the creators free to create. Yves Saint Laurent had Pierre Bergé; Valentino had Giancarlo Giammetti; and, more recently, Miuccia Prada turned the running of her family's company over to her husband, Patrizio Bertelli. The advantage of having a "partner" instead of a CEO is that a partner is going to allow an artistic personality to express itself—no matter the cost. But as partners get old, or want to cash out, they have to sell or float their companies.

In the 1990s, the suits arrived. At first the new CEOs were men who had worked at lower levels in the brands, but as the industry got larger, the talent pool of people with experience in luxury became small by comparison. The brand owners had to search wider and wider to find executives. When McQueen arrived at Givenchy, Arnault hired a CEO from Nike to work with him. Later managers were lured from Procter & Gamble. McQueen complained that the managers Arnault had hired didn't really understand fashion. "You can have the business savvy, but you have to know about fashion," he said in 2002. "It was like I was a stallion that was being held back by a two-ton truck. I wanted to make it work, but it was like fighting a battle." After two years he renewed his contract, but not without misgivings.

"I never smoked in my life until I started at Givenchy," he said. "And I was on forty a day. That was the one sweeping thing that shocked me. I was twenty-six when I started, and I'd never smoked in my life. Every six months you do a show and get publicity and they sell perfume," he said. "But it's between those six months when there [aren't] those shows that it deteriorates. No one in the fashion press or the buyers actually sees the trauma you go through in order to get things done."

In May 1999, Isabella stumbled upon a way to get him out. She was at a dinner sitting next to the new creative director of the Gucci Group, Tom Ford. Gucci Group had been founded earlier that year when, in order to thwart a takeover by LVMH, the CEO of Gucci, Domenico De Sole, sold 40 percent of the company to François Pinault's conglomerate PPR (Pinault-Printemps-Redoute). Suddenly, instead of being a takeover target, they were in line to be the second biggest luxury group in the world. The deal left Gucci Group with some €3 billion to spend on acquisitions—money they were looking to spend on brands and people to join them. "You should look at Alexander," Isabella told Tom Ford at the dinner in London.

"He might be someone interesting for you to buy." Ford replied, "Do you think so? I quite fancy him." The next morning she was on the phone to McQueen. "Get your arse out of bed and ring Tom Ford. He fancies you!"[14]

In June, McQueen met Gucci Group's other half, CEO Domenico De Sole, at a *Vogue Italia* party in Monte Carlo. McQueen introduced himself and asked if he could have his picture taken with De Sole, who agreed. After the deed was done, De Sole asked McQueen what he intended to do with the photo. "Send it to Bernard Arnault," he said, letting De Sole know he was open to other offers. McQueen didn't send Arnault the photo—instead, he kept it for a time in his office safe—but he began serious talks with Gucci Group when they were both back in London. "I knew I had to put into action what I wanted to do," he said. "I saw Domenico and I made a beeline for him."

The deal was announced in December. Not only had McQueen sold his business to someone other than his boss at Givenchy, but he had sold it to Arnault's archrival. "Talk about bite the hand that feeds you," McQueen said. "I bloody chewed it up and spat it out. And there's a lot of gristle on that meat." Arnault cancelled McQueen's next two Givenchy shows, but despite his requests to be fired, they kept him bound to his contract. Asked why he didn't just fire McQueen, Arnault said, "Because we are polite." Some of the things LVMH executives said off the record were not polite. "[McQueen] was very frustrated because of the success of John Galliano," said one, referring to the designer at Christian Dior. "The fact is what he does doesn't have the same level of taste. He was very jealous." Another said, "The problem with Mr. McQueen is that he is always on drugs."[15]

Here, anyway, they were right. McQueen had developed a ferocious cocaine addiction. Beyond what people would consider casual use, he'd order multiple grams, and stay up for days. When the resulting paranoia ensued, he'd become terrified that people were coming to get him. He'd lock the door, and ask Isabella to hold the key. He later admitted the problem and said he'd get clean. But he never did. Told about what the executives at LVMH were saying, McQueen replied, "It's just bitchy. LVMH is a multinational conglomerate that's worth billions, and they're saying such pitiful things. It shows they're an insecure company. I find it really bizarre."[16]

Isabella found it really bizarre that despite another big deal for Alexander—despite the millions Gucci Group paid McQueen for its 51 percent stake in his brand—there was still no deal in it for her. In the fashion world, friends speculated that she was simply too unorthodox, her style too raw, to fit in at a corporate group. De Sole said that, for his part, had McQueen wanted Isabella on the payroll, it would have been done. This time Isabella complained vocally—to her friends and to the press. But although she would later fall out with McQueen, the job was not the reason.

The Hilles
Are Alive

CHAPTER TEN

After a dinner of fish soup and roast chicken cooked by Loïc, the French chef at

Hilles, Isabella decided she'd like to smoke a joint. She phoned the local drug

dealer, known as Pom Pom, who arrived by horse. She invited him—and his

horse—into the long room at Hilles, where the giant Shire horse with furry legs

waited comfortably on the original William Morris carpet. At dinner were the

artists Tim Noble and Sue Webster and the photographer Donald McPherson,

with Hen Yanni, his model girlfriend who was also a friend of Isabella's. One

joint led to another, and Isabella decided that Hen must be photographed in the

house, on the horse, naked. "Oh," Isabella said throughout the shoot, "if Det-

mar knew, he'd have a heart attack!"

Isabella had always lived her life as if it were a story—it was her
way of avoiding emotion. "Feelings were things in the British
Empire that would get in the way of success," said Geraldine
Harmsworth. "So you tucked them under the carpet. Our generation was the fag end of the empire. It builds a lot of character,
and that's what Isabella had loads of in the real sense of the word. She
lived a narrative."

Living her life as if it were a work of fiction had long been one of Isabella's ways of surviving and not letting things get her down. It also had
the effect of making her intoxicating to be around. As she got older, and
life became more interesting, the stories became more elaborate. She'd

return from travels with all sorts of tales—with varying degrees of veracity. It was something that everyone was happy to overlook in the interest of sheer entertainment.

Her social behavior was similarly nonconformist, but it made for some awkward interactions, as she often revealed details about people present that they may not have wanted aired publicly. "This is Lucy, apparently she's amazing in bed." "This is Joe. You wouldn't believe what he gets paid for putting someone in a white T-shirt." "This is Geraldine. She's an heiress." "This is Donald. He has an enormous cock." "This is A. She's had a face lift." Isabella threw out these gems with careless abandon, not in the slightest bit concerned about the ramifications—usually not even aware of them, as she'd whisk off immediately afterward.

When she married Detmar and gained some control over Hilles, she also gained a fantastic stage from which she could cast her own life. Sophie Dahl, Philip Treacy, Alexander McQueen, Julien Macdonald—even Detmar—were not just friends, they were actors in her play, and she expected them to behave accordingly. Everyone's memories of Isabella seem to begin in the kitchen: Issie making porridge, rare-breed hens running amok at her feet, dressed in a monkey fur coat, or a black evening dress, or vestments—and always, always in Manolos. This was the mixture of the sublime and the mundane that characterized every aspect of her life.

It was at Hilles where her imagination could truly run free. She hired Bannerman's, the royal gardener, to draw up plans. "She was always talking about box hedges and dry stone walls," said Philip. Isabella had arranged for a government grant to fix up the place, and paid for what it didn't cover herself, spending thousands, for example, on revamping the oak doors. The sounds of Saturday morning, according to Philip Treacy and Lucy Birley, were of work: hammering, banging, and Isabella issuing directions.

Hilles was also a place she could show off to her parents with pride. She had managed to do what they had not—establish herself in a stately home. Once, when her father came for a visit, Isabella put on a Thai feast, to be eaten outside. A giant table was laid, with a cloth from India, and everyone was commanded to "make an effort." Unfortunately, Evelyn, then nearly eighty, was grumpy because the weather was hot. He had to sleep in the drawing room, as they could not get him upstairs because of his lost leg. "He used to get drunk at parties and wave his leg around," remembers one of Isabella's friends. Detmar and Evelyn would talk to each other the way men did fifty years ago: "Do have another glass of port." Selina Blow, Detmar's sister, remembers watching a video of the movie *Splash* with Evelyn in the library at Hilles. "I was about twenty-four and wearing shorts. I said, 'Evelyn, that's Daryl Hannah,' and Issie said, 'He's not interested in the film. He's looking at your legs.'"

As an additional source of income, Detmar and Isabella had been renting the cottages on the estate. One was rented to John Bryan, the Duchess of York's financial adviser who was famously caught sucking her toes, another to the designer Jasper Conran. Detmar said of the prospective tenants, "Well, they can't be dull. I mean, one of the cottages was rented to a barrister, but he had to be dispatched. He was just too boring."[1] The five-bedroom farmhouse in which Detmar had spent his earliest years with a nanny was offered for $5,000 a month.

As years went by Isabella's life was slowly becoming divided. On one hand she had her oldest friends, those she met during her school days and the heady days afterward, when she was rushing between Oxford and London. Most of them had now married and had children. A surprising number of them had also been through rehab, which meant they no longer partied the way they did in their youth. On the other hand, she had cultivated a group of more hard-partying, young friends, such as Alexander McQueen, Stuart Shave from Modern Art, and the photographer Donald McPherson.

Weekends at Hilles reflected the division in her life. Some weekends it would be early nights and long walks with Lucy Birley; other weekends it would be late nights with Tim Noble and Sue Webster, or with Alexander McQueen. Although she didn't do hard drugs—on one occasion she even flushed McPherson's precious pink cocaine down the toilet—Isabella loved both kinds of weekends. But she kept the more sordid details of the wild weekends from her oldest friends, who had put that kind of thing behind them and were far more conventional.

No matter who was on the guest list, the weekends were organized with Isabella's usual love of networking. If Tim Burton and Lisa Marie Presley were going to be there, then so also should Sean Ellis, who might like to take a portrait. Lucy Birley would get calls saying that she really *must* make an effort, because some royal figure would be dropping by. When Prince and Princess Michael of Kent were expected one weekend, Isabella entered the kitchen and announced to the hungover guests assembled there trying to dull the morning suffering that they would be expected to curtsey. They grimaced, but they did. On another occasion, Princess Margaret came to stay, and the staff complained that Isabella made them wear all-white uniforms.

Isabella's inclination to direct the activities didn't stop at formalities; indeed her enthusiastic matchmaking could be terrifying. On one occasion she urged the gay McQueen to take the son of a friend upstairs. On another, one of her assistants from the *Times* locked herself in her bedroom, lest she have to let in the lesbian with whom Isabella was desperately trying to set her up.

Bedrooms would be allotted according to a hierarchy in Isabella's head. If there were only a few people, Sophie Dahl would get a room with a four-poster bed. If there were many, she would get one of the little back bedrooms.

The cost of an average weekend was regularly over £600 just for the food and drink. "We need cooks now," Isabella informed Detmar not long after they married. Given his love of food, it was one expense with which he was okay.

Costume requirements were less frightening than the matchmaking, but no less demanding. "Isabella had a cozy side, but was capable of being Machiavellian," said Sophie Dahl. "She saw people as caricatures of themselves, forgetting sometimes that you were a real person, because she had a Fellini version of you in her head. If I didn't look really immaculate, she'd say, 'What are you doing? Go put on some lipstick.' She had no patience for frumpiness."

Isabella had no tolerance for frumpy, but eccentric, strange, and naughty were to be encouraged. Alexander McQueen decided that he liked one of the tapestries in the blue bedroom at Hilles so much that he rolled it up and took it home. Isabella found it hysterical—and managed to retrieve it before Detmar found out. When her mother—who, despite her advancing age, continued to flirt—came to visit, Isabella seated her next to an unsuspecting male, leaving him to wonder what, exactly, was the polite way to reject the advances of a horny septuagenarian who kept inviting him to her bedroom. Rona, her stepmother, made an equally comic impression on guests. Once, when asked by one of the chefs if she had enjoyed her meal, she is said to have replied, "I've had better food on British Rail."

On some weekends, Hilles was used to support the talent of Isabella's disciples. She hired Nigel, a local mechanic who trained birds as a hobby, to teach McQueen the art of falconry. It was, she said later, the most exciting time she had with him. McQueen, it seems, was a natural—meaning he was very good at getting the birds back. When he was looking to make a statement with a collection at Givenchy, they decided that hats of horns should do the trick, and one of the estate's Soya sheep met an early demise. The designer Anthony Price gave Isabella some rare Japanese chickens, which also met an early demise when they were discovered by a fox. But before their death, Philip Treacy and Isabella plucked so many feathers for hat embellishments that guests wondered how they still could have any left.

But despite existing as a setting for Isabella to inspire her protégés, Hilles was better known for the outrageous anecdotes provided by a combination of colorful characters and Isabella's daring antics. "You'd hear the clip-clop of shoes on the wood of the stairs," a frequent visitor said. "And then it would go silent, and you'd think, whose door is it? And then you'd hear the door to your bedroom open and, clip-clop, and you'd say, 'Issie, what's the time?' She'd of course lie and say it's nine a.m., and you'd look and it would be seven thirty, and she'd get into your bed." One Christmas, when Philip Treacy was there, Isabella invited the local fire department up to Hilles for drinks to thank them for putting out a fire there the week before. There was one condition: they had to come in uniform. No uniform, no drinks. They agreed. When the engine came off the dirt road leading to Hilles, they feared the party would have to be cancelled but, after several hours, the firemen were able to get it right and make it to the front door. Upon entering, in addition to spotting the medieval accoutrements that always decorated the main hall, they found a Christmas tree covered in cobwebs, looking as if it had been standing there for the past century. (Isabella had asked Philip to decorate it, and that was his vision.) But even stranger was the hostess herself. Isabella came into the room in a low-cut lace dress wearing a neon green and hot pink cloud on her head. The firemen did not know where to look. Isabella spent an hour or so nudging Philip whenever one of the better-looking of them looked their way but eventually tired of their presence and began wondering how they would get them to leave. When the chef began making noises about dinner the firemen took their cue and said their goodbyes.

Visitors to Hilles would go to midnight mass or play games like charades. Isabella's taste for dramatic scenery and over-the-top costumes provided incredible visuals, which stayed with guests as the years passed. "We went out one night to find some berries," said Lucy Birley. "And [Issie] was wearing a white silk dress. A flurry of snow came up from the valley and it was incredibly beautiful."

When candle wax spilled on the William Morris carpet during one weekend party, the first priority was to keep it from Detmar. A guest told Isabella the way to get it out was to put brown paper on the wax and then iron it so that the wax was drawn to the paper. Isabella started the task, but as usual, got distracted. The smell of burning carpet soon filled the air. She panicked and began to look for a place to hide, climbing into bed with a friend and burrowing beneath the duvet. Amaury, Detmar's brother, wearing Moroccan robes and wielding a sword, began searching the bedrooms, calling for her. When he came into the room where she was hiding, he could see the feathers of her hat sticking out of the duvet quivering and he began to prod her with the sword.

Between weekends, the house was largely uninhabited. One group of visitors was warned by Isabella that she had not had time to clean up after a lunch some three weeks earlier. They arrived to find a cinematic tableau: a rat scurrying across the dining room table eating the food that had been decadently left on the plates as though the guests had been kidnapped mid-meal.

Despite the fun and frivolity of gatherings at Hilles, Detmar's precarious position with regard to the house was taking its toll on the couple's relationship. He was stuck between an overbearing mother and a wife he could not control. Although he expected that he would inherit the house one day, it was not yet his. This fact was made clear from the beginning: in their earliest days at Hilles, he and Isabella were given rooms in the attic, while Helga's bedroom, which featured smoked mirrors and a brown dressing table like that of an aging film star, was kept as a shrine between her visits. Although his father had given him every indication that the house should one day be his, according to the traditions of the country, Helga had done nothing about seeing to this. Under UK law, if the property wasn't transferred to Detmar at least seven years before her death, there would be an enormous amount of estate tax due. Such a large amount that much of the land surrounding Hilles would have to be sold to pay the bill.

Helga's visits also made it quite clear who was in charge. When her mother-in-law arrived, Isabella's friends observed that Isabella went into a state: "Oh, my god! Helga is coming!" she'd say. During those visits, Isabella seemed to regress. She told Selina that she liked having an adult in the house, but that she also felt obligated to bring Helga breakfast in bed and run her errands. She worried about getting in trouble with her, as though she were the naughty child. Helga's attire—turbans, long nails, dark glasses, big jewelry—was as dramatic in its own way as Isabella's was in hers, but "she wasn't fun," said a friend of Isabella's. "You felt you were having an audience with a foreign princess." Isabella had always known that Detmar was a mommy's boy, but what she thought would be a boon was becoming a bore. Once, when they were visiting Sri Lanka, Detmar took the seat at the head of the table, assuming that Helga would not be joining them. When he heard her on the stairs, he fairly flew, gathering up his plate, cup, and silverware and leaping to another seat before he was spotted. "You've never seen anyone move so fast," said Stuart Shave. It must have been amusing, but one suspects that Detmar's deference came off as somewhat emasculating as well.

Detmar may not have known about all of the weekend goings-on at Hilles, but enough stories were trickling back to Helga in Sri Lanka that she became concerned. "I was on occasion alerted to various wild parties taking place at Hilles, our home in Gloucestershire," she said. As a result, notes began appearing around the house warning unnamed persons not to use certain pieces of china or asking them not to move things. Isabella, who grew up in the shadow of Doddington Hall, a far, far grander house, took particular joy in using those very items when she and her friends had the place to themselves.

Helga's concern eventually led her to say that perhaps the house was better suited for Selina, who was married to a doctor and had two children. The idea of losing Hilles shook Isabella and Detmar to the core, but they reacted differently. "I'm staying and fighting," Detmar said. "This is my home."[2] There was another house on the estate, Spoon Bed Farm, which Isabella and Detmar could have moved into and made their own but Detmar felt the big house was rightfully his.

Meanwhile Isabella, painfully reminded of her family's expulsion from Doddington Hall, said she'd rather just go—even after the years of money and effort she'd put into renovating Hilles. The house had always been a crucial element in her relationship with Detmar, and losing it seemed to be a marker that their marriage had come to an end. Although she said she loved him, she had grown increasingly frustrated with him. And although her obsession with sex had not waned—instead of joking about how she and her boyfriend were having it, she had begun joking about how she and her husband were not having enough. Sean Ellis said to her, "You love talking about sex, but you never do it." She replied, "I know! I know! I find it far more interesting to talk about it. It is always such a disappointment when you do it." In one interview, she described one of her hats as "a penis with a hard-on. Not that I would know what they look like . . . I haven't seen one for so long."[3] Weekends when Detmar was at the house were becoming increasingly uncomfortable for the other guests. He and Isabella bickered constantly. She would accuse him of being cheap, and he'd turn on her as well, calling her a bitch. Things about her that Detmar used to find charming, such as the way she was constantly in contact with a million people, became annoying.

The promise of an idyllic life at Hilles had masked for a long while many of the couple's inherent problems. Namely, that Isabella and Detmar each had their own tendencies toward narcissism and excess and both suffered from depression. For Isabella, beautiful and expensive things and places distracted her from feelings of inadequacy. "It's hard to be an aesthete today," she said. "It's a lonely life. These details mean something to you, but nothing to anyone else."[4]

Both of them were always complaining about not having any money, but this rang on deaf ears to the struggling art crowd with which they were now hanging out. (It is difficult to feel sorry for a couple pleading poverty when their laundry, being sent out to the same service as the Queen's, arrives weekly, cleaned, in tissue paper and cardboard boxes.) "She told me she earned as much as a plumber," said Webster. "I don't remember the amount, but it sounded like quite a lot." Still, Isabella's friends agreed with her assessment that Detmar was just cheap. If she wasn't at Hilles, dinner would consist of a ready-made meat pie from the supermarket. At a party at the Carlyle in New York, Isabella reprimanded her husband in front of her friends, "Oh, Detmar, do offer them some nuts. Don't be so cheap." Adding for effect, "You'd never know he was a millionaire, would you?"

On September 10, 2001, things seemed to have reached a point of no return for Isabella. She told a friend that she phoned their gallery partner, Stuart Shave, from New York and said, "Let's make a deal. You don't leave me with Detmar and I won't leave you with Detmar." Isabella had begun regularly talking about leaving her husband altogether—and her friends began to encourage her.

But before she could make a break, in October 2001, Isabella got some bad news. Jeremy Langmead had left the *Times*, and his successor, Robert Johnson, had been told by his new bosses to make dramatic budget cuts at the magazine. Both Isabella and her deputy were fired.

Though angry with the way she'd been given notice, Isabella was not lacking for things to do. Having added a couple of contracts to her Swarovski deal, she still had some work in place. At this time she was working for Corian and Du Pont, and she had been doing an increasing amount of work with a young American photographer, Donald McPherson. "When I met her for the first time she greeted me with, 'Hi, sexy,'" said McPherson. "She was very good at making you feel important." When the *Times* job fell through, the two began doing shoots for *V,* an edgy New York fashion magazine. When McPherson came to Paris, Isabella insisted he stay in the flat, for which Swarovski was now paying. They soon decided to share it. "We agreed I'd pay something like twelve hundred euros a month," McPherson said. "I was pretty sure I was paying the entire rent, but I didn't care."

Isabella began to spend more and more time in Paris. "She was great in Paris," said Michael Roberts, who was living there at the time and working for *The New Yorker*. "She blossomed. She felt she was amongst her peers and felt they spoke the fashion language that she spoke: that slightly more erudite or intellectual mixed with inspiration." For the shows, she'd travel with Roberts in his car, "I would only go to those things if she wanted me to go," he said. "I'd be like the flunky, the supporting act. But it would always be my car." In the city at night, she'd also dine with him, piggybacking on the largesse of Condé Nast. "She loved Caviar Kaspia," he said of the ultra-expensive Left Bank restaurant. "As we all do. Especially if you don't have to pay."

In the Paris flat, she slept in a silver bed that once belonged to the lead singer of Queen, Freddie Mercury—but never alone. Her distaste for being alone was becoming more and more consuming. She would sleep either with McPherson or with Hen Yanni, his girlfriend. Being needy of company, however, made Isabella no less demanding. In the flat, she had a beautiful round white sofa. McPherson and Hen came home after a night out and got into a fight, and in the commotion, a full ashtray spilled all over it. Isabella was furious; they had ruined one of her beautiful things. "She screamed at me, 'Fix it!'" said McPherson. "I said, 'How?' and she said, 'Just graffiti it.'" McPherson tried to placate her and asked among friends until he got the name of a well-known French graffiti artist. He gave the man £500 and a bag of pot to come and spray-paint the sofa. In the morning they awoke to find the artist asleep on the newly decorated sofa with the spray can in his hand. Isabella later took the sofa to London, saying that now that it was art, she wanted to have it sold at Christie's.

The more time she spent in Paris, the less she spent with Detmar. "I'd have to remind her to ring him," said McPherson. She would be in Paris for weeks at a time without getting in touch. "Issie would always say, 'Poor Detmar,' " he said. Paris was a lot more fun for Isabella. McPherson would go out and bring back croissants in the morning and she was allowed to eat and smoke in bed. "Detmar would kill me!" she'd exclaim. Although he was willing to wear the clothes, Detmar didn't have Isabella's adventurous soul and was becoming increasingly threatened by it. "I think her situation with Detmar . . . had become very strained," said Michael Roberts. "She had become diminished in a way. Like a timid housewifey person almost. I think she tried to turn herself into something that wouldn't cause too much fuss." Detmar was in denial. He blamed the split on his mother. "It was all Issy [sic]," he explained later. "She got fed up with my mother."[5]

In July 2003, Isabella traveled to Italy to judge a student design competition sponsored by DuPont. Although she was still technically living with Detmar and was still legally his wife, she considered herself to be a free woman. And she was eager to meet eligible men. In Venice she met one she'd later dub Casanova. "I was doing a job for DuPont textiles in Venice," she said. "And I had to go there for the night. I didn't know anybody. Philip Treacy said he knew someone. This man picked me up in this speedboat and he was wearing these white trousers and he sat with his legs apart. I couldn't look at the palazzos, I could only look at him."[6] Casanova became her lover. In October 2002, when she was back in Venice for the fortieth birthday party of Elton John's boyfriend, David Furnish, she looked up Casanova again—despite the fact she was there with Detmar. She and David LaChapelle, who had also been invited to the party, went to see him at the antique store he ran with his father.

Despite—or perhaps compounded by—a new love, Isabella's issues with money surfaced before long. She got audited, and the men from the

Inland Revenue came to Waterloo to go through her books with her accountant from Hilles. As McPherson passed through the room, Isabella called out, "Donald, can you please explain to these men how this business works?" Before he could even reply, she pointed to the lingerie photos of Sean Ellis's that were now framed and hanging on her wall. "Do you see those knickers?" she asked. "The ones that the models are wearing. Do you think those knickers can be returned?" The shocked accountants didn't know what to think—or where to look.

One afternoon, Sir Desmond de Silva, Detmar's uncle, was walking past a Mayfair gallery when he saw a portrait of Lady Vera Delves Broughton, Isabella's grandmother, in the window. It had been painted in 1922 by Philip de Laszlo, a painter famous in his day for his portraits of high-society figures. De Silva rang Isabella to tell her she should buy it. "But I'm selling it," she replied. She would later give the money from the sale to Casanova.

Creatively, however, she continued to work. She began to plan a book and exhibition celebrating her thirteen years with Philip Treacy. *When Philip Met Isabella* launched at the Design Museum in London, and traveled the globe. For the exhibition, Treacy asked artists to create portraits of Isabella. Tim Noble and Sue Webster had Isabella over to Rivington Street to create one of their shadow sculptures out of trash. "We'd never made a portrait of anyone other than ourselves," said Webster. Isabella gave them a box of her things to use in the sculpture. It held a couple of pairs of Manolo Blahnik shoes, bangles, and lipsticks. Treacy provided feathers he used in making hats. "We thought it was too glamorous," Webster remembers. "Our impression of Issie is incredibly gothic, because we'd been to Hilles. She was obsessed by English history, the Tower of London, and all that business. We made a sculpture based on what our idea of Issie was." In addition to designer shoes and red lipstick, they used a black rat like the kind that caused the Black Plague and a raven from the Tower of London. Isabella adored it.

After the launch of the exhibition, Isabella hosted a party at her house on Theed Street—and borrowed the butler of Prince and Princess Michael of Kent to preside over it. "I love staff, I'm afraid," Isabella said. "I feel quite nouveau riche about it. Oooh, it takes the sting out of everything."[7] When an uninvited editor from *Vanity Fair* tried to come in, Isabella stopped her at the door. "Michael," she said to the butler within earshot of the entire room, "will you please get this lady a taxi." When McPherson confronted her about the incident, she defended herself. "But, Donald," she explained, "she wasn't invited!"

The exhibition and book brought renewed attention to Isabella, and with it another job offer, this time back at the place where she had really begun: *Tatler*. Michael Roberts was at Claridge's to meet Geordie Greig, then editor of the magazine, about the vacant position and suggested that Isabella come along. Ronnie Newhouse, the wife of the international CEO of Condé Nast, Jonathan Newhouse, also recommended Isabella for the job. Isabella made an impression that the other candidates did not. "I remember interviewing fashion directors and nineteen girls with long blond hair came in with identical views about Tod's shoes," said Geordie Greig, one of the most socially connected men in London. "Issie was not into that. She didn't do dull." Still, Isabella wasn't about to be had easily. "They had to haul me back," she said. "I didn't want to be here of course, not one bit. I worked at the *Tatler* sixteen years ago, and I'd worked for American *Vogue* and the *Sunday Times*, and, well, I wanted to be free, I wanted to be me! But Geordie summoned me to Claridge's and I said: 'Geordie! I don't want it!' and then he said: 'Come and see Nicholas Coleridge [Condé Nast's managing director].' So I did, and I'd just been to buy some diamonds, so I took them off and threw them at Nicholas and said: 'No! I don't want to do this.' But they got me drunk and so I said 'yes.'"[8]

Tatler *Tales*

CHAPTER ELEVEN

The Turkish artist Haluk Akakce was a little bit drunk when he got off the Eurostar at Gare du Nord in Paris at 4:00 p.m. (He'd been much, much drunker—and pretty high—the night before, which is why it took him three tries, three tickets, and all of his money to finally get onto a train from London that afternoon.) Even so, he knew the vision at the end of the platform was not an apparition. There was a man in a suit holding a sign with his name on it. That much he had expected. When he had phoned Isabella and explained his post-Eurostar transport dilemma—no cash, and little time before his 4:15 meeting to discuss his doing a special project for the luxury label Louis Vuitton—she had told him that, if at all possible, she'd arrange a car to take him from the train station to Louis Vuitton. But why the two other men holding Turkish flags? And—he blinked—was that two French police officers? He shuffled forward a few more steps, clutching his fake nylon Lancel bag with one hand and patting the pocket of his parka with the other to push the half-empty bottle of red wine he'd taken from the train's bar car into its depths. When he got closer, all became clear. He could now make out more of the sign the driver was holding up. Under his name, it read, "President of Turkey." Even for Isabella, this was a bit much. He walked up to the men, his hand outstretched, and said, "I am Haluk Akakce." He paused and then continued: "I am not the president of Turkey," he said, searching for something more plausible. They stared, their faces impassive. "I am the cultural minister." They gave a Gallic shrug, and the whole party departed. As Akakce was driven through the streets of Paris in the back of a Mercedes with blacked-out windows, led by a motorcycle police escort with sirens wailing, he phoned Isabella. "President? Issie, Turkey doesn't even have a president." "Darling," she said. "How did you think I was going to get you a car on such short notice? I told them ["them" being the French office of Condé Nast] that I had an exclusive interview with the Turkish president." When Akakce arrived at the offices of Louis Vuitton with his bottle of wine, his fake Lancel bag, a beret sliding off his head, and his full motorcade, a group of executives standing outside stopped and stared. Then the one he was meeting approached him and paid him the ultimate compliment. "You know," he said, "the way you look, you could be French." He got the job.

When Isabella arrived back at *The Tatler* (as she and now Philip Treacy called it) in the fall of 2002, the internal workings of the magazine had changed considerably. No longer was it the hotbed of whoopee cushion fun that it had been when she worked there for Michael Roberts in the mid-1980s. The long lunches consisting primarily of liquids and liaisons had been replaced by 10 a.m. meetings. "Where's Issie?" was the morning revelry trumpeting from editor Geordie Greig's office. Isabella, with her stacks of Smythson's stationery, Montblanc fountain pen, and pink ink, was confounded by the amount of time her new assistants spent on their computers sending e-mails. It was a sight that both frustrated her, because she didn't really know how to work a computer, and annoyed her, because it wasn't the way she thought a fashion department should work. "Why are you all just sitting at your desks?" she'd say. "You've got to be inspired. Go to an art gallery!" Their protestations that there was work to be done, work that necessitated their sitting at their desks, fell on deaf ears. "I don't care," she'd say. "We are going to a gallery." When she wasn't in galleries, she was often on the phone to them issuing directives. "She'd call us and just start spouting names," said Anna Bromilow, her first assistant there. "You wouldn't have a clue what she was talking about, and by the end, you'd have scribbled all over your desk. Her mind worked at quite a frenetic pace."

Productivity had come to rival pedigree in the Condé Nast pecking order, and the new generation of Condé Nast staffers was being hired not just for their connections or their creative spirits, but also for their ability to get work done. These were mostly beautiful, hardworking women who were serious about their careers. The arrival of Isabella into this new corporate culture was endlessly amusing. When smoking in public buildings was made illegal, Isabella stared blankly at anyone who dared to point this out to her. Around her desk were burn marks from stubbed-out cigarettes, and at least once a day her assistant had to sacrifice some of her Evian water to douse the trash can fires caused by Isabella's discarded cigarettes. "She was incredibly naughty," said Bromilow, now the fashion director at *Tatler*. "And I absolutely loved it."

When Isabella met her new team, she quickly assigned them her own set of nicknames—Bromilow, who had once studied art history, became the Art Historian; another girl who had spent a summer working in a casino became the Croupier. Then she promptly began getting them to raise their standards of dress. Not for the models in the shoots, but for themselves. "When she arrived, we all suddenly clocked that if we got dolled up we'd bet better treatment from her," said Bromilow. "So we'd all come in looking more and more glam. The heels got higher and higher." Once properly attired, she'd whisk them off to Claridge's for meetings and introduce them as "the next Anna Wintour" or "the famous film star." They found it mildly embarrassing—particularly when Isabella would then disappear and they were left to explain that although they'd studied drama, they had never been in a film. But it was infinitely preferable to how she introduced her old friends to them. "This is X," she'd say. "X used to be a junkie. Remember, X, when Alexander and I came to your house and found you passed out on the bed? Poor junkie." The office was soon filled with the sound of her throaty laugh and her graphic descriptions of sex. When she and David LaChapelle were heard talking about pearl neck-laces, it wasn't jewelry they were discussing. One of her favorite pastimes was trying to pimp her young assistants out to rich and/or famous men. When Mick Jagger came into the building, Issie dragged him around the floor saying, "I want you to meet this foxy girl I work with." As before, soon there was a long list of antics ascribed to Isabella:

> "Get this. Isabella's knickers came untied at the couture shows and when they fell to the ground, she just stepped out of them and kept walking."

> "You won't believe it. Isabella sat through an entire lunch with the PR from Prada with her breasts resting on the table. They'd popped out of her corset and she seemed not to notice."

> "Did you hear? Isabella spent £35,000 to charter a yacht in Turkey."

Isabella's first official undertaking was to ring Greig and say that the fashion cupboard, where the clothes for upcoming shoots were stowed, needed to be redecorated with silver foil and blue paint. Greig, amused, okay'd it.

Next, she and Donald McPherson concocted the most elaborate shoot in *Tatler* history. It was an homage to one of her oldest friends, Manolo Blahnik, who was having his own exhibition at the Design Museum. An array of personalities from singer Grace Jones to Sarah Ferguson, the Duchess of York, would be photographed all over the world wearing Manolos for the feature entitled "Kiss My Feet." When they photographed Ferguson, Isabella introduced her to the photographer by saying, "This is Donald. He has an enormous cock." They decided she should be photographed in Alexander McQueen and Manolos, sitting by the side of a pool. In the background, naked boys jumped into the pool. During the shoot, Isabella, remembering the 1992 photographs of Ferguson having her toes sucked by her financial adviser, told McPherson to make sure he was getting her toes in the picture, to reference the famous tabloid shot. After the shoot, in a blatantly flirtatious move, the Duchess of York sent McPherson tapes of the Scottish folk song "Donald, Where Are Your Trousers?" (Thanks to Isabella, McPherson and his cock were starting to develop a reputation among the English royals. Isabella invited him to join her for a dinner at a royal residence. She was late, but when Isabella finally arrived, she introduced an already awkward-feeling McPherson to the hostess and then whispered into her ear, "He has the most enormous cock." "I'll sit next to him" was the instant reply.)

When the Manolo Blahnik feature was finished, it was the talk of fashion editors throughout London. Not only was it the most expensive shoot in *Tatler* history, but, at £45,000, it also ate up the Fashion Department's entire annual budget. (When Grace Jones arrived in Paris she found that no one from *Tatler* had booked a hotel room for her. So she booked her own—a €3,000-a-night suite for three nights.) When the massive bills for the shoot started coming in, Greig went to Nicholas Coleridge to break the news. Neither was shocked, given Isabella's reputation for largesse. "It was an amazing shoot," Greig explained. "Those images, one hopes, over time will pay for themselves. It was an incredible lifting, changing moment for *Tatler*."

For their next shoot, Isabella and McPherson breathed life into Liverpool. The port town hadn't been called a happening destination since the Beatles departed. But an influx of highly paid footballers led to a gaggle of young girls dressing to impress them. "I think it's wonderful," said Isabella. "It's all miniskirts, high heels, cleavages, and a massive attitude."[1] On a research trip to the city, Isabella had decided it was as much fun as Brazil at Carnival time, and a feature was planned. Of course, it didn't hurt that the Duke of Westminster was spending £750 million to regenerate the city's shopping center and that he was connected to Isabella through his niece Eloise Anson, one of Isabella's modeling discoveries and goddaughter to her friend Daphne Guinness. Isabella and McPherson were planning to take the train from London to Liverpool. But in the taxi on the way to the station, she decided it made more sense for the driver, with whom she'd made friends, to take them all the way to Liverpool, some four hours away—with the meter running. When they arrived, she asked the driver to stay overnight so he could take them back to London when the shoot was over.

Although she was excited about the project, she was already beginning to show signs of weariness. She told McPherson he could pick out the clothes—she'd just select the hats. When it came time to return home, she found that the mother of two of the girls in the shoot had commandeered her driver. Isabella was furious. "The nerve!" she said. When the driver got pulled over for speeding on the trip back to London, it turned out his license had been suspended. Everyone in the car had to go to the police station, to the great amusement of Isabella.

Taxis, suites at the Ritz, dinners out—even by Condé Nast's relatively generous standards the expense involved in Isabella's shoots was beginning to become more of a concern. Assistants were instructed to rein her in wherever possible. Despite her rank on the masthead, when Isabella traveled, it wasn't in business class. "Geordie's very kind and supportive and Scottish, and of course fantastically intelligent and it's impossible to work for stupid people. And he'll let me do anything I want as long as I fly easyJet," Isabella said, referring to the budget airline that flies to and from remote airports to keep costs down. "I just got the Bulgari yacht for a shoot, a Mrs. Howard Hughes half-naked on a boat thing, and Geordie said: 'Fine, but will you fly easyJet?'"[2] Isabella's expenses were an exercise in creative writing. She'd get a bit tipsy at the nightclub Annabel's and write a filthy story on the back of her receipt. Or she'd say to whichever friend she was dining with, "Who is in town?" If Mel Gibson was in town, then she'd write "dinner with Mel"—never mind that she'd never met him. "She got away with murder," said one assistant. "No one else would have gotten away with it, but everyone absolutely loved her."

That December, she, Donald McPherson, and Daphne Guinness went to Kuwait to photograph members of the royal family there. "It was the first time the al-Sabahs had let a photographer into their homes and shoot them in their own jewels," said McPherson. Isabella pulled off the coup after meeting Majed al-Sabah, one of the nephews of the emir, backstage at a Valentino show. He had opened a luxury store in the outskirts of Kuwait City and had been making an impression at the shows with his fur coats and handsome smile. "You're the real deal! Not like some of them," she said when they met, referring to the many Middle Easterners merely pretending to have royal roots. With their shared love of luxury, the two became fast friends. Isabella decided that al-Sabah warranted a place on the *Tatler* masthead as contributing editor, and when she heard that he was having designers such as Prada, Dolce and Gabbana, and Pucci design custom kaftans for his store, she decided a shoot was in order. She and McPherson decided to stay on afterwards and celebrate Christmas with him. Despite being a devout Muslim, al-Sabah gave McPherson four Prada suits and three pairs of Dior boots. He had a French chocolatier make a full-size bust of Isabella; it had taken fifty hours to make. His uncle gave her a Cartier watch, and she promptly gave it to her Casanova.

Al-Sabah's generous gestures were all the more impressive given that the shoot had not gone off seamlessly. When McPherson said he'd like to shoot one of the models in a sheer kaftan and draped over a 1967 convertible Corvette belonging to one of al-Sabah's cousins, it was decided that it was best done outside of town, so as not to attract attention. So they drove some thirty miles from the Iraq border, where they could see the military helicopters preparing for the Iraq War flying past, and staged the photograph. "The girls were wearing very little clothes and we were urging them to take those off," said Daphne Guinness. Suddenly two men drove by in a pickup truck and shouted, "Respect our country!" When they came back with machine guns, Isabella decided the shoot was over and ushered the model, another British aristocrat, into the car.

In January 2003, for her debut haute couture week at *Tatler*, Isabella wanted to make a statement. She asked David Bartlett, a well-known industrial designer and the father of Philip Treacy's boyfriend, Stefan, to make a pop-up photo booth. Then she, David LaChapelle, and Daphne Guinness, whom she made fashion editor on the project, traveled to Paris with the aim of shooting the models backstage after each show, still dressed in the designer's clothes—before they had time to take off the dresses and makeup. "We get there first!" she said. "While Anna Wintour is waiting in the front row. It's take-away couture."[3]

It turned out not to be as easy as it sounded. The first problem was Isabella's wardrobe. She had arrived in Paris for the haute couture shows to find that her luggage had not. Michael Roberts had suggested that she look at the work of a Japanese designer called Jun Takahashi at a label called Undercover. He was showing semi-sheer burkas in unusual colors, such as fuchsia. "I was kind of thinking it was something she might use in a shoot," Roberts said. Instead, she borrowed one and put it on for the Dior show. It was in the days leading up to the American invasion of Iraq, and so this kind of behavior was interpreted as a political statement. When she arrived at the show with David LaChapelle, French journalists started shouting at her. "I told her to say she was showing solidarity for the oppressed women of the Middle East," LaChapelle said. "She wasn't, of course; she was just covering her face. But she thought it sounded good." The next day Isabella told reporters, "Firstly, at Dior it was worn for practical reasons, as I had not been made up or had my hair done, but then I decided that I would wear one in a different color to every show. For me it was also a statement against war. I am not a fan of Bush, he has a muscle for a brain." [4]

Then a model at the Valentino show didn't know who LaChapelle was and refused to stay behind to be photographed. At Chanel, the threesome was evicted by security. Guinness thought it was the fault of the model from Valentino, who had spotted them again. "She was very skinny and high strung," said Guinness. "I spent the rest of the week trying to keep her away from David." LaChapelle thought it was because they were laughing during the show. Either way, Isabella felt humiliated. Amanda Harlech, Karl Lagerfeld's muse, had to tell security to let them back in. In the pictures, each girl is holding a prop, say, a FedEx envelope, with a word on it. When the photos were laid out together in the magazine, the message read, "All you need is love." "It was a sublime take on fashion," said Guinness.

And love—or at least infatuation—was something Isabella knew about. She was completely enthralled by her new lover and arranged to meet Casanova in Paris during the haute couture shows. Isabella invited him to the post-party following Philip Treacy's fashion show at the Pink Paradise Club and introduced him to Lucy Birley. "She was all over him," Birley said, "sitting on his lap, and I just took one look at him and thought 'gigolo,' I suppose. She was absolutely completely head over heels." Like her earlier boyfriends, Casanova was good-looking, with thick wavy brown hair and a come-hither look and, as before, Isabella began raving to her friends about his prowess in bed, in the most graphic terms. From the beginning she knew he wasn't going to be a faithful replacement for Detmar, but knowing it and accepting it were two different things. "I thought it would be good for her to have sex with Casanova so long as she did not fall for him," said LaChapelle. "I'm pro-love. I knew she'd been lonely." Isabella made only the flimsiest efforts to keep the affair a secret from Detmar. She even took Casanova to Detmar's barber—one he shared with his uncle Desmond de Silva. When de Silva went for a haircut, the barber told him about the young Italian Isabella was squiring around town. When de Silva asked Isabella about it, she admitted the affair but said, "Please don't tell Detmar." Detmar found out anyway, and was despondent.

To make matters worse, in London the tabloids were reporting that Isabella had told her friends that her marriage to Detmar was over. Although Detmar had tried to convince her to stay. ("I wrote her these letters saying I was heartbroken," he said. "I love you so much, I can't bear it, blah blah blah.")[5] Isabella wasn't listening. She said she hadn't received his letters, so he began sending copies of them to her sisters. It didn't make any difference to her. "Samo," she'd say, quoting her old friend Jean-Michel Basquiat: "Same old shit."[6]

Isabella was far too engrossed with Casanova to consider a reconciliation with Detmar. "[She] thought if she got [Casanova] jobs, he'd stick around," said McPherson. After the haute couture, she took Casanova to Moscow with her when she and David LaChapelle went to photograph a rich Russian woman, naked, in the taxidermy room of the National History Museum. Initially they were booked into a "monstrous, ugly hotel," said LaChapelle. Isabella took one look and marched out. "I can't stay here!" she said. "I'm an ugly woman, and all I have is my eyes." Instead they checked into one of Russia's grandest hotels, the National, across the street from the Kremlin. "Every night we were eating caviar and drinking vodka," said LaChapelle. "It was very decadent." So were Isabella's evenings with Casanova. She arrived very, very late the day of the shoot. When she appeared at the door of the Winnebago where LaChapelle, the aristocrat model and her husband, and the rest of the crew were waiting, she promptly launched into every detail of the sex she had had the night before. She explained in giddy tones how Casanova had ingeniously employed one of Treacy's most famous hats in a sex act. "It wasn't dirty because it was so childlike," said LaChapelle. "It was like she was talking about her first trip to Disneyland." She also asked LaChapelle to photograph her and her lover in action—with Casanova dressed in an old Russian military costume for added effect. LaChapelle would later tease her that he'd sold the pictures to *Rolling Stone* or was going to use them in his next exhibition.

Isabella then tried to convince Geordie Greig to let Casanova write a story about the Manchester United football team. Donald McPherson had come over from New York to shoot Keira Knightley for *Tatler* at the same time, in the spring of 2003. When Casanova arrived from Venice for a match, bringing with him fresh mozzarella, Isabella was, said McPherson, "nervous like a schoolgirl." She'd been on the phone all morning with her assistants, trying to get Harrods to send over a free fois gras picnic basket for the journey to Manchester. By now, people were more suspect of Casanova's motives. When Isabella and Casanova left for the train to Manchester, Isabella in one of Philip Treacy's Andy Warhol-esque hats with David Beckham's likeness, complete with a £10,000 diamond earring in Beckham's ear, McPherson cleaned her house as a favor and threw away things he found belonging to Casanova. "I thought 'he's coming into my family,'" McPherson said. "Everyone knew he was bad news." Soon thereafter, McPherson ran into Detmar at a pub near Theed Street. He'd lost a noticeable amount of weight and seemed overcome by the new turn of events.

Although McPherson usually stayed with Isabella when he came to London for work, when Casanova arrived for that visit, the photographer moved into a room at the Portobello Hotel to give the couple privacy. That evening, when they came back from the soccer match, he had a few of the people he worked with, including Isabella, back to his hotel for an impromptu party. At around 1 a.m., Isabella wanted to leave. Casanova didn't. He stayed and flirted with McPherson's friends until 4 a.m. "It was devastating to her," McPherson said.

The pressures of starting a new job and trying to end her marriage, and the disappointment of the new affair, had taken their toll. Isabella was exhausted. She and McPherson retreated to Sarah St. George's house in the Bahamas. "She was so loving," McPherson said of Isabella. "Like a puppy, but so depressed. I kept saying to her, 'You can't love anyone unless you love yourself.' She kept asking, 'What do I have to live for?'"

It soon became apparent to the people closest to her that Isabella needed more than a vacation. "Do I look tired?" she asked a writer from the *Daily Mail* at a party in London in May 2003. "I'm exhausted. Every day is like deadline day. It never stops. I need a holiday, but I've only just got back from one in the Bahamas. I'm worse than when I went."[7] That June, Isabella and Treacy went to a *Tatler* party to celebrate the launch of the new £250,000 German luxury Maybach car. Isabella looked fantastic in a black dress with a low-cut back crisscrossed with straps and a black-and-white disc hat, but she felt miserable. "It was the first time she couldn't hide her feelings," Treacy said. "She just looked like there was something wrong. I said, 'Let's just get on with it and pretend.' And she couldn't. She was trying, but she couldn't help showing how she felt on the inside."

Although she wasn't suicidal, she was depressed to the point that Alexander McQueen also began to become seriously concerned. He agreed to pay for her to do a stint in The Priory Hospital, provided she promise one thing: never to get back together with Detmar, whom McQueen saw as the cause of her problems. McQueen, Treacy, and the jewelry designer Shaun Lane then drove Isabella—wearing a McQueen glitter corset with a diagonal fuchsia stripe—to the farthest reaches of West London to The Priory Hospital.

From a distance, The Priory in Roehampton looks like one of the stately homes that Isabella and her friends grew up in. It was built as a private home in 1811, in Strawberry Hill Gothic—a style that mixes turrets and battlements with the arched windows of Gothic cathedrals. It sits like a white castle at the end of a long drive, behind a plush green lawn. That day, as the group walked from the parking lot to the building, Treacy noticed that in the green grass were thousands and thousands of cigarette butts. It was a sign, he thought, of the level of anxiety of the people housed inside. When they got to Reception, the party of four was called into a room for Isabella's assessment. Priory staff asked how she felt and if there was a history of suicide in her family, and then they told her she should be admitted. "She was very fragile and childlike," said Treacy. "She was looking for reassurance that things would get better." They checked her in and the three men drove back to London in silence.

With Detmar out of the picture—McQueen also didn't want him to visit her—and Donald McPherson back in America, Stefan and Philip became Isabella's primary caregivers. On Treacy's first visit, Isabella introduced him to a friend she had made, a young girl with dark hair. "Oh, Philip," she said. "You'll love this. She calls me 'Miserabella.'" The following year, Treacy was drinking in the pub next door to his studio when he saw the girl singing on television. It was Lily Allen, who released her first best-selling album, *Alright, Still*, after her stay at The Priory.

Isabella was allowed out on the weekends, and rather than stay alone at her house on Theed Street she stayed on Elizabeth Street with Stefan and Philip. Stefan painted a room in their house lilac, her favorite color, and on Friday afternoons he would go collect her in the red postal van Treacy's company used to deliver hats. Their weekends consisted of a calm routine. "She was trying to get better," Treacy said. "There were no visitors. I don't remember her being on the phone. She wasn't catatonic, just fragile." Saturdays they'd go to the farmers' market in Pimlico with a basket for food, Treacy's dog in tow. They'd go for walks to the Berkeley Hotel to swim in its pool. In the evenings, she and Stefan would cook. Sunday mornings, Isabella and Philip would go to the Bourne Street Church. "It's a High Anglican church, but for years I thought it was Catholic," Treacy said. It had all the rituals—and the visuals—that they loved. "The high mass they gave was religious high theater—and she loved it," Treacy said. She was also trying to dress more calmly—in running shoes and even jeans. On Sunday evenings, Stefan would drive her back to The Priory. "She was sad," Treacy said. "But in a sweet, considerate way. It was about thanking us. There was nothing pathetic about it."

Jumping from best friend and pal-around-town to caregiver was never going to be easy. But it was made even harder for Treacy by the assessment given at The Priory. Part of the therapy revolved around getting Isabella to stop wearing hats. It seemed The Priory's doctors thought she suffered from an addiction—to millinery. They instructed her to stop hiding, to come out and show the world the "true" Isabella. "Can you imagine?" she said to McPherson. "They told me not to wear hats." All her friends were shocked. "They tried to disassociate her from the thing that she was most passionate about," said Daphne Guinness. "Would they tell a writer not to write? I told her, 'Don't let them change you.' She wasn't an accountant. She had a philosophical problem with life."

But Treacy, thrust into the role of pusher of illicit millinery, was conflicted. "They were saying she had to find herself, but not necessarily within a hat," he said. "In retrospect, we shouldn't have listened, because the hats made her feel powerful. But I'm not going to interfere in their prognosis [sic] by turning up with all these hats. I didn't want it to seem like 'I don't give a fuck as long as she wears the hats.'"

Isabella was released in September, but she wasn't cured. Instead, she'd moved on to a much more elaborate course of medication, including lithium, which had a noticeable effect on her. "She was like a zombie," said McPherson. She had been taking antidepressants since the mid-1990s, so now she had a drawerful of them. "We used to call them her Marilyn Monroes," said Treacy. After years of hearing her complain about the effect they had on her, Philip tried one of her pills on the way to a party and was amazed by how strong they were. An older doctor she was seeing in London suggested a more radical course of therapy: electric shock. Although it was used frequently in the 1940s and '50s, by the time Isabella had it, only about one million people a year worldwide were receiving it. It is usually restricted for the most severe cases of depression—those that don't respond to other treatment or for people who are catatonic. At this point, Isabella was neither, and her friends begged her not to do it. "There was a part of Isabella that enjoyed being wired up," said Lucy Birley. "But I felt this was something done in Tennessee Williams films, and that it wasn't necessarily the best for her." After each treatment, she'd enter a manic phase, but then she'd crash. And as time went on, the periods between the crashes became shorter and shorter.

Back at work in the fall of 2003, Isabella attended not only the shows in London and Paris but also Milan. Milan was her least favorite stop on the fashion calendar, filled as it was with designers whose collections were more commercial than fantastical. So far in her fashion career, Isabella had been pretty much able to attend the shows as and when she wanted. But her job at *Tatler* was different. As fashion director she was expected to make the full rounds of New York, Milan, London, and Paris, to be the face of the magazine and show to the advertisers that someone important from the editorial team was there to see the new collection. Watched on TV or over the Internet, a fashion show seems like a glamorous party with a very specific form of entertainment. And, if you only have to attend one show a day, that description fits the bill. It is hard to explain to the uninitiated, but to cover all the shows for six weeks twice a year is uniquely soul-destroying—even for the strongest of souls. Take the tedium of being away from home for such a long stretch, add to it the pressure to look one's best day after day (after all, those are professional critics sitting across the aisle), and sprinkle in the fake pleasantries and perceived snubs inherent in any industry convention and you have the recipe for any number of break-downs. Stronger women than Isabella have emerged from the collections desperate for some real human contact. Or contact with humans who seem more real. For her birthday in November, Isabella went back to Italy, not to Milan but to Venice and into the arms of Casanova.

"Whatever her passion, it would envelop every part of her life, so if it was feathers, it was going to see all the stuffed bird museums in the world," said Birley. And if it were a man from Venice then "it all turned into capes and masks and embroidery." Isabella started to entertain the idea of moving to Venice and running a hotel with Casanova.

But in the short term, while casting about for stories to shoot, she and her lover decided upon "Nipples in Naples." "Nipples in Naples," or "See Nipples and Die," was planned to be "No Muff Too Tough" and would feature naked English aristocrats holding fur muffs. But when Geordie Greig and the other *Tatler* bosses nixed the idea, Isabella decided she'd shoot swimsuits in the Italian city of Naples instead. "Naples rhymes with nipples," Isabella explained. "And nipples, I notice, have been out in other magazines but not *Tatler*. So that was the concept for the shoot. A nipple had to be out in each shot."[8] Unfortunately, the girls in question hadn't been told this before the shoot. Jessica Andrews, Isabella's twenty-year-old unpaid intern, had been called to Naples to bring a Chanel swimsuit that had been left behind in London. To her horror, Isabella instructed her to strip. When she balked, Isabella told her if she didn't, she'd be fired. Andrews thought, "I'm way in over my head. For one thing, it was freezing." So Isabella stripped first. "As my uncle had to lead the troops in Dunkirk," she said. "I had to lead these girls into it, otherwise they wouldn't have done it."[9] "I did it and I got the job," said Andrews. "As soon as I got back I was put on the [*Tatler*] payroll."

Andrews noticed that Isabella would become manic around Casanova. Not content with her usual sly, witty innuendos, together Isabella and her lover put on a performance that no one nearby could miss. "She'd start singing opera in a restaurant and he would join in," she said. "She was really sexual with him." Andrews wasn't impressed.

Back in London, Detmar had inadvertently come up with the perfect solution to Isabella's housing crisis. Although he'd rented an apartment in Shoreditch, a part of East London filled with young artists, he was refusing to sell their Theed Street home, making it hard for Isabella to come up with the money to begin divorce proceedings. Since neither of them was living in the house, Detmar had decided to rent Theed Street. Through his art world connections he was introduced to Haluk Akakce, a Turkish artist who had a fellowship from the Delfina Studio Trust to work in London for nine months. The fellowship had come to an end before Akakce's visa expired, and he had begun asking around for a place to live. Some artists introduced him to Detmar, who said he could rent Theed Street for the very reasonable amount of £100 per week, so long as he didn't mind if Isabella or he came by from time to time. Akakce agreed and made plans to return to New York to sublet his apartment there. As he was packing, he got a phone call. It was Isabella. "Do you mind if I move back into the house?" she asked Akakce.

Detmar had told her that he'd found someone to live in Theed Street—an artist—and she saw it as a way to move out of Philip and Stefan's without having to live alone. Confused, Akakce pointed out that it was in fact her house. And then he realized that she was proposing that they live there together. "You're an artist," she said. "And to live with an artist would be interesting." "Shouldn't we meet first?" he asked. They arranged to meet the following evening at Baltic, a Polish restaurant. "Do you know what I look like?" Isabella asked. "No," said Akakce, who had never heard of her. "I am not a psychic." Isabella replied that she'd be wearing a white feather headdress that had been inspired by Warhol's wig. Moments after he hung up, his phone rang again. This time it was Detmar. "You have to give the £100 to me," he said. "Not to Isabella."

Although she was thirty minutes late, there was no mistaking Isabella when she arrived at Baltic. Akakce, cherubic with curly brown locks, watched as the bartender, who had been mixing the artist's second gin and tonic, poured the tonic until it spilled over the rim of the glass and onto the floor. He looked to see what the bartender was staring at. It was Isabella, in a long chain mail dress, a white mink coat, and the aforementioned headdress. She came over to him and said, "You must be Haluk. Please zip my dress. Fucking McQueen; his zippers are shit." Then she said, "You've been doing coke, haven't you?" He had. They moved to a table and, after Isabella ordered caviar, she began to question him about his work. When he explained he was making sculptures of wood, she said, "You must meet this man I'm with. His father has a workshop. He was the first person to fuck [a famous female singer] in the ass."

At that moment, Detmar arrived, spotted the caviar, and shouted, "You cunt! He's a tenant. It was supposed to be a drink. We're here to earn money." Isabella responded, "Can't you see he's a great artist? What does one hundred pounds mean?" When Detmar stormed out, she said to Akakce, "Let's make this easy. You don't have to pay [rent] at all." Then she told him that she would work for him and help him promote his art. Akakce pointed out that Isabella had never seen his work. "That's okay," she said. "I know a star when I see one. Get your gallery in New York to send me a fax. I want to know everything about you."

When Akakce returned from New York he arrived at Theed Street well past midnight. From the house came the sound of the Sex Pistols. Isabella opened the door wearing a maid's uniform. "Darling!" she said, "I've been cleaning the house for you." "It was like we already knew each other," Akakce said. A few days later she showed him a list that Detmar had written of what he saw as the reasons for their split. Number one was Alexander McQueen. Number two was hats.

As Akakce was settling into Theed Street, Detmar was consoling himself with a new love affair. Although he'd had plenty of dates since the split (he once said "because I was married to Issie, I got much prettier dates than I ever could on my own"),[10] he'd so far failed to seduce a woman who could rival Isabella. He'd traveled to Miami for the Art Basel–Miami Beach Fair, and was staying at the house of Gianni Versace, which was open to the public for the first time since the designer's murder on its front steps. One morning he came downstairs to find Stephanie Theobald, a columnist for *Harper's Bazaar*, having a breakfast meeting with Maureen Paley, a New York gallerist. "He seemed like a character from *Brideshead Revisited* and didn't seem to have made it to the twenty-first-century yet,"

Theobald said. "This fey character in a pink coat." Because Theobald had been dating only women for the last fifteen years, she wasn't as put off as she might have been. After breakfast they decided to go to look around the fair together and, that evening, to go to the launch of the Muhammad Ali tribute book *GOAT* (Greatest of All Time).

"He's fun," Theobald said of Detmar, "like a child. He'd finish smoking and then say to me, 'Stef, what should I do with my cigarette?'" She told him to look out for women for her, and then selected one for him. "I want you," he said. "If he'd been rough and tough I wouldn't have been interested," said Theobald. "I thought he was gay. But I got drunk and thought, 'This is going to make a pretty interesting story. I may as well go with it.'" In the morning, Detmar rang Stuart Shave at Modern Art. "Stephanie and I are in love," Theobald heard him say. It was news to her, but together they retrieved her belongings from her hotel and moved her into the Versace mansion.

It was another house, Hilles, said Theobald, that was the big topic on Detmar's mind. Isabella was the other. "I thought they were getting divorced," Theobald said. "He kept talking about the lawyer and how expensive it was. He was very bitter about Isabella, but it was also as if he was so embroiled with the story that he couldn't let it go either."

Isabella was having her own money problems. In order to raise money, Isabella had sold back to Shave the *Excessive Sensual Indulgence* fountain by Sue Webster and Tim Noble, and although she'd acquired the piece in a trade, Detmar wasn't at all pleased: having the work of your artists on the open market is not good for business. Shave gave her £40,000 for the work. She also borrowed money from McQueen—£10,000 in exchange for a sculpture of a golden cow that would be collateral. The terms were set out in a contract sent over from his lawyers. Despite the financial strain of life as a single woman, Isabella was amused by what Detmar was getting up to with Theobald. When word of his new lover trickled back to Isabella, she told everyone, "My husband is dating a lesbian!"

Akakce by now was as entranced with life in Isabella's shadow as everyone else. "I'd awake in the morning and find these lists," he said. "Number one would be 'Please pick up toilet paper,' with brand and quality noted. Number two would be 'Please design a crystal shower curtain.' Number three would be 'Let's think about a butterfly curtain.' And Number four would be 'Meet me in Venice.' I would choose one of them," Akakce said. "Meet me in Venice." It was a mutually beneficial relationship. "When I first moved in, she was very dependent," he said. The two took to sleeping together, platonically, in Isabella's bed. "I had to buy her pajamas," he said. "We used to say our relationship transcends true love. She made me feel I was the most precious thing. The only one who made me experience unconditional love."

Isabella would complain to him that she couldn't really help him the way she had helped Treacy and McQueen, because she no longer had the drive. "But our conversations changed my perspective," said Akakce. "That was more important than 'you can introduce me to Sheik Majed or to Bernard Arnault.'"

More than career advice, Akakce was in need of nurturing, and it was in Isabella's nature to comply. The result wasn't without its comedic moments. After one particularly late night, Akakce slept until four in the afternoon. When he awoke, he found Isabella on the phone in the kitchen. (Isabella was always on the phone. Akakce once saw her put it through the x-ray machine at the airport still connected to a caller.) "Would you like a cup of tea?" he asked her. "Julia, I have to go," Isabella said to her sister. "It's easier to bring the Pope from the Vatican for a fuck than it is to get Haluk to do anything."

What Akakce and Treacy and Bartlett and McPherson had all begun to do was to warn her to be wary of Casanova, who seemed to still be continually on her mind. "But she'd say, 'Why doesn't anyone want me to be happy? I deserve to feel that I am a woman and I'm alive and I don't care what it costs,'" Akakce said.

It cost a lot. In addition to accompanying her on trips to Moscow and

Paris, Casanova convinced her to give him the £15,000 she got from the sale of her grandmother's portrait to redecorate Theed Street. Casanova shared her lavish tastes, at least in the abstract. He promised glass sculptures to hold her hats, a bath shaped like a gondola (saddling him with another nickname, "The Gondolier"), Egyptian chocolate to bathe in, furniture from a countess's palazzo, which would be covered in rabbit droppings to give it "the greeny gilt color of a river," and a pink sitting room, like the light of St. Marks' Square.[11] All she got was the pink sitting room. "[Casanova] arrived with one can of cheap pink paint," Akakce recalled. "And then he put all her furniture in the garden. The weather was shit and it was all ruined. Then he said he'd have it recovered and we never saw it again." Isabella's assistant Jessica Andrews remembers it slightly differently. "He charged an absolute fortune for something I could have bought [at auction], left it in the rain, and then wanted her to pay more to have it re-done. And on this day Issie was really in a bad place. She would shake quite a lot. Andrews stepped in and said, 'You cannot talk to her this way. You ruined it and you need to pay for it.' Casanova started screaming at her, 'You're the devil! You're a devil woman.' Isabella was in tears, and I bundled her into the car and took her to work."

It was now a year after she, Daphne Guinness, and David LaChapelle had made such an impression at haute couture with their pop-up photo booth, and Isabella was stuck as to what to do next. LaChapelle, increasingly fed up with the fashion world, had said he didn't want to do the shows again. From Isabella's point of view, there was just one alternative: Haluk Akakce. There was only one problem—Akakce had never taken a professional photograph. "I'll get you assistants," she said. The artist wasn't convinced. Surely Isabella would be better off taking one of the other photographers she worked with? "They're starting to realize I'm not well," she said of her bosses at Condé Nast. "I have to go with someone no one has ever heard of. Either I take the world's best or I take someone new.

Don't complain. I'm offering you an amazing opportunity—a fabulous week in Paris." Akakce considered the proposal and decided just one thing was missing. "What will I wear?" he asked. "I'll call the Japanese," Isabella said. She phoned over to Yohji Yamamoto's office: "I have a challenge. There's an elephant I am bringing to couture." She outfitted Akakce in a black jacket held together by a giant safety pin, which she would grab on to to pull him from place to place.

Paris was everything she'd promised. They stayed at a flat belonging to the owner of Harrods, Mohamed al-Fayed, above the Cartier store on Place Vendôme, and were driven in the Bentley that came with the apartment. At the Christian Dior show, the publicist Karla Otto tried to tell Isabella that John Galliano would choose the models Akakce would be photographing, but Isabella was having none of it. "Haluk is an artist!" she exclaimed. "No one will tell him whom to shoot." Demanding to see Galliano herself, she then turned to Akakce. "Stop smiling," she ordered. "If you say, 'May I' or 'Please,' they will drop you." When Isabella got her audience with Galliano, she did with him as she did with Karl Lagerfeld for Philip Treacy so many years before. She introduced her new protégé as if she were doing Galliano an enormous favor. "This is Haluk. He's never taken a photograph before and you're going to be his first. Isn't that wonderful?" Galliano agreed that it was. "It was so chaotic," said Anna Bromilow, who was also there. "You have to be pretty demanding to get what you want backstage at couture, other-wise forget it. She was screaming at Gwen Stefani to get out of the way and [Gwen Stefani] was practically crying. But the shoot was a huge success."

While smoking and waiting outside the Ritz for the Versace show to begin, Isabella, in her dollar sign hat, complained to Akakce that the show was late because they were waiting for "fifty pounds or twenty dollars to come." It was the rapper 50 Cent who was due to arrive. When three limos with blacked-out windows pulled up, Isabella said to Akakce, "This looks more like five million." When 50 Cent reached out to try to touch her hat, she pulled back, horrified. "It's couture!" she admonished.

Although her friends had tried to intervene several times, it was Casanova who finally made the break with Isabella. Fed up with the stories she was telling about him, he began to ignore her phone calls. For the first time in fifteen years, Isabella was officially without a man in her life. And, thanks to an item in the *Daily Mail* in March announcing that Detmar was having an affair with a lesbian, it was now very public knowledge. For any woman of forty-six to suddenly find herself single would have been a major adjustment. With Isabella's need for attention and craving for security, it could have been completely crippling. Fortunately, she quickly found a new diversion.

That Valentine's Day, Isabella had gone to a party at Daphne Guinness's house. There she met Matthew Mellon, the strong-jawed scion of the Mellon Bank fortune who was wearing red suede shoes of his own design. Good-looking, with an old name and a rich family legacy, he was everything Isabella had always dreamed of in a man. At the time, Mellon was launching a new shoe business of his own, and Isabella and her connections held an added interest for him. "Matthew is very easy," said Lucy Birley. "Turn up at his [house] and it's 'Darling, do you want some 1952 Veuve Clicquot?' Life is difficult and we all have things that make us feel better about ourselves. And for Issie it was glamour." She was immediately entranced. She felt in Matthew a kindred spirit. Although his family wasn't as old as hers it had certainly been as rich in its day. The affluence in their pasts would link them together. Isabella even became convinced that Matthew owned a boat that had once belonged to Lord Moyne, her grandmother's lover.

What started as a potential business relationship quickly grew into a passionate love affair. "She was the love of my life," Mellon told friends. And she felt the same. When Isabella discovered that Detmar's architect grandfather designed the kitchen in Mellon's Eton Square duplex, she decided they should have sex there—on the stove—as revenge of sorts against Detmar. Isabella had grand plans about what her life would be like when she and Mellon married. Her pride and joy became a Fendi bag that she thought looked like a slice of melon. One day, she went to Philip Treacy and asked him to make her a melon-shaped hat. Not in favor of the coupling, he refused. "We were all against Matthew [at first]," said Akakce. "But he treated her like a woman. He opened the door for her. With Detmar she paid 50/50."

In May, Mellon, eager to spoil her, chartered a plane and took Isabella for a romantic week in the south of France. There they attended Naomi Campbell's birthday party in Saint Tropez. Isabella was proud to promote the company her new lover had launched: "Do you know Harry's Shoes?"[12] she asked all the partygoers, speaking of the line of men's shoes he'd invented with comfortable rubber soles that he'd named for his grandfather. But there was a fly in the ointment. Detmar was crushed by the news of her affair with Mellon and had been ringing her daily throughout the trip. On the plane ride home, Mellon urged Isabella to consider reconciling with Detmar. "I said she had to get it cleaned up," Mellon said. "I suggested that she get back together with Detmar. I'm very conventional at heart. I'm not a home-wrecker. I didn't want to be the reason their marriage broke up." Isabella reluctantly agreed to try for a reunion.

On May 28, 2004, Stephanie Theobald got an e-mail from Detmar telling her that he was reuniting with Isabella. She was surprised, not least because the night before he'd come to her book launch with Tracey Emin and Bryan Ferry. But Isabella and Detmar had recently run into each other at the Cy Twombly opening at the new Gagosian Gallery in King's Cross and decided to get back together.

Isabella's relationships with men had been another part of her self-constructed fantasy. They came not as individuals, but as packages that involved a life she craved. In that, she was not unique among women. But the tumultuous and disappointing affairs with Casanova and Mellon sent her already delicate self-confidence plummeting. "She wanted to love someone," said Harmsworth. "When you haven't been loved you really want to love someone. All that love that you couldn't express for your mother because she would slap you down. For a child an important thing is to give love. And you think it's because they want to be loved, but they want to be allowed to love. So with Issie she loved too much and it was people who couldn't love her back properly." Her friends began to think that even if a reunion with Detmar wouldn't repair her confidence, at least it would give her a base from which she could try to relaunch herself. Even those who would never say that Detmar had been a positive force in her life had to admit that he was at least a stable force—and compared to Casanova—a loyal one. They were united in many ways by their weaknesses—by their need to be the center of attention, by their fantastical tendencies. It wasn't a foundation for what most people might consider a "normal" relationship, but after fifteen years they were bound at the very least by their shared peccadilloes. When it seemed she was unable to find happiness elsewhere, a return to the status quo didn't seem so bad. Detmar said he received a call from one of Isabella's therapists saying, "You are the key to her."[13] He felt he had to try to reconcile.

Even to Detmar and Isabella, it didn't seem the most wholehearted of reunions. "In the end it just seemed easier to stay with Detmar," said Grenfell. "But she was angry about it." After breaking the news, Detmar wrote to Theobald that he'd still like to go to the Hay Literary Festival with her that weekend, to help her promote the book, if it was appropriate. He also told her she was "a wonderful person and a very good cook." One of Isabella's therapists asked if she really wanted to be married to Detmar. "At this point I'd settle for a hamster," she said.

That June, she and Detmar went together to the Serpentine Summer Party, an annual fund-raising gala for the Serpentine Gallery, prompting reports in the press that they'd reconciled. Isabella played these down.

"Let's just say we are on a trial period. I am very happy at the moment, but I am keeping my options open. You never know, there might be another knight in shining armor around the corner."[14]

If the knight in shining armor was meant to be Matthew Mellon, the arrival in his life that September of a young actress named Noelle Reno crushed those illusions. Reno was Mellon's new girlfriend and had moved from Los Angeles to live with him. Isabella did not approve. "She thought Noelle was not worthy," said a friend of Noelle's. "She would sit and flirt with Matthew as if [Noelle] were not there." The presence of his girlfriend did not even stop Isabella from lavishing praise on intimate parts of Mellon's anatomy in public.

It seemed Isabella hadn't fully given up on Mellon herself. Reno may have had age and beauty on her side, but Isabella proved to be a worthy adversary. "Isabella would talk circles around Noelle," said a friend who dined with them both. "She'd be there with the cigarette and the hat and, well, it was like watching a Broadway show." When Mellon relapsed into cocaine use, Isabella thought she saw a way back in. When Reno would leave the flat, Isabella would come over. Although she always hated when others used drugs—and in particular cocaine, which she found made people boring—she would stay up with Mellon, comforting him, and telling him it was all going to be okay. She'd also take him by the shoulders and shake him asking, "What are you doing with her? She's so boring!" Eventually Reno told Mellon she couldn't take it anymore—that she had too much self-respect to be treated so shabbily by Isabella—and Mellon reluctantly agreed to limit his contact with her.

Despite keeping up appearances, it was clear to her friends that Isabella was not getting better—only worse. But when they suggested that she stop working, she'd reply that Detmar didn't think that was a good idea. "He thought work was good for her," said Lucy Birley. "He was totally adamant that she keep her job, that as long as she keeps working she'll be all right." He also wasn't keen for her to stay in at night. "One of the problems was that Detmar was never going to say, 'Darling, you look tired. Let's stay in and watch telly,'" said Birley. At the period when she was most vulnerable, she was now going out and drinking a lot.

Isabella's daytime behavior was also worrying. On her lunch hour, she had taken to sitting in Hanover Square, in a small green park in front of Vogue House, smoking cigarettes with the homeless people who lived there. She asked them all to tell her their stories, insisting that one day she, too, would be where they were. When she was in the office, she was increasingly preoccupied with what she saw as her failings and spent most of her time discussing them with her colleagues. "She was charming, but not at all strong," said Nicholas Coleridge. "Being with Issie was like having someone around who was always slightly drunk. Your heart went out to her, but as it went on longer and longer it got harder."

The course of her treatment did not make the people around her have faith that she'd soon improve. Although she said she loved the shock treatments—and spoke of them the way one might speak about going to a spa—they were making her wildly unpredictable—often to undeniably hilarious result. This probably contributed to the circumstances of her next trip.

Isabella had been invited to present Philip Treacy with an award at the Shanghai Fashion Awards and wanted to add on a photo shoot in Beijing. But she didn't want to be jet-lagged. Shortly after an electroshock treatment she decided the only logical answer was to fly to Moscow and take a train to China, to mitigate the effects of the time difference. "It was impossible to get her out of this idea," said Margarita Wennberg, a wealthy Russian friend. Wennberg had her assistant book the trip for Isabella—"it was all first, first, first," she said—but there was no getting around the fact that the Trans-Siberian Rail was not the Orient Express. On November 13, Wennberg's driver took Isabella to Yaroslavsky Station at 11 p.m. It was almost winter in Russia, and at night the temperatures were below freezing. Still, Isabella wore her Prada platform shoes without stockings. "My driver followed her with all her Vuitton bags and said he had never seen such a thing."

The next day, only twenty-three hours into the six-day journey, Isabella phoned Wennberg and said, "Get me off this train. No one speaks English, there are no showers, and I want some tea." "What could I do?" said Wennberg. "I said, 'Put the attendant on the phone,' then I said to the attendant, 'This lady wants some tea!'" That accomplished, she set about trying to find a way to get Isabella off the train. Isabella was in Ekaterinburg, famous only for being the rural place where the Romanov family, the last royal family of Russia, was murdered.

Back in London, Jessica Andrews was at the *Tatler* offices single-handedly packing all of the clothes for the shoot and most of Isabella's clothes as well. Finding clothes for Isabella had become a feat, as designers, including Alexander McQueen, were increasingly reluctant to loan things to her knowing they were unlikely to get them back. At 2 a.m., Andrews got a phone call. It was Isabella, who, through her tears, explained to her assistant that she was in the middle of Siberia. She'd gotten off the train. Andrews phoned Isabella's rich friends, until a solution was found. "Someone put her on Siberian Airways," said Wennberg.

As Jessica Andrews was flying alone to China for the shoot, Condé Nast had to pay thousands of pounds in excess baggage fees to get her there with all the clothes. She arrived exhausted, and no sooner did she lie down on the bed than her phone began to ring. It was Isabella. "How dare you forget my birthday! How dare you not plan anything!" she said. An hour later, Andrews was careening around Beijing in a rickshaw with Alexandra Spencer Churchill, the model for the shoot, and Isabella. After the shoot, Isabella's mania seemed to drop off and she became almost helpless. She complained to Donald McPherson that Geordie Greig wouldn't buy her a ticket from Beijing to Shanghai for the awards ceremony (giving an award to Treacy wasn't technically part of her job). "She kept saying, 'How will I get there? How will I get there?'" McPherson replied that he would buy her a ticket himself.

Once there, McPherson tried to lift her spirits—insisting she exercise, and putting her into a tanning booth—and to help her accomplish what she had gone there to do. He even helped her write her speech. Backstage at the ceremony, when the moment came for her to give the award, she froze. McPherson had to push her out onto the stage.

That night, Isabella's state of mind only worsened. She insisted that Andrews sleep in her bed, once again desperate not to be alone. But Andrews, a young assistant in a new city, wanted to go out. Once Isabella fell asleep, the girl sneaked out, returning, a bit drunk, at 6 a.m. But Isabella was awake, and upset at finding herself alone in bed. "Where have you been?" she asked. In her mind, there were no personal or professional boundaries to her working relationship with her assistants. "I just went to the bathroom for a drink of water," Andrews replied. She knew there was no reasoning with Isabella at this point.

Isabella hadn't lost her knack for transforming her misadventures into comedy, and, ultimately, she managed to turn the Trans-Siberian train trip into one of her funniest stories. She would have people in stitches describing how she'd been reduced to trading her Manolos and Philip Treacy hats for food. "Imagine the sight—all of these Chinese people getting off the train wearing Manolos and McQueen," she said to Akakce. The story she spun was amusing, but the reality had not been. In truth she had been terrified.

Back in London, Stuart Shave was to confront his own reality. He had begun to see that he couldn't run the gallery the way he wanted with Detmar and, to a lesser extent, Isabella, involved. But Detmar wasn't keen to go. They discussed various scenarios, including dividing the artists and asking each which partner they'd rather stay with. But the answer to that was clear. Detmar explained to his cousin Simon Blow, "I could have fought it, but I would have been left with a gallery and no artists." Shave and Detmar settled on a price of £100,000 for Detmar and Isabella's shares, and the gallery, which was about £150,000 in the red when Detmar left, was turning a profit within six months. "Art, aside from the opening parties, is a deeply critical environment," said Shave. "The fashion connection ultimately did not feel an authentic part of how I wanted the gallery to develop. It felt integral to my work to remove myself from the partnership. But I never regretted going into business with them."

Undeterred, Detmar teamed up with artist, Pablo León de la Barra, and opened another gallery, Blow de la Barra, this time in Mayfair. Again, Isabella was at the center of it. She was with de la Barra and Detmar when they approached artist Stefan Brüggemann about being part of the gallery. "She was really the soul of the gallery and the reason I wanted to be represented by them," Brüggemann said. "She said to me that I must use her mouth, as this was her biggest tool." Although she was barely able to function herself much of the time, she launched herself into the job of promoting others. It was a necessary diversion from the sense of gloom growing inside her. Undoubtedly Detmar, who thought she was happiest when she was working, encouraged her in this, but perhaps Isabella also thought that if she worked hard for others one day someone would step in and rescue her. But the root of Isabella's problems lay within herself and only she could fix them.

"I kept saying 'You can be like a phoenix,'" said Harmsworth. "You have done it before and come out of the ashes and you can do it again. We're all middle-aged now and we have to reinvent ourselves. We have to make that transition and of course it is painful." Ultimately it would prove too painful for Isabella to bear.

Miserabella

CHAPTER TWELVE

In June 2005, the annual Royal Ascot horse race was moved to York, the far-
thest corner of northeast England, while the usual grounds in Windsor were un-
dergoing renovation. The event's host that year, the Duke of Devonshire, had invited
Philip Treacy to come and judge the "best turned out horse." He, Stefan Bartlett,
Lucy Birley, and Isabella made the journey by train. In the stables they found the
queen, who was inspecting her own horses. Isabella, in an Alexander McQueen
kimono and a hat from Treacy's Warhol collection, featuring a dancing couple,
went as close to the sovereign as she could manage without appearing conspicuous.
After the race, they went to a lunch thrown by the Duke of Devonshire and then
began their journey home. It had been, Philip thought, a spectacular day. Midway
through the journey, Isabella announced, "I've been thinking. Things are great, but
I have just been feeling that maybe it would be better if I killed myself." "We were
dumbfounded," Philip said. "It seemed like quite a radical solution."

I sabella could talk about madness in the sanest—and funniest—
ways imaginable. In 2005, she became fixated on the idea of killing herself and would regale anyone who would listen with the
stories of her somewhat half-hearted attempts. "I finally found a
vet who will give me Ketamine," she said, referring to the tran-
quilizer used to calm horses. "The problem is, now he wants to see my

horse." She went to Virginia Woolf's house, to drown herself in the lake there as Woolf had done, but said she went at the wrong time of year so that when she arrived the lake was dry. In Milan, she asked her Italian driver to "take her to the river," so she could throw herself into it. But she was confusing Milan, which has a canal, with Florence, which banks the flowing Arno. "River? What river?" her Italian driver kept asking. He finally took her to the canal. Isabella got out of the car, looked at dank water in the shallow canal, realized she would only end up wet and muddy, got back in the car, and said, "Take me to dinner."

The problem, Isabella said, was life. She just simply didn't see the point of going on anymore. She was able to break it down into categories: sadness over her inability to have a child, fear of winding up destitute, frustration with the commercial turn the fashion industry had taken, and confusion over the fact that others had become so financially successful while she had not, but the root of it all was that Isabella could find no reason to live, therefore, she figured, she may as well die. "In life you begin with a charm bracelet," Isabella said. "And gradually the charms drop off. Being charming, being charmed I adore it all . . . You need charm more and more as you get older." [1]

"We are all searching for meaning in our lives and we have to invent it," said Harmsworth. "Our jobs give us meaning or people give us meaning. What she felt was she had no meaning." Grenfell agreed. "She was disillusioned," she said. "It was her inability to break away from her marriage and the fashion world—all of that which she knew was not satisfying. She didn't know how to find a new path at that point. And the fact that she couldn't change it pulled her down low." Isabella couldn't, wouldn't be convinced that there were other viable alternatives available to her.

Although she was coherent in discussion of her problems, her behavior was becoming more and more disjointed and extreme—starting with the requests she was making. For a holiday in the Maldives with Mc-Queen, she wanted milliner Stephen Jones to make her a bathing cap covered in Swarovski crystals. When her assistant Jessica Andrews tried to point out to her that she'd drown under the weight of it, she ignored her. Returning from holiday, Isabella acted as if Andrews had never warned her of such a thing. Instead she seemed to lay the blame on her assistant, telling her pointedly: "I couldn't wear it, I almost drowned." She also wanted an emerald-encrusted Vertu phone, like the one Majed al-Sabah had, and phoned Andrews in the middle of the night to tell her so. Andrews explained that the phone was made of crystals, not emeralds, but Isabella wanted one anyway. And she wanted a real Turkish flying carpet to use in a shoot, like the one Haluk Akakce had described to her. She refused to listen when Andrews tried to explain that no such thing existed: magicians use a metal frame that bends around the body. "She went mental," Andrews said. Eventually Bryan Ferry, whose girlfriend was being photographed in the shoot, had to be enlisted to convince her that her assistant wasn't just inept.

Some of her stunts were more worrying as they taxed her already precarious finances. On a trip to Istanbul for Akakce's birthday, Isabella decided that she had to hire a boat to do a photo shoot, "Turks in Tartan." Her plan was to have Turkish fabric companies make tartan. Although she recently was able to pay off her overdraft, thanks to a contract for an Isabella Blow lipstick for MAC (she wanted to call it Blow Job, but it was finally called Blow and has since been discontinued), she had Andrews phone her bank in London and insist that they extend her a £30,000 loan to hire the boat. "McQueen is coming and we're going to buy the factory," Isabella explained. But McQueen didn't come. He was still not speaking to her because she had gone back to Detmar. She wanted Matthew Mellon to come, but he was in Los Angeles. Philip Treacy also passed. He felt that showing up would be a tacit endorsement of the crazy plan. It was just Isabella and Akakce—and a boat so large that it came with a staff to operate it. The captain of the boat wanted to be paid in cash. Isabella went to the bank in a small village on the same day its elderly residents were able to pick up their pension money. Akakce arrived to find her in the bank surrounded by elderly Turks, trying to cajole the bank manager into emptying the safe to give her the full amount. She would later describe it as the best holiday of her life.

Back in London Isabella begged Nicholas Coleridge and Geordie Greig for a raise. "Lack of money was a big obsession in her life," said Coleridge. "She'd talk to Geordie and me and we'd give her advice." On one occasion they gave her a raise as well. The next day Coleridge saw a security guard standing outside Isabella's office. "She had S. J. Philips, the expensive jeweler on Bond Street, showing her pieces that cost £25,000, £30,000, £40,000—more than the entire raise. I think she thought it was naff to understand money. She considered it beneath her."

Isabella was still going to work and covering the shows, but for the people working with her, an increasing amount of time was spent trying to console her. She'd sit in a corner of the *Tatler* offices shaking, crying, and saying again and again that that she just didn't see the point of going on, that she was sure she was going to end up destitute, with no place to live, like the eccentric early twentieth-century arts patroness, the Marchesa Casati. "She was incredibly vulnerable," said Anna Bromilow, "like a crushed little bird." When she wasn't talking to someone face-to-face, she was on the phone—sometimes ringing a single person ten times a day to go over again and again how dire she felt. During the shows, Andrews's main job had become trying to keep her safe. In Paris, she had to pull Isabella out of oncoming traffic after she had taken too much lithium. In Milan, Andrews was left with an incensed designer after Isabella skipped a meeting at Bottega Veneta. When given the phone to explain her absence, Isabella told Tomas Maier that she was in bed having an orgy—and described it in the most graphic details. He promptly pulled all of the company's advertising from *Tatler*. "Oh, God, Geordie, what should I do?"

Isabella said when her boss called her on it. "Should I go and see him? Am I going to get fired? Oh, that's terrible. Did I really do that?" She did, and a variety of Condé Nast executives, right up to the international CEO Jonathan Newhouse, were enlisted to make amends. When she was found sleeping in the park in front of the Principe di Savoia Hotel in Milan her bosses decided to send her home.

In the summer of 2005, Andrews quit. She'd spent one morning going through documents with Isabella and popped down the hall to drop something off at the Editorial Department. When she returned, Isabella said, "Where the fuck have you been all morning?" Andrews explained that she'd been with her, going through paperwork. "Don't lie to me" was the reply. "She'd completely changed," Andrews said. "I just thought, 'I don't want to do this anymore.'"

Instead of hiring another full-time assistant, the company decided they'd give Isabella assistants on six-month rotations—to keep things fresh. Privately, she continued to rely on two young men. Instead of Philip Treacy and Alexander McQueen, who were both now so occupied with their own businesses that they couldn't devote the constant attention she required, she had Haluk Akakce and Kamel Belkacemi.

Isabella met Kamel Belkacemi at Waitrose grocery store in 2004, when she was living with Philip Treacy following her stay at The Priory. He was a young handsome French boy who once wanted to be a designer but was now working at the trendy fashion emporium Dover Street Market. He had long been an admirer of hers and approached her to tell her so. She was on the phone, but grabbed his wrist and, upon hearing his accent, said, "You pick the wine. You're French." Belkacemi, afraid to admit that he didn't drink, picked the bottle with the best label. To whomever she was speaking with on the phone, she said, "I'm with the most beautiful boy. He's your type." Belkacemi gave her his phone number, thinking he'd never see her again. But that December, Isabella rang and invited him to tea at Vogue House. They met—she in a white fur coat by Alexander McQueen—at the café on the ground floor, and she began to cry. "If you had met me before, I would have shown you a better person than the one in front of you now," she said. Belkacemi was sweet and infinitely patient, and Isabella quickly came to depend on him.

After her shock treatments it was usually Belkacemi who would collect her from the hospital. "She wasn't scared," he said. "But she couldn't remember what had happened in the two previous days." She would be up, nevertheless. "She was a diva afterward," he said. "It was do this—right away!" He'd go with her to the fashion shows and, if she had a shoot in, say, Amsterdam, he'd travel with her—often on his own dime—and sleep with her in her bed, despite her snoring and despite the fact that she'd take little liberties like using his toothbrush and not even rinsing it afterward.

Isabella was not improving. She tried residential stays at a few other mental health facilities, but to no avail. Matthew Mellon tried to get her to go to a place in the U.S. that specialized in bipolar disorders, but she refused to go. Part of the problem was that she refused to commit to the kind of time that real therapy needed to be effective. "At some of the [mental-health hospitals] they said she really had to do a lot of work," said Grenfell. "I remember her saying to me, 'I just can't do this introspective. I don't want to go there. I just want to carry on.' "

What she carried on with were suicide attempts. In 2006, she went from talking about killing herself to actually trying to do it. The attempts, though more serious, still had a cry-for-help feel to them, not least because Isabella would usually tell someone what she was up to in time for her attempt to be thwarted.

On March 20, Treacy and Bartlett were on their way to Dubai when they decided to stop off at Isabella's flat on Eaton Square to give her some flowers that had been delivered to them that day, lest they die in their absence. When they arrived she opened a bottle of champagne and went to fetch her grandmother's scrapbook. In her black ballpoint pen, not her signature pink, she inscribed the book to the two. Treacy tried to stop her, saying, "What are you doing?" Isabella told him that she'd taken 118 pills. Treacy didn't believe her, so she told him to look in the trash can. Indeed, it was filled with pill containers. Treacy told Bartlett to phone an ambulance, and he phoned Lucy Birley. When Birley arrived, Isabella was on the sidewalk refusing to get in the ambulance. Known among her friends for her cool demeanor, Birley screamed, "Isabella, *get in the fucking ambulance!*" A shocked Isabella did as she was told. For the next eight months Isabella refused to speak to Bartlett, blaming him for calling the ambulance.

From then, the attempts began to run into one another. She phoned Philip Treacy one night to say she was in Cheshire, and that she'd taken another overdose. She spoke very calmly about the room, the music playing, the candles she'd lit. Treacy phoned her sister Julia Delves Broughton and had someone at *Tatler* ring the company car service to find out where exactly Isabella was. He then rang the front desk at the hotel in Nantwich where Isabella had been left off and told them to check on her. When Isabella rang again, Treacy put the call on speakerphone. Her tone had changed. She was now sitting in the back of a police car between two officers. "I am *furious* with you," she said. Philip and Julia, who was with him, couldn't help but laugh.

On another occasion Isabella drove her car into a Tesco grocery store delivery van in Stroud, later saying that she always hated Tesco. Akakce once got a call from a stationmaster who had stopped Isabella from jumping in front of a train. "It was a prolonged period of difficult things to process," said Treacy. "You were never irritated by it, you were just a bit stunned by it all. You were prepared for anything. Anything could happen."

Throughout the last year of her life, Isabella had been surreptitiously reaching out to the two mother figures in her life: Rona and Helga. "She wrote me a lot of letters in the last year," Rona said. "She was expressing unhappiness in all areas of her life." When Rona heard that Isabella was making her way to Cheshire, she rang the farm manager to warn him that Isabella might try to drown herself in the lake in Doddington Park. "The poor girl must have gone through agonies in her mind," Rona said. "She'd tell me she was afraid that she'd become a bag lady or a tramp. I said there's no need at all. She had prospects. I said that I'd make sure that none of my family would ever end up like that."

She also rang Helga frequently in Sri Lanka, looking for support. "I asked her why, with so many around her, that she was unable to talk," Helga said. Isabella told her, "They have all had enough and have their own problems and do not understand." Helga, who had been through it before with Jonathan, knew how exhausting it was to talk to someone suffering from severe depression—someone who was "caught on a repeat record" and spent hours trying to reassure Isabella of her worth—and trying to jolly her out of her mood. "I told her, 'God is not ready for his expense account, Izi (*sic*), for you to style the heavens and have your next adventure.'"

On April 23, 2006, Isabella made the most serious attempt to date. She leapt off a motorway overpass. The day had begun fairly normally. She was going to be allowed out of the Bowden Hospital in Harrow for a day. She sent Belkacemi a text at noon saying she was on her way to him, but that she would take a taxi at 5 p.m. to meet Bryan Ferry. (Usually Belkacemi would take her back to the suburban hospital himself.) They had lunch together at Maroush, a popular Lebanese restaurant, and then had a drink at Harrods. Then Isabella said she had to go see Ferry. "I just put her in a taxi, stupidly," said Belkacemi. "She looked so happy." She never saw Bryan Ferry that day. Fifteen minutes from Harrods, she got out of the taxi and jumped from an overpass. Belkacemi found out when he got a text message from Detmar the next day saying that Isabella had fractured her ankles—just after leaving him. It was the last part that stung Belkacemi. It was particularly unfair given he was the most loyal of Isabella's visitors, going to see her in hospital nearly every single day.

Isabella was taken first to Ealing Hospital, a general medical hospital near where she jumped. Matthew Mellon came to visit and she said he told her she was "the shag of his life." Her cousin Benjie Fraser was another regular visitor. Belkacemi came and brought her a DVD player and the film *Some Like It Hot*. Isabella thanked him and said, "The funeral scene is amazing." She then began ringing friends and assistants plotting her next attempt. She rang Akakce and asked him to find out which bridges in London had nets beneath them, because, she said, "You don't want me to be stuck like a fish in a net in couture." She rang Anna Bromilow at *Tatler* and gave her specific instructions to bike over "her MAC lipstick, her Vertu phone, a few foreign fashion magazines, and some of that rope from the maintenance department." She had a length of rope delivered to Belkacemi's house and asked him to bring it to the hospital. (He didn't.) When Tim Noble and Sue Webster came to visit, she tried to get them to help her escape. When they refused, she tried to throw herself over a wall. As darkly comic as Isabella made it, the situation was becoming increasingly serious and increasingly hard for those around her to handle.

On Belkacemi's visits, he would listen as Isabella would argue the case for suicide to the staff of the hospital. He recorded some of the conversations on his phone. "I can't die here in the hospital obviously," Isabella said, dressed in a blue robe with white piping. "There's nothing to die with. There are no bridges—it's impossible." The nurse said, "You need a good long sleep." Isabella continued: "I'm very, very, very depressed. Very. I refuse to accept that I am a cripple and I refuse to be on the pills. I have got to kill myself. I have got to." Belkacemi pointed out that her ankles would heal. "Don't you understand? I couldn't live before, why would I suddenly want to live now?" Isabella said. "I don't want to be here on this earth. I'm not enjoying anything at all. I don't want to be here with no shoes on . . . So many people kill themselves, it's not unusual. It's just unusual to have someone who wants to die so much to have been left here."

The nurse said it would be hard on her family and Isabella had an answer to this, too: "I had eight suicides in my family. It comes like that to us." She snapped her fingers. "It's like bacon and eggs. It's like cheese and toast. I just have to make sure it happens the next time." Then she got up to make herself a cup of tea.

Although the attempt was the most serious to date, she told Belkacemi that at the last minute she had scooted over to a place where the bridge was lower—and shredded her fingernails when she changed her mind and tried to hang on. The attempts, it would seem, had become part of the performance. In another video, Isabella goes into great detail about the staging of her death. "I dream it's going to happen," she said. "I'm in Eaton Square, there are candles, candelabra, pills, an aria in the background, lipstick, makeup, McQueen oyster jacket, high shoes—no accident or anything horrible like that—incense, a large bunch of roses at my feet. A funeral car comes to collect the body, tears of joy running down my face . . . and off to Hilles, on the top of the hill and into a grave. Glory be God, that is what I want. I cannot tell you how much I'm dying . . ." Belkacemi laughed as he waited for Isabella to say, "I'm dying to die" but, the reverie broken, she looked at him and stuck out her tongue.

Up until now, Condé Nast had been paying for much of Isabella's private treatment, but the costs were becoming a problem. "She'd exhausted the resources we had," said Nicholas Coleridge. "Condé Nast had paid for three places, and she'd gone beyond the amount of corporate Medicare we had in place and we had already contributed a lot more beyond our insurance limit, too. She needed something long term, and not expensive." When her ankles had healed enough for her to leave Ealing Hospital, she was transferred to The Gordon, a state-run hospital near Victoria Station.

The Gorden was free, and the doctors there were good (most of the doctors in private practice in the United Kingdom also work for the National Health Service, which provides free care), but it wasn't pleasant. Lucy and Julia were horrified to visit and find Isabella reduced to crawling to the toilet. She complained that the other patients were stealing her money and her cigarettes. The two decided that she had to get out.

On June 29, Birley sent Belkacemi a text: "Can we meet at 9:30. Bring B&H [Benson and Hedges cigarettes] for Issy." She and Julia arrived at the hospital in Birley's Mercedes station wagon. Belkacemi rustled Isabella, screaming, into the backseat and they took her to a private hospital in North London where the rooms resembled the luxury hotel suites Isabella so loved. During the journey Isabella kept trying to get out of the car, forcing Birley to put on the child lock on the back doors. A round robin of phone calls had taken place in the weeks prior, trying to raise money for further treatment. The Gordon was opposed to her leaving—saying she'd get no better treatment in private care, but Ferry was sure that having her own room, better food, and one-on-one therapy with a single doctor would make a big difference. In the end, Daphne Guinness and Alexander McQueen paid, on the condition that Isabella never find out.

Detmar was noticeably absent for much of this time. "Detmar did not behave well at that point at all," said one of Isabella's friends. "He had his own demons with his father's depression and suicide, and he didn't know how to cope." Undoubtedly, life with Isabella was hard. Particularly hard given the memory of his father's decline. But even so, many of her friends will never forgive him. Other friends also could not face a visit, either because they'd been through it before with someone else or because they, too, suffered from depression and it hit too close to home. "There were not hundreds of people coming," said Treacy. Anna Wintour came, brought Isabella a Fracas scented candle, and reprimanded her for using the company account to take a taxi to Cheshire. Matthew Mellon also visited nearly every day, often bringing dinner for two.

Rupert Everett came to visit. He had been covering the men's wear shows and, he said, needed some advice. "Why do the collections make you feel so empty?" he wrote in *Vanity Fair*. "What is it?" "Money," Isabella replied. "It's McDonald's these days. You go in. You get photographed. You think you're watching beautiful people in wonderful clothes, but actually you're in a sausage grinder. You forget who you are. You might have a luxury brand name written over your tits, but is that enough? In the end I was just a hat with lips, and that's not chic."[2]

B y August, Isabella was out of the hospital, but she was still not well. People at *Tatler* remembered her pushing Geordie Greig against a wall and a Human Resources officer having to intervene. Greig says he doesn't recall the episode, but that if it happened, it must have been in jest. One thing was clear: Isabella wasn't able to continue working. On August 23, she was moved to the contributing editor's line on the masthead and stripped of her responsibilities.

But it didn't stop her traveling. Within days, she was in India, visiting an old friend, Prince Tikka Singh, and going to the shows in New Delhi. "She loved the warmth of India," Singh said. "She loved the madness of India, the fashion, the colors, the fabrics." She also loved the shopping. In an earlier visit Isabella commissioned a Swarovski–crystal studded sari and had a Rigby & Peller bra sewn inside, because, she said, "They're not big on support in the subcontinent. I can't think of a better example of East meets West."[3] Alarmed by her behavior—particularly the way she was spending money—Tikka rang Nicholas Coleridge at Condé Nast to ask who was paying her bills. He explained she no longer worked for them, but arranged to have her brought back. "It felt like it was never going to end," Coleridge said. "Her life was never exciting enough for her."

Without a real job, Isabella had become fixated on finding new ways to make money, lots of money, fast. Earlier in her life she'd considered such oddities as a line of cutlery with celebrity heads, based on an ivory set at Hilles, which featured a fork with Napoleon's head and a knife with Wellington's. Now she considered a line of handbags and a book about her life, and a documentary about AIDS research for the Arab television station Al Jazeera. In early December, she flew back to India, this time with Rupert Everett, on a trip paid for by ICI Dulux, a Euopean chemical company that makes paint. She was going, she said, to start interviewing Bollywood stars for the project. "Bollywood stars are known to be uncharitable which I disapprove of," she told the *Times of India,* in a comment that made head-lines. She added, "When we talk about Indian fashion, I see a whole lot of potato sacks. There is a long way to go."[4] Then she walked out of a Dulux-sponsored fashion show, despite the fact they'd paid for the trip, saying she was bored. At the end of the month, she and the fashion publicist Karla Otto planned to spend Christmas together in Goa, relaxing. There, Isa-bella again tried to kill herself, taking sedatives and walking into the surf to drown. She passed out before she reached the water and was rescued by a taxi driver who found a hotel key in her pocket and took her, uncon-scious, to Karla Otto. Otto had her taken to a local hospital where she spent New Year's Eve, sending her wishes to friends in London by text message.

The attempt was followed by what appeared to be a restored will to live. Her therapist in India said Isabella was devoting all her time to her project in Kuwait and that "she is progressing quite all right and is 90 per-cent well."[5]

Back in London, on January 25, 2007, many of her old friends agreed with the assessment. It looked as though Isabella had turned a corner. She attended a dinner party in honor of painter Anselm Kiefer, arriving late, as usual. Lucy Birley, who was sitting next to Kiefer, watched her walk in wear-ing a black satin jacket and a headdress. Kiefer turned to Birley and said, "Who is that fabulous creature?" "Everyone's attention was on her," said Birley. "It was like the old Isabella." Isabella sat next to John Maybury, a Brit-ish film director, who once accidentally overdosed himself. "Looks like they've put all the suicides at the same table," he joked. She laughed, and when the music started, she and Maybury were the first to hit the dance floor. It was the last time Lucy saw Isabella. "In a way, I'm happy," Birley said. "Because she was herself."

But the remission was short-lived. That March there was another disastrous trip abroad, this one to Kuwait. Majed al-Sabah had hired Isabella to do a special project for him—a series of books called *Arabian Beauty*. The project turned out to be a bitter disappointment for Isabella. Al-Sabah, rightly, wanted final control over the images and the clothes the models would wear. "I cannot put our women in . . . dresses with total transparency," he said.[6] Isabella bristled at being directed. She overdosed in Kuwait and was taken to hospital there. In the hospital they discovered a cyst on her ovary they feared might be cancer. Although Majed was in Milan, his sisters tended to her. "She couldn't stop crying," said Donald McPherson. "They took care of her for ten days." She was flown back from Kuwait with two nurses.

Back in London after her trip, Isabella had surgery to remove an ovarian cyst and recovered enough to go to a party. At a charity auction she announced to a journalist her intention to launch a line of accessories. "The first thing I'm going to design is a very versatile handbag," she said. "It will be based on a rotating marble statue of Krishna—that's the sort of opulence and intensity I want to convey. The only problem is finding a place to sell it as it will be quite expensive."[7] Indeed, part of her plan was a strap made of diamonds that could be removed and worn as a necklace.

Isabella was now living at Hilles full time. She told her friends that she was happy there, working in the garden and trying to take it easy. In early April, she rang McQueen and asked him to come to Hilles. She wanted to make peace with him, she said. She had her assistant take down Detmar's pride and joy—the portrait of his grandfather done by Augustus John that hung over the kitchen door in the Great Hall—and in its place put a photograph of McQueen framed in neon lights. The message was clear: *This is how much I love you.*

McQueen later said that they sat down and talked for three hours. "We talked about things we had been through and . . . God, I'm hoping things are all right. I said, 'You look so good,' and I said, 'You're not talking about death—no, are you?' And she said, 'No, no.' She really fucking shamboozled me, didn't she? She knew what she was doing. I was just—she convinced me that she was fine, that she had come through the worst of it."[8] Isabella told friends that she'd been upset by the weekend, that McQueen had come with friends and they'd sat around smoking pot and not wanting to do any of the things she had planned.

On April 28, back at Hilles, she threw a dinner party for friends. Two days later, she and her sister Lavinia went to London together so that Isabella could pose for pictures that were meant to accompany a *Vanity Fair* story on English eccentrics and to talk about photo shoot ideas with Geordie Greig. "She wanted the photographs to be modern, erotic, naughty, the story of a badly behaved aristocrat, a bit like herself," said Greig.[9] But the strong woman who appeared in the photographs taken by Steven Meisel in the late 1980s was gone. The armor she was wearing in the photograph by Tim Walker could not mask the frailty that showed on her face. Instead of a feature on eccentrics, the portrait accompanied an article on her death.

On May 5, a sunny Saturday morning at Hilles, Isabella went outside with a bottle of Paraquat—the same poison her father-in-law used to kill himself thirty years earlier—put the bottle to her mouth, and drank. Did she really mean to die? It's hard to say for sure. Certainly Isabella knew that since it had killed Jonathan, the threat was real. Detmar and other people living at Hilles had previously found bottles of the poison hidden around the house, but disposed of them before Isabella had a chance to drink from them. But this time they were not fast enough. After taking a swig, she made her way back inside Hilles and called Lavinia. "I knew something was wrong," Lavinia told a friend. "But she didn't say what."

When Lavinia got home she found Isabella curled up on the bathroom floor. She'd been sick and her vomit was blue. Paraquat is a far more powerful poison than Isabella may have realized. It takes as little as two tablespoons to be fatal. On the way to the hospital, Isabella admitted to Lavinia what she'd done. "She was worried that she didn't drink enough," Lavinia said at the inquest. "I don't know if that was said to reassure me, or in disappointment." Philip, Stefan, and Julia had been on their way to Hilles for a visit—instead they went to the hospital. Helga told her brother Desmond de Silva what had happened and he also made his way to her bedside.

The next day, the doctors told Isabella that she would not recover. She had in fact drunk ten times too much. Taking the news in stride, Isabella chose to keep it to herself. She changed out of her hospital gown into a vintage silver lamé shirt then rang the people closest to her for a final chat and to tell them the things she wanted them to have—not mentioning that she knew she was dying. She wanted Haluk to have her hats, Desmond's daughter to have her 410 shotgun, which she said she'd have sent to his club in London. There was no inkling in her voice that anything was seriously awry. "She carried on the conversation in a way that convinced me she was going to be all right," de Silva said. Though every so often, she'd turn away—presumably to grimace at the pain in her gut.

At the end of the day, she told de Silva her fate and said, "You musn't tell Detmar. I want him to go back to Hilles. I don't want him to know." Detmar and the rest of the party departed. Although she'd confessed to de Silva, after so many failed previous attempts, he didn't believe her. "I thought she was just being theatrical," he said. "It came as a great surprise when Detmar rang the following morning and said she was dead." Isabella died during the night, quietly and alone. The story of her life had come to the end she said she wanted.

A f t e r w o r d

In the wake of Isabella's death, newspaper columnists in the UK
said, with staggering authority, that fashion was largely to blame
for her demise. "The sense is strong that the death of the fashion
stylist Isabella Blow is just another of those frequent glimpses
beyond the surface of the fashion industry into something pretty
dark," said Deborah Orr in *The Independent*.[1] "How vile the fashion industry
is," declared India Knight in the *Times*. "Fashion eats people up and spits
them out in a way that sends shivers down your spine: no wonder so many
of its former stars end up unhinged." The consensus seemed to be that
fashion doesn't do enough to look after its own when things get tough. As
evidence Knight pointed to the work Isabella did to promote Alexander
McQueen. "Fast-forward, and McQueen is a global brand, a squillionaire,
and Blow is, well, dead,"[2] she wrote.

Fast-forward even more, to February 2010, and Alexander McQueen
is, well, also dead, and also by his own hand. Isabella's death had
impacted McQueen greatly. The pain he felt showed clearly on his face at
her funeral. Did he feel responsible, the way that people in the industry

were implying he should? Perhaps. Shortly afterward he and his close friend, the jewelry designer Shaun Leane, went to India for a month. It was the longest that McQueen had ever been away from home. Later, after his fall/winter 2008 show, inspired by his trip and called *The Girl Who Lived in the Tree,* he told a journalist that the trip had been a "pilgrimage"[3]—he had embraced Buddhist culture as a way to heal his pain. And, he said, it had worked. He came back refreshed and renewed, and adamant that neither he—nor the industry in which he toiled—was responsible for Isabella's death.

The Girl Who Lived in the Tree told the rags-to-riches story of a girl who lived a life of sadness inside a tree until she found true love and emerged from the shadow of the tree into light and love. The first half featured models in tight black suits and short dresses with flared skirts and petticoats that *W* magazine called "Victorian Goth ballerinas," as well as long, hooded knit dresses with sparkling snowflakes on the side. In the second half of the show the girls were wearing Gem Palace jewels, embroidered military jackets over draped chiffon skirts, white tights, and silk prints featuring images of Brittania. *W* said, "That both of these characters should move into the light is not an accident; they're merely manifesting the mood of the designer who, after an extended dark period, both personally and professionally, has embraced the light."[4]

McQueen's next show was an even more direct account of his feelings for Isabella. *La Dame Bleue* was a sort of greatest-hits number, with special attention paid to the pieces Isabella loved most. As the models walked the runway, behind them stood a giant metal light-encrusted sculpture of a flapping creature—an Icarus. The reference to the Greek myth—which recounts the story of the boy who flew too close to the sun—was not lost on many.

At the time of the *W* interview in June 2008, the first time McQueen had spoken about her death to the press, he insisted that Isabella's death gave him reason to live. "I learned a lot from her death," he said. "I learned a lot about myself. [I learned] that life is worth living. Because I'm just fighting against it, fighting against the establishment. She loved fashion, and I love fashion, and I was just in denial." (He said this referring to his particularly bleak collection, *In Memory of Elizabeth Howe, Salem 1692*, based on the Salem witch trials. *W* called it "a study in vitriol expressed via fashion."[5])

The following year, in September 2009, he defended fashion again—this time from Isabella herself—in an interview with the *New York Times*. "She [Isabella] would say that fashion killed her, but she also allowed that to happen in a lot of ways. She got herself some good jobs and she let some of them go. You could sit Isabella down and tell her what she should do with her life. But she would never understand that all it came down to, 'You just are, Isabella. And that is your commodity.' "[6]

Despite his stated optimism about what he had learned from Isabella's death, in the early hours of February 11, 2010, Alexander McQueen locked himself in his Mayfair apartment and, after taking what the coroner called a "substantial" amount of cocaine and sleeping pills and then trying to slit his wrists, he hanged himself in his wardrobe with his favorite brown leather belt. At his inquest, his doctor—the same one Isabella had been seeing when she died—said that McQueen had previously tried to overdose twice, in May and in July of 2009. On the back of a catalog of images found in his bedroom called *The Descent of Man* by the artist Wolfe von Lenkiewicz, McQueen had written: "Please look after my dogs. Sorry, I love you. Lee. PS Bury me in the church." It was just part of the full note, which has never been released. People close to him said that he was despondent over the death of his mother earlier that year following a prolonged illness and had been trying to steel himself for her funeral the next day. Sam Gainsbury, who produced many of his shows, said, "I think Lee got to a really dark place and could not get out of it. It was in that instance on that night. On another day maybe he would have gone to sleep and gotten out of it."[7] David LaChapelle is fairly convinced that McQueen had been waiting until after his mother had died to do something he had long thought about but that he knew would destroy her.

The pundits, meanwhile, said the predictable: The problem was fashion. "The fashion industry that he [McQueen] dominated is one of the least attractive legal activities on earth, populated by weirdo artists, freakish PRs, and emaciated and mentally disordered models . . . It is a disgusting place to make a living," said George Pitcher in the *Telegraph*.[8]

D id toiling in fashion kill Isabella and Alexander? Of course not. According to a 2008 article in the *British Journal of Psychology*, "Patterns of Suicide by Occupation in England and Wales: 2001–2005," the odds of committing suicide by trade are much higher for health professionals, agricultural workers, and (for women) secretaries. It's just that workers in those trades don't make the headlines much—even when they're not killing themselves.

Isabella and Alexander McQueen toiled in a high-profile industry. (These days, even magazine stylists are household names thanks to the onslaught of reality TV shows.) The deaths of Isabella and McQueen made news because they were recognizable names, not because they were an example of an industry-wide epidemic. The fashion industry is just that—an industry—but people seem to hold it to a higher standard than they would another industry. Would people complain that not enough farmers came forward to help when one of their own was in trouble? Some people are better equipped to deal with the obvious hypocrisy in the industry, just as some lawyers are able to deal with the hypocrisy in theirs. And those who can't, leave. David LaChapelle stopped taking fashion photographs four years ago, at a time, he said, "when it was raining money." He thought he'd move into something like farming, but then art galleries began calling him. He had hoped that Isabella would be able to make the same shift, but even if she had, a change of career alone would not have saved her.

What the fashion industry has (somewhat ironically for an industry focused on creating images) is an image problem. Because photographs featuring young and beautiful people are used to sell fashions that change rapidly, people assume that the fashion industry also churns through the old in favor of the new when it comes to those who toil in its ranks. This isn't helped by the fact that workers in the industry tend to wear mostly black, the color of death, making them all too easy to mock. But the history of the industry is filled with *jolies laides* like Isabella who work happily until their twilight years. Carrie Donovan from *The New York Times* and Diana Vreeland at *Vogue* and then the Metropolitan Museum of Art are just two famous examples. The front row of any major fashion show is filled with more than its fair share of colored-over gray coiffures. Photographers Bruce Weber and Patrick Demarchelier were both born in the 1940s, and Helmut Newton was working right up until his death at the age of eighty-four. The ages of Karl Lagerfeld (seventy-seven), Oscar de la Renta (seventy-eight), Diane von Furstenberg (sixty-four), and Carolina Herrera (seventy-one) do not stop them from creating clothes that young women still dream of wearing. Of course, not every fashion student who gets touted as "the next big thing" makes it, but the same can be said of young musicians, actors, writers, and even fund managers. The fashion industry is not alone in being a fiercely competitive industry but it is uniquely singled out as the root of the problem when one of its workers trips up.

When Isabella was born, it was unthinkable that a woman from her class would have to work for her living. But work she did—and it was work she enjoyed. This did not kill Isabella Blow, but neither could it save her. The business *did* value what she brought to it, and she was rewarded with ample opportunities for financial independence. But it could not provide her with what she needed. Isabella wasn't looking for just a career when she began to work, she was looking for a place she could feel at home. She once said to a client, "Let me speak to Donald. He's my artist. He's shooting for you, but he belongs to me. Eloise [the model] belongs to me. This is how I work. They're my family and I work with my family. I work very, very closely with the people I'm with."[9] And the problem was not that Donald and Eloise didn't feel the same—likely they did. But trying to extract that kind of love from a job is too much to ask of any occupation—even one filled with equally passionate people.

Alexander McQueen also surrounded himself with a surrogate family at work but, in fact, he put real family, his mother, at the center of it. When the models were coming out covered in fake blood and wearing ripped dresses in his 1995 *Highland Rape* show, his mother was backstage making tea and offering sandwiches.

While others were blaming the industry in which she worked, a key member of Isabella's family, Detmar, came out and, strangely, announced that Isabella had died of cancer. Six months later, the woman he was dating, Mara Castilho, became pregnant. When his son was born, he had him christened in Gloucester Cathedral. Detmar said, "Being present at a birth is more positive than being present at a death. I hope the birth breaks the chain of despairing deaths in the family."[10] Isabella's friends were shocked not just by the suddenness of the announcement, but by the resemblance between Castilho and Isabella. In July 2010, Detmar announced that he had proposed to Castilho. "Now I've finished the book about her [Isabella], I feel somehow released to remarry," he said. "The day I finished it, I . . . got so smashed on champagne that I decided to ask my girlfriend to marry me."[11]

Detmar may have moved on, but Isabella's sisters were still grappling with the effects of her death. Isabella frequently said that wearing one of Philip's hats did more for her self-esteem than plastic surgery or a line of cocaine could possibly do.

After she died, Isabella's wardrobe became the property of her sisters. Isabella had named them as executors of her will, and they were the sole beneficiaries of her estate. But because it was a joint asset, when the Eaton Square flat was sold for £535,000, Detmar was able to keep the profits. "Issy left me her heart," Detmar said. "That was more than enough for me. I already had the proceeds from our Eaton Square flat, so there is no problem."[12]

But there was a problem. Aside from a museum-worthy wardrobe, Isabella also left debts. According to figures released by the probate office in the UK, the debts totaled £88,000. Meanwhile, Isabella's clothes were quietly cataloged and locked away in a storage facility owned by Christie's. With no other means of paying the debts, her sisters were faced with the realization that they would have to sell what people considered the very soul of her—her clothes. They approached several institutions and various friends to no avail. Three years later, her sisters announced that the collection would be sold at auction in September 2010.

A last-minute reprieve came when Daphne Guinness stepped forward in July 2010 to buy the entire collection, which reportedly contained some ninety McQueen outfits, fifty Philip Treacy hats, and multiple pairs of Manolo Blahnik shoes. Guinness wrote an essay in the *Financial Times* explaining her motives:

> *I shall never get over Issie's absence, and when I heard her estate needed to be settled so that her sisters could pay off its debts, the realization of what that would entail was really the last straw. The planned sale at Christie's could only result in carnage, as souvenir seekers plundered the incredible body of work Issie had created over her life. . . . Indeed, in many ways, the auction would not be merely a sale of clothes; it would be a sale of what was left of Issie, and the carrion crows would gather and take away her essence forever.*

While clothes were not the essence of Issie—although worn by anyone else they would have none of the same impact—they are the most tangible part of her that is left. In her essay, Guinness continued:

> *Isabella was my friend when she was alive, and that fact is unchanged by her death, and as her friend I did not want anybody misappropriating her*

vision, her life, and her particular genius. . . . It [the collection of her
clothes] is like a diary, a journey of a life, and a living embodiment of the
dearest, most extraordinary friend.[13]

Guinness has hired Kamel Belkacemi, Isabella's most loyal visitor
when she was in hospital, to work with her on building some sort of memorial for Isabella around the clothes. It's a daunting task. Exhibitions of
clothing are notoriously difficult to pull off. Without context, without a
human body, they are lifeless things devoid of meaning. The real genius of
Isabella wasn't what she wore, it was how she wore it. It was her spirit. To
do her justice they will have to find a way to show that she was more than
just her collection of clothes.

Notes

INTRODUCTION: DRESSING ISSIE

1. Daisy Garnett, "Mad as a Hatter's Muse," *New York Times Fashions of The Times Magazine,* February 22, 2004.
2. Philip Treacy, *When Philip Met Isabella,* London: Assouline, 2002.
3. Rachel Cooke, "The Interview: Detmar Blow. Enduring Love," *The Observer,* May 13, 2007.

1. THE CHATELAINE OF ELIZABETH STREET

1. André Leon Talley, *A.L.T.: A Memoir,* New York: Villard, 2003.
2. Lisa Armstrong, "The Mad Hatter with Genius," London *Times,* January 10, 2000.
3. Tamzin Lewis, "Hats On," *The Journal,* Newcastle, November 28, 2006.
4. Daisy Garnett, "Mad as a Hatter's Muse," *New York Times Fashions of The Times Magazine,* February 22, 2004.
5. Tamsin Blanchard, "Isabella Blow, Style Queen and Promoter of Fledgling Designers," *Observer Magazine,* June 23, 2002.
6. Beverly D'Silva, "Relative Values: Selina Blow and Her Brother Amaury," *Sunday Times,* February 3, 2008.

2. THE STATELY HOMES OF ENGLAND ARE MORTGAGED TO THE HILT

1. Lisa Freedman, "Property Guide: Hall of History and Headlines," *Times,* April 30, 1988.
2. Unpublished video footage by Anthero Montenegro.

3. Ibid.

4. Freedman, "Property Guide."

5. This and all historical conversions figured using per capita GDP. Lawrence H. Officer, "Five Ways to Compute the Relative Value of a UK Pound Amount, 1830 to Present," MeasuringWorth.com, 2008.

6. Freedman, "Property Guide."

7. Ibid.

8. "Doddington Estate," *Crewe and Nantwich Observer*, October 9, 1920.

9. Cyril Connolly, "Christmas at Karen," *Sunday Times Magazine,* December 21, 1969.

10. Tina Brown, *The Diana Chronicles*, New York: Doubleday, 2007, Chapter Three.

11. Mary Soames, *Clementine Churchill*, New York: Doubleday, 2002, Chapter Seventeen.

12. Connolly, "Christmas at Karen."

13. James Fox, *White Mischief*, London: Jonathan Cape, 1982, Chapter Nineteen.

14. Ibid.

15. Ibid, Chapter Two.

16. Errol Trzebinski, *The Life and Death of Lord Erroll*, London: Fourth Estate, 2000, Chapter Seven.

17. Evelyn Delves Broughton, Letter to the Editor, "Thwarted Diana Guilty of White Mischief," *Daily Telegraph*, February 15, 1988.

18. Fox, *White Mischief*, Chapter Nineteen.

19. Ibid, Chapter Five.

20. Ibid, Chapter Twenty.

3 . Loving Your Parents Is Common

1. Larissa MacFarquhar, "The Mad Muse of Waterloo," *The New Yorker*, March 19, 2001.

2. Stanford Cliff, *Home: 50 Tastemakers Describe What It Is, Where It Is, What It Means*, London: Quadrille Publishing Ltd., 2007, p. 142.

3. Liza Campbell, *A Charmed Life: Growing Up in Macbeth's Castle*, New York: St. Martin's Press, 2006, Chapter Ten.

4. Emine Saner, "My Husband Ran Off with a Lesbian, So I Fell for a Gondolier," *Evening Standard*, August 31, 2005.

5. Richard Kay, "Family Feud at Isabella's Funeral," *Daily Mail*, May 10, 2007.

6. Saner, "My Husband Ran Off with a Lesbian, So I Fell for a Gondolier."

7. Karl Plewka, "The New Surrealists," *Interview*, September 1, 1998.

8. Saner, "My Husband Ran Off with a Lesbian, So I Fell for a Gondolier."

9. Issy von Simson and Alice Rose, Tatler Schools Guide 2010, London: Condé Nast.

10. "Obituary of Isabella Blow: Stylist who discovered Philip Treacy and whose distinctive hats were landmarks in the world of fashion," *Daily Telegraph*, May 8, 2007.

11. Colin McDowell, "Isabella, Queen of Fashion," British *Elle*, November 1999.

12. Linda Watson, "Obituaries: Fashion Agent Provocateur Whose Discoveries Included Alexander McQueen and Philip Treacy," *The Independent*, May 9, 2007.

13. McDowell, "Isabella, Queen of Fashion."

14. Tamsin Blanchard, "Isabella Blow, Style Queen and Promoter of Fledgling Designers," *Observer Magazine*, June 23, 2002.

15. "Bullingdon Club Too Lively for Prince of Wales," *New York Times,* June 1, 1913.

16. Isabella Blow, "How Do I Look?" *The Independent*, September 9, 2005.

4. BITING THE BIG APPLE

1. Joe McKenna, "Look: Girl in a Brouha-bra," *Sunday Times*, July 27, 1986.

2. Stanford Cliff, *Home: 50 Tastemakers Describe What It Is, Where It Is, What It Means,* London: Quadrille Publishing Ltd., 2007, p. 142.

3. Stephen Doig, "In Memory of Isabella Blow," Hintmag.com, July 23, 2007.

4. Jerry Oppenheimer, *Front Row: Anna Wintour: What Lies Beneath the Chic Exterior of Vogue's Editor-in-Chief*, New York: St. Martin's Press, 2005, Chapter Twenty-six.

5. Doig, "In Memory of Isabella Blow."

6. Stephanie Clifford, "Cuts Meet a Culture of Spending at Condé Nast," *New York Times*, September 27, 2009.

7. Oppenheimer, *Front Row*, Chapter Twenty-six.

8. André Leon Talley, "Life with André, Blithe Spirit; Gilded Age," *Vogue*, July 2007.

9. Christopher Mason, "When an Office Strikes a Pose," *New York Times,* February 18, 1999.

10. Doig, "In Memory of Isabella Blow."

5. LA VIE EN ROSE

1. Maurice Chittenden, "Terror Attack Costs First Lady of Lloyd's £2m," *Sunday Times*, July 14, 2002.

2. "Lady Rona Delves Broughton Seeks Appointment to Lloyd's Ruling Council," *Daily Mail*, October 20, 1989.

3. Chittenden, "Terror Attack Costs First Lady of Lloyd's £2m."

4. Nicholas Coleridge, *The Fashion Conspiracy*, London: William Heinmann Ltd., 1988, Chapter Twelve.

5. Larissa MacFarquhar, "The Mad Muse of Waterloo," *The New Yorker*, March 19, 2001.

6. Liza Campbell, *A Charmed Life: Growing Up in Macbeth's Castle*, New York: St. Martin's Press, 2006, Chapter Fourteen.

7. Karl Plewka, "The New Surrealists" *Interview*, September 1998.

8. Joe McKenna, "Look: Girl in a Brouha-bra," *Sunday Times*, July 27, 1986.

9. David Jenkins, "The Editors," *Tatler*, November 2009.

6. True Loves: Detmar and Hilles, Philip and Hats

1. Amy Larocca, "The Sad Hatter," *New York*, July 16, 2007.

2. Simon Blow, *No Time to Grow*, London: John Murray, 1999, Chapter Two.

3. Simon Blow, "Fatal Blows," *Tatler*, May 2009.

4. Blow, *No Time to Grow*.

5. Blow, "Fatal Blows."

6. Blow, *No Time to Grow*, Chapter Fifteen.

7. Rosie Millard, "The Issy & Detmar Show," *Times*, September 4, 2005.

8. Beverly D'Silva, "Relative Values: Selina Blow and Her Brother Amaury," *Sunday Times*, February 3, 2008.

9. Ibid.

10. McDowell, "Isabella, Queen of Fashion," British *Elle*, November 1999.

11. Rachel Cooke, "The Interview: Detmar Blow. Enduring Love," *The Observer*, May 13, 2007.

12. Ibid.

13. Eve MacSweeney, "Over at Hilles and Far Away," British *Vogue*, November 1992.

14. McDowell, "Isabella, Queen of Fashion."

15. Ibid.

16. Philip Treacy, *When Philip Met Isabella*, London: Assouline, 2002.

17. Ibid.

18. Isabella Blow, "What Are You Wearing Today?" *The Guardian*, September 12, 2005.

7. The Making of a Queen

1. Alix Sharkey, "The Real McQueen," *The Guardian*, July 6, 1996.

2. Nicholas Coleridge, *The Fashion Conspiracy*, London: William Heinemann Ltd., 1988, Chapter Six.

3. Ibid., p. 128.

4. Shane Watson, "Mad as a Hatter," *Evening Standard*, July 1, 2002.

5. Bridget Foley, "Hail McQueen," *W* magazine, June 2008.

6. Sharkey, "The Real McQueen."

7. Alex Bilmes, "The Interview: McQueen," *GQ*, May 2004.

8. Sharkey, "The Real McQueen."

9. Jess Cartner-Morley, "Boy Done Good," *The Guardian*, September 19, 2005.

10. Sharkey, "The Real McQueen."

11. Cartner-Morley, "Boy Done Good."

12. Sharkey, "The Real McQueen."

13. "McQueen of England," *The Face*, November 1996.

14. Ashley Heath, "Bad Boys Inc.," *The Face*, April 1995.

15. Bilmes, "The Interview: McQueen."

16. Heath, "Bad Boys Inc."

17. Sharkey, "The Real McQueen."

18. Tamsin Blanchard, "Isabella Blow, Style Queen and Promoter of Fledgling De-signers," *Observer Magazine*, June 23, 2002.

19. Unpublished video footage by Anthero Montenegro.

20. David James Smith, "Fashion Victim; Isabella Blow," *Sunday Times*, August 12, 2007.

21. *Women's Wear Daily*, "Alexander McQueen, a True Master," February 11, 2010.

22. Colin McDowell, "Shock Treatment," *Sunday Times*, March 17, 1996.

23. Olivier Bernier, *Pleasure and Privilege*, New York: Doubleday and Company, 1981.

24. "Bite into It," *Straits Times,* November 24, 2001.

25. Michael Roberts, "Alexander McQueen (1969–2010)," obituary, Vanity Fair.com, February 11, 2010.

26. Ibid.

27. Plum Sykes, "25 Years of London Fashion Week," *Vogue Daily*, Vogue.com, September 25, 2009.

28. Heath, "Bad Boys Inc."

29. McDowell, "Shock Treatment."

30. Stephen Doig, "In Memory of Isabella Blow," Hintmag.com, July 23, 2007.

31. Larissa MacFarquhar, "The Mad Muse of Waterloo," *The New Yorker*, March 19, 2001.

32. Blanchard, "Isabella Blow, Style Queen and Promoter of Fledgling Designers."

33. Amy Spindler, "In London, Blueblood Meets Hot Blood," *New York Times*, March 5, 1996.

34. Grace Bradbury, "Fashion's Strangest Muse?" London *Times*, November 21, 1996.

35. Toby Young, *How to Lose Friends and Alienate People*, New York: Little, Brown, 2001, Chapter Twenty.

36. David Kamp, "Alexander McQueen and Issie Blow, You Will Be Missed," Vanity Fair.com, February 2010.

37. David Kamp, "London Swings! Again," *Vanity Fair*, March 1997.

38. Colin McDowell, "Isabella, Queen of Fashion," British *Elle,* November 1999.

39. William Middleton and James Fallon, "McQueen Hasn't Decided He Wants Givenchy Post," *Women's Wear Daily*, September 27, 1996.

40. Vassi Chamberlain, "Lean, Mean McQueen," *Tatler,* February 2004.

41. Mimi Spencer, "Animal Magic," *Evening Standard*, July 8, 1997.

8 . Sniffing for Truffles

1. Larissa MacFarquhar, "The Mad Muse of Waterloo," *The New Yorker*, March 19, 2001.
2. Unpublished video footage by Anthero Montenegro.
3. Paula Carson, "Fashion — Dressed to Kill," *Creative Review*, August 3, 1998.
4. Dana Thomas, "A Man for One Season," *New York Times*, February 21, 1999.
5. Melanie Rickey, "Move Over McQueen—Here Comes the Kansas Ranger," *The Independent*, December 29, 1997.
6. "The History Plays," *Women's Wear Daily*, March 16, 1998.
7. Thomas, "A Man for One Season."
8. "The History Plays."
9. MacFarquhar, "The Mad Muse of Waterloo."
10. Ibid.
11. Jeremy Langmead, "It's Hauge, the Hook of Holland," *Sunday Times*, November 22, 1988.
12. MacFarquhar, "The Mad Muse of Waterloo."

9 . The Tragedy of Success

1. Christopher Mason, "Playhouse for a Mad Hatter," *New York Times*, September 16, 1999.
2. Ibid.
3. Sarah Mower, "Young Master," *Sunday Times*, September 5, 1999.
4. Ibid.
5. Isabella Blow, "Apocalypse Now," *Sunday Times*, July 18, 1999.
6. Bill Cunningham, "Caught in Their Acts," *New York Times*, March 22, 1998.
7. Stephen Doig, "In Memory of Isabella Blow," Hintmag.com, July 23, 2007.
8. Shane Watson, "Mad as a Hatter," *Evening Standard*, July 1, 2002.
9. Isabella Blow, "Avant Guard—Fashion," *Sunday Times*, February 7, 1999.
10. Isabella Blow, "Sáo Paolo Chic," *Sunday Times*, April 30, 2000.
11. Larissa MacFarquhar, "The Mad Muse of Waterloo," *The New Yorker*, March 19, 2001.
12. Ibid.
13. Tamsin Blanchard, "Isabella Blow, Style Queen and Promoter of Fledgling Designers," *Observer Magazine*, June 23, 2002.
14. Christa D'Souza, "McQueen and Country," *The Observer*, March 4, 2001.
15. Lauren Goldstein, "The Guys from Gucci," *Time*, April 9, 2001.
16. Ibid.

10. The Hilles Are Alive

1. Rosie Millard, "The Issy & Detmar Blow Show," *Sunday Times,* September 4, 2005.

2. Amy Larocca, "The Sad Hatter," *New York,* July 16, 2007.

3. Tamsin Blanchard, "Isabella Blow, Style Queen and Promoter of Fledgling Designers," *Observer Magazine,* June 23, 2002.

4. Cathy Horn, "Ford Shines, but Stars Come Out for Slimane," *New York Times,* January 30, 2001.

5. Rachel Cooke, "The Interview: Detmar Blow. Enduring Love," *The Observer,* May 13, 2007.

6. Emine Saner, "My Husband Ran Off with a Lesbian, So I Fell for a Gondolier," *Evening Standard,* August 31, 2005.

7. Larissa MacFarquhar, "The Mad Muse of Waterloo," *The New Yorker,* March 19, 2001.

8. Polly Vernon, "The Entertaining Mr. Sloane," *Observer Magazine,* May 1, 2005.

11. Tatler Tales

1. "The Insider: The Birds Who Want to Bag a Footballer," *Liverpool Echo,* November 5, 2002.

2. Polly Vernon, "The Entertaining Mr. Sloane," *Observer Magazine,* May 1, 2005.

3. "Fashion Scoops: Working Girl," *Women's Wear Daily,* January 13, 2003.

4. Simon Chilvers, "Mind Blowing," *The Guardian,* January 24, 2003.

5. Rachel Cooke, "The Interview: Detmar Blow. Enduring Love," *The Observer,* May 13, 2007.

6. Amy Larocca, "The Sad Hatter," *New York,* July 16, 2007.

7. "PS Blow, by Blow," *Daily Mail,* May 14, 2003.

8. Ruth Addicott, "Tatler's Blow Leads from the Front in Naples," *Press Gazette,* February 12, 2004.

9. Ibid.

10. Larocca, "The Sad Hatter."

11. Daisy Garnett, "Mad as a Hatter's Muse," *New York Times,* February 22, 2004.

12. Melanie Rickey, "It's My Party," *Sunday Times,* June 6, 2004.

13. Cooke, "The Interview."

14. KiKi King, "SPY: Detmar and Isabella Together," *Telegraph,* June 19, 2004.

12. MISERABELLA

1. Lucy Siegle, "This Much I Know: Isabella Blow, Stylist, 46, London," *Observer Magazine,* May 29, 2005.
2. Rupert Everett, "Lips Together, Knees Apart," *Vanity Fair,* September 1, 2006.
3. London Fashion Salutes Indian Designs," *Times of India,* July 20, 1999.
4. Mandvi Sharma, "Indian Stars Are Uncharitable," *Times of India,* December 3, 2006.
5. "Fashion's Quirky Icon in Goa Hospital," *Indian Express,* January 3, 2007.
6. Edward Helmore, "Final Blow," *Vanity Fair,* September 2007.
7. Katie Nicholl, "Shane Bowls Over Jemima, But Hugh's Not Out Yet," *Mail on Sunday,* March 25, 2007.
8. Bridget Foley, "Hail McQueen," *W* magazine, June 2008.
9. Hilary Alexander, "Beautiful and Outrageous but Doomed," *Daily Telegraph,* May 8, 2007.

AFTERWORD

1. Deborah Orr, "Isabella Blow's Death Revealed the Dark Heart of the Fashion Industry," *The Independent,* May 12, 2007.
2. India Knight, "Fashion Has a Rotten Heart," *Sunday Times,* May 13, 2007.
3. Bridget Foley, "Hail McQueen," *W* magazine, June 2008.
4. Ibid.
5. Ibid.
6. Cathy Horn, "General Lee," *The New York Time Style Magazine,* September 11, 2009.
7. Ingrid Sischy, "A Man of Darkness and Dreams," *Vanity Fair,* April 2010.
8. George Pitcher, "It's Sad That Alexander McQueen Has Died, but 'Fashionistas' Are Just Freaks: There, I've Said It," *Daily Telegraph,* February 15, 2010.
9. Unpublished video footage by Anthero Montenegro.
10. Richard Kay, "Blow's Baby to End Cycle of Tragedy," *Daily Mail,* August 14, 2008.
11. Richard Kay, "Blow's Man to Wed Issy Lookalike," *Daily Mail,* July 19, 2010.
12. Ibid.
13. Daphne Guinness, "Why I Stopped the Sale," *Financial Times,* July 3, 2010.

Index

Hagens, Gunther von, 152
Hall, Jerry, 97
Halley, Erik, 169
Halston, 70
Hamnett, Katharine, 104, 131–32
Harlech, Amanda, 143, 205
Harmsworth, Geraldine, xxi, 96, 98,
    150, 221
  daughters of, 115
  on feelings, 181
  on life's meaning, 230
  lifestyle of, 45
  on mothers, 47
  on transition, 226
Harmsworth, Vere, 96–97
Harris, David, 141
Harrow, Eton v., 107–8
Haslam, Nicky, 99
hats
  lobster for, 169
  for memorial service, 3
  mistreatment of, 175–76
  for Parker Bowles, 15
  sex and, 189, 206
  therapy and, 210
  traditional, 14
  from Treacy, 1–3, 11, 13–15, 18–19, 25,
    114–19, 129–30, 133–34, 175–76, 210
  for wedding, 13–14, 115–16
Hay, Idina, 33
Hay, Josslyn, 32–33
Heath, Ted, 46–47
Heathfield, 47–50
Helen. *See* Delves Broughton, Helen Shore
Helga's Folly, 113
Hempel, Anouska, 92
Herbstein, Winnie, xiii
Herrera, Carolina, 251
Hickinson, Hugh, 36
Highland Rape, 137
Hilles, xvii, 6–7, 9, 15–16, 106
  accidents at, 186–87
  Birley, L., on, 111, 186
  clothes at, 112, 123
  description of, 110–11
  Detmar J. and, 105
  Detmar v., 111–13, 189

Doddington Hall v., 110–11
drugs at, 181
Evelyn at, 182–83
fashion supplies from, 185
firemen at, 186
as gallery collateral, 158
Isabella and, 20
Macdonald's visit to, 123
Perera and, 107, 113, 187–88
rentals at, 183
repairs at, 182
social divisions at, 183–84
as stage, 181–82
suicide at, 243–44
Treacy on, 111
Vogue story on, 129–30
weekends at, 139
worth of, 158
Hillson, Bobbie, 124
Hirst, Damien, 78, 141, 156
Hitchcock, John, 127
Hogg, Pam, 109
Hogg, Quinton, 47
Holloway, Julian, 151
Holloway, Sophie. *See* Dahl, Sophie
Home, 41
Home Chance, 157
Hughes, Fred, 64

Icarus, 137
ICI Delux, 241
Les Incroyables, 92, 125
The Independent, 247
India, trips to, 172, 240, 241
inheritance
  Issie and, 130–31
  of Jock, 27
  marriage and, 66
  primogeniture for, 42–43, 44
  Rona and, 130–31
Inner Temple, 40
Iraq, war in, 204
Issie. *See* Blow, Isabella Delves Broughton
Issie/Detmar
  engagement of, 112
  as "it" couple, 160
  Silva on, 111, 159

Brit circle in, 69
fashion shoot in, 167–68
London v., 78
residence in, 63, 68–69
New York Times, 8, 54, 140, 155, 165–66, 170, 249, 251
The New Yorker, 155, 191
feature article in, 175
Newhouse, Jonathan, 194, 233
Newhouse, Ronnie, 194
Newhouse, Si, 71
Newton, Helmut, 251
Nihilism, 131–32
Nipplegate, 167, 168
Noble, Tim, xxiii, 157, 181, 193, 237
Nuthurst Primary, 44–45

Ogilvy, Augusta, 150
Ogilvy, David, 64
Orr, Deborah, 247
Otto, Karla, 218, 241
Oxenberg, Catherine, 63–64
Oxford
beautiful people at, 53
drugs at, 54–55
raucous behavior at, 54
secretarial college in, 52–53
Ozbek, Rifat, xxiii, 16, 131–32
clothes from, 93
at wedding, 115

Paley, Maureen, 214
Palmer, Iris, 139, 150, 152
Paris, 191–92
for Akakce, 217–18
haute couture shoots in, 204–5, 217–18
Treacy and, 118–19
Parker Bowles, Camilla, 15
Perera, Helga de Silva Blow, xviii
background of, 106
clothes for, 113
Detmar and, 108, 114, 187–89
first marriage of, 106, 107
Helga's Folly for, 113
Hilles and, 107, 113, 187–88
home of, 15, 17
Issie and, 113–14, 188, 192

remarriage of, 108
suicide attempts and, 236
at wedding, 116
as widow, 108
Piers Gaveston Club, 54
Pilkington, Celia, 40
Pinault, François, 177
Pitcher, George, 250
Pleasure and Privilege (Bernier), 133
Plymouth, Lady, 105
Prada, 200
Prada, Miuccia, 176
Presley, Lisa Marie, 92, 184
Price, Alison, 44
on Issie's childhood, 45
Price, Anthony, 185
primogeniture, 42–43, 44
Priory Hospital, 208–9

Rabanne, Paco, 153
Reno, Noelle, 222
Renta, Oscar de la, 251
residences, 81–82. *See also* Doddington Hall; Elizabeth Street house; Midland, Texas
with Akakce, 213–14
with Metcalfe, 60
in New York City, 63, 68–69
in Paris, 191–92
in Scottish Highlands, 98–99
after secretarial school, 57
on Theed Street, 165–66
Rich White Women, 154–55
Rigby & Peller, 94
Right Said Fred, 134
Roberts, Michael, xxiii, 13, 194, 204
analysis of, 87
Brazil trip with, 171–72
on Detmar, 192
fashion shoots of, 86, 89–90
on hiring Issie, 85
on Issie's fame, 169
McQueen and, 136, 145
on office attire, 93
on Paris, 191
Scott, J., and, 155
on *Tatler* promotion, 117–18
Rocksavage, David. *See* Cholmondeley, David